an ITC *publication in*

MATHEMATICS

SET THEORY
AND THE
NUMBER SYSTEMS

Set Theory

and

INTERNATIONAL TEXTBOOK COMPANY

the
Number Systems

MAY RISCH KINSOLVING

Chairman, Department of Mathematics
Ithaca College, Ithaca, New York

Scranton, Pennsylvania

To
Walter

Preface

The word "mathematics" is derived from the Greek $\tau\grave{\alpha}$ $\mu\alpha\theta\eta\mu\alpha\tau\iota\kappa\acute{\alpha}$, which means "learning" or "knowledge." Today, "mathematics" is applied not to knowledge in general but to knowledge of a particular kind. Still, there is some misunderstanding as to exactly what sort of knowledge is involved. Often, the layman thinks of mathematics as arithmetic, and of the mathematician as one who is very quick and clever at performing computations. The scientist may think of mathematics as another science of which arithmetic is only a very small part. Most professional mathematicians, however, regard their subject as neither of these things. (Indeed, it is commonly said, by mathematicians, that they can seldom add two numbers correctly or balance a bank statement.) Present-day mathematicians generally regard their subject as the study of logical consequences of systems of axioms, where the axioms are completely arbitrary statements made about completely abstract objects. Thus, one could argue that mathematics is more closely related to philosophy or the arts than to the sciences.

The purpose of this book is to acquaint the reader with some of the basic concepts and techniques of mathematics, and to illustrate how these concepts and techniques may be applied to an axiomatic development of various number systems and to a study of cardinal numbers. Along the way, many properties of the real numbers and of the cardinal numbers will be investigated.

The book is intended for a one-semester course. Such a course might be taken by students who are not planning to specialize in mathematics but who, nevertheless, wish to learn about the nature of mathematics; by students who do plan to specialize in mathematics and want a foundation for their later studies; by prospective mathematics teachers; and by those preparing to teach "modern" mathematics. The book is also intended for the general reader—whether he be a curious adult or a curious high-school or college student.

Very little previous knowledge of mathematics — at most, some elementary algebra — is required for an understanding of this book. Exercises are provided at the ends of various sections. The reader is strongly urged to carry out these exercises so that he may have adequate preparation for handling the ideas that follow.

The author sincerely thanks the staff of the International Textbook Company for their help in the preparation of this book and in particular, wishes to thank John W. Lindsay, San Fernando Valley State College, for his many valuable comments and criticisms.

MAY RISCH KINSOLVING

Ithaca, New York
December, 1966

Contents

Contents

SET THEORY
AND THE
NUMBER SYSTEMS

1 / *Logic*

1-1. INTRODUCTION

In order to understand some of the examples in the first two chapters, one should be familiar with the following notions, which are developed more thoroughly in Chapters 3 through 6.

1. The numbers $\cdots, -3, -2, -1, 0, 1, 2, 3, \cdots$ are called integers. An even integer is an integer which is a multiple of 2, that is, a number which can be expressed in the form $2n$, where n is an integer. The even integers are $\cdots, -4, -2, 0, 2, 4, \cdots$. An odd integer is a number which can be expressed in the form $2n + 1$, where n is an integer. The odd integers are $\cdots, -3, -1, 1, 3, 5, \cdots$. The integers $1, 2, 3, \cdots$ are called positive integers. The integers $\cdots, -3, -2, -1$ are called negative integers. The integer 0 is neither positive nor negative. An integer a is said to be divisible by an integer b, where b is not 0, if there is an integer c such that $a = bc$; that is, a is the product of b and c. For example, 6 is divisible by 2, but 2 is not divisible by 6.

2. Numbers of the form $\dfrac{p}{q}$, where p and q are integers and q is not 0, are called rational numbers (ratios of integers). For example, $\dfrac{3}{4}, \dfrac{-2}{27}$, and $\dfrac{10}{-9}$ are rational numbers. Moreover, any integer n is a rational number, since n may be expressed in the form $\dfrac{n}{1}$.

3. Numbers such as $\sqrt{2}, \sqrt[3]{2}$, and π, which cannot be expressed as ratios of integers, are called irrational numbers.

4. All the rational numbers together with all the irrational numbers constitute the set of real numbers or the real number system.

If x is a real number, then x^2 denotes the product of x with x, x^3 denotes the product of x^2 with x, and so on.

For any two real numbers m and n, either m is greater than n, m equals n, or m is less than n. If m is greater than n, we write $m > n$; if

m equals n, we write $m = n$; if m is less than n, we write $m < n$. For example, $5 > 3$; $3 = 3$; $3 < 5$. The notation $m \geq n$ or $m \leq n$ indicates that m is greater than or equal to n, or that m is less than or equal to n, respectively; for example, $5 \geq 3$; $5 \geq 5$; $3 \leq 5$; $5 \leq 5$. The notation $3 \leq x \leq 7$ indicates that x is a number between 3 and 7 and that x may equal 3 or x may equal 7. The notation $3 < x < 7$ indicates that x is a number between 3 and 7 but that x may not equal 3 or 7. The notation $3 \leq x < 7$ indicates that x is a number between 3 and 7 and that x may equal 3 but not 7.

The symbol ∞, called infinity, does not denote a real number. To assert that $0 < x < \infty$ is to assert that x is a real number which is greater than 0; to assert that $-\infty < x < \infty$ is to assert that x is any real number.

The absolute value of a real number x, denoted by $|x|$, is defined as follows:

$$|x| = \begin{cases} x \text{ if } x \geq 0; \\ -x \text{ if } x < 0. \end{cases}$$

For example, $|5| = 5$; $|-5| = 5$; $|0| = 0$.

5. A complex number is a number of the form $a + bi$, where a and b are real numbers and i is a number (not real) with the property that $i^2 = -1$. For example, $2 + 3i$, $5 - 2i$, and $6i$ are complex numbers. Any real number is also a complex number, with b equal to 0.

1-2. AXIOMS, THEOREMS, AND VALIDITY

In the logical development of any branch of mathematics, certain undefined (or primitive) concepts must be introduced in order to avoid circular definitions. As an everyday example, suppose that someone wishes to learn the meaning of the word "parasang," and in his dictionary he reads that a parasang is a farsakh. Never having heard of the word "farsakh" before, he consults his dictionary again only to read that a farsakh is a parasang. Surely our poor man has learned nothing from these (circular) definitions. In geometry, "point" and "line" often are taken as undefined concepts, for defining a point as the intersection of two distinct lines and a line as a join of two distinct points clearly is a meaningless procedure. Indeed, with a little thought, one will be convinced that it is impossible to define *every* word in a language.

After certain concepts have been chosen as undefined, all additional concepts will be precisely defined in terms of these undefined ones.

A mathematical statement is a declarative sentence about one or more undefined concepts.

Examples 1. "Two points determine a line" is a mathematical statement.

2. "Construct a line joining two given points" is not a mathematical statement.

Certain mathematical statements are designated as axioms. Axioms are assumptions, and they state *everything* that is assumed to be known about the undefined concepts. A statement is considered valid if it is an axiom or if it can be proved from the axioms and definitions, in accordance with the rules of logical deduction, to be described in Sec. 1-4. A proof of a statement consists of reasoning by which one justifies the validity of the statement from the axioms and definitions.

It is important to note that the validity of a statement is completely unrelated to the truth of the statement. Since the axioms are unproved statements about undefined concepts, it certainly can make no sense to speak of the truth of the axioms, let alone of any statement derived from them. Bertrand Russell once said[1] that mathematics may be defined as the subject in which we never know what we are talking about or whether what we are saying is true. This is a sound observation for, since the basic concepts are undefined, one does not know what he is talking about when he speaks of these concepts, and, since the validity of a statement depends upon unproved axioms, one can never know whether the statement is true. Indeed, "true" can have no meaning when applied to a statement containing undefined concepts.

A theorem is a valid statement of importance; that is, an important logical consequence of the axioms or definitions. A corollary is a valid statement which is an immediate consequence of, or a special case of, a preceding definition or theorem. A lemma is a valid statement which is proved preliminary to proving a theorem. It may be of interest only in that it is needed to establish a certain theorem.

A theorem (or corollary or lemma) may be expressed in the form, "If P, then Q," where P and Q are statements.

Examples   **1.** If two angles of a triangle are equal, then the sides opposite the angles are equal.
                2. If an integer a is less than an integer b, then $a + 1$ is less than or equal to b.

Here, the statement "P" is called the hypothesis, the word "if" indicating that P is assumed to be valid. The statement "Q" is called the conclusion, the word "then" indicating that Q must be proved valid in order to prove the validity of the theorem. The axioms are understood to be assumed throughout the development of the mathematical theory and,

[1]"Recent Work on the Principles of Mathematics," *International Monthly*, Vol. 4 (1901), p. 84.

hence, generally are not repeated in the hypothesis. Because of this, a theorem (or corollary or lemma) may simply have the form "Q."

Example. The sum of the lengths of two sides of a triangle is greater than the length of the third side.

In this case, the conclusion only is stated, and the theorem asserts that the conclusion holds, providing that the axioms hold.

EXERCISE

State whether each of the following is a mathematical statement and give all reasons for your answers.
  a) 6 is greater than 2.
  b) 2 is greater than 6.
  c) What is a number?
  d) Why is 6 greater than 2?
  e) Multiplying by 66,548,989.237 is a lot of work.
  f) Curses on these numbers with many digits.

1-3. MATHEMATICAL USAGE OF CERTAIN WORDS

Certain words are used frequently in mathematical discourse. We shall now consider some of these words and how their use in mathematics differs from their everyday use. In order to give concrete examples of some of the notions introduced, in this discussion we shall assume some of the elementary properties of the real numbers.

The capital letters P, Q, R, and so on, will be used to denote statements. For example, P might be the statement "$1 = 1$" or the statement "$1 + 1 = 2$."

The word "and" may be placed between two statements "P" and "Q" to form a new statement "P and Q." The statement "P and Q" is valid only when both P and Q are valid.

Example. Let P be the statement "2 is an even number." Let Q be the statement "5 is an even number." Then "P and Q" is the statement "2 is an even number and 5 is an even number," which is not valid, even though P is.

The word "or" may be placed between two statements "P" and "Q" to form a new statement "P or Q." In mathematics, this compound statement is understood to mean that either P is valid or Q is valid and *possibly both are valid*. Thus, "or" is used in the "and/or" sense (one or the other or both). One should contrast this with everyday usage, where "or" frequently means one or the other, but *not* both.

Examples   **1.** Let P be the statement "4 is an even number." Let Q be the statement "5 is an even number." Then "P or Q" is the statement "4 is an even number or 5 is an even number," which is valid, since P is.

               2. Let P be the statement "4 is an even number." Let Q be the statement "6 is an even number." Then "P or Q" is the statement "4 is an even number or 6 is an even number," which is valid, since both P and Q are. (In everyday usage, one might argue that "P or Q" is not valid simply because *both* P and Q are valid.)

The word "not" may be placed before a statement "P" to form a new statement "Not P." This new statement is called the negation of P.

Example.   Let P be the statement "4 is an even number." Then "Not P" is the statement "Not 4 is an even number" or "4 is not an even number."

The negation of the compound statement "P and Q" is "Not P or not Q," for to deny that P and Q are both valid is to assert that at least one of them is not valid.

The negation of the compound statement "P or Q" is "Not P and not Q," for to deny that either P or Q is valid is to assert that both P and Q are not valid.

The negation of the statement "Not P" is "Not (not P)"; that is, "P."

The word "equals," denoted symbolically by $=$, may be placed between two expressions to indicate that the two expressions are names of the same identical object. Hence, if we know that $a = a'$, then we also know that $a' = a$, since, if a and a' denote the same object, then a' and a denote the same object. By the same argument, if $a = a'$ and $a' = a''$, then $a = a''$, for all three expressions are names of the same object. If two expressions a and b are *not* equal, we write "$a \neq b$."

Mathematical statements often concern sets of objects rather than a single object. A quantifier is a word or phrase telling how many (quant-) of the objects of the set are involved in the statement.

The quantifiers "each," "any," "every," and "all" may be used interchangeably.

Example.   Each integer is a number; any integer is a number; every integer is a number; all integers are numbers.

The word "any" may sometimes be used in a way in which the other three words cannot. For example, suppose that we want to prove that for all real numbers x, x^2 is positive. We might start by saying, "Let x be any real number," indicating that we are choosing an unspecified real number x in an arbitrary fashion. Then we would proceed to show that x^2 is positive, where x is our arbitrary unspecified number. From this, we would conclude that all real numbers have positive squares, since our arbitrarily chosen number does. The word "any," used in this way, cannot be replaced by "each," "every," or "all."

The quantifiers "some" and "there exist" may be used interchangeably.

Example.   For some number x, $x^2 = 1$; there exists a number x such that $x^2 = 1$.

Consider the statement "All integers are numbers." To deny this statement, one would assert "There exists an integer x such that x is not a number." To deny the statement "There exists an integer x such that x is not a number," one would assert "All integers are numbers."

If P and Q are any two statements, one may form the compound statement "If P, then Q," or its equivalent, "P implies Q." This is denoted symbolically by $P \Rightarrow Q$.

The statement "$Q \Rightarrow P$" is called the converse of the statement "$P \Rightarrow Q$." The converse of a valid statement need not be valid.

Examples   **1.** Consider the statement "If an integer is divisible by 6, then it is divisible by 3." Its converse is "If an integer is divisible by 3, then it is divisible by 6." The original statement is valid; the converse is not.
   2. Consider the statement "If a triangle is equilateral, then it is equiangular." Its converse is "If a triangle is equiangular, then it is equilateral." Both the original statement and its converse are valid.

The statement "Not $Q \Rightarrow$ not P" is called the contrapositive of the statement "$P \Rightarrow Q$." It will be shown, in Sec. 1-4, that if a statement is valid, then its contrapositive is valid, and, conversely, if the contrapositive of a statement is valid, then the statement itself is valid.

Consider the statement "P and $Q \Rightarrow S$." Its converse is "$S \Rightarrow P$ and Q." Its contrapositive is the statement "Not $S \Rightarrow$ not $(P$ and $Q)$"; that is, "Not $S \Rightarrow$ not P or not Q."

If P implies Q, then P is said to be a sufficient condition for Q, for, if P is valid, then Q must be valid also. That is, the validity of P is sufficient for the validity of Q. Similarly, it is said that Q is a necessary condition for P, for, if "Not Q" were valid, then "Not P" would be valid also. That is, it is necessary for Q to be valid in order for P to be valid.

The statement "*P* if, and only if, *Q*" means "*P* if *Q*, and *P* only if *Q*." Now "*P* if *Q*" is just another way of asserting "If *Q*, then *P*." "*P* only if *Q*" means that *P* is not valid unless *Q* is valid; that is, if *P* is valid, then *Q* must be valid, or, "if *P*, then *Q*." Therefore, "*P* if, and only if, *Q*" means "If *P*, then *Q*, and, if *Q*, then *P*." This situation is described by saying that *P* is equivalent to *Q*, or simply that *P* and *Q* are equivalent. The equivalence of *P* and *Q* is denoted symbolically by *P* $\longleftrightarrow$ *Q*. Since "*P* $\Longrightarrow$ *Q*" means that *P* is a sufficient condition for *Q*, and since "*Q* $\Longrightarrow$ *P*" means that *P* is a necessary condition for *Q*, it follows that the assertion "*P* $\longleftrightarrow$ *Q*" is the same as the assertion "*P* is a necessary and sufficient condition for *Q*." By the same reasoning, asserting "*P* $\longleftrightarrow$ *Q*" is the same as asserting "*Q* is a necessary and sufficient condition for *P*."

To prove that *P* $\longleftrightarrow$ *Q*, one must prove that *P* $\Longrightarrow$ *Q*, and also the converse, *Q* $\Longrightarrow$ *P*.

EXERCISES

1. Negate the following mathematical statements:
    a) 5 is less than 7.
    b) 5 is less than 7 and 5 is less than 9.
    c) All real numbers are positive.
    d) Whenever a number is real, it is positive.
    e) No real number is positive.
    f) Some real numbers are positive.
    g) 5 is greater than 3, or 5 is less than 3.
2. Give the converse of each of the following statements (neither the statements nor their converses necessarily being valid):
    a) If two lines do not intersect, then they are parallel.
    b) If $x = 5$, then x is a solution of $x^2 - 5x = 0$.
    c) The diagonals of a parallelogram bisect each other.
    d) An even number is divisible by 4.
(HINT: First rewrite the statements of part c and part d in the form "If *P*, then *Q*.")
3. Give the contrapositive of each of the statements in Exercise 2.
4. Rewrite each of the following, using the words "and," "not," "or," and "if . . . , then."
    a) *P* if *Q*.
    b) *P* otherwise *Q*.
    c) *P* but not *Q*.
    d) *Q* whenever *P*.
    e) Neither *P* nor *Q*.

1-4. RULES OF LOGICAL DEDUCTION

The following rules of logical deduction are commonly used in proving that a statement is valid.

1. *Rule of Inference.* If P is valid and if "$P \Rightarrow Q$" is valid, then Q is valid.

2. *Rule of Transitivity of Implication.* If "$P \Rightarrow Q$" and "$Q \Rightarrow R$" are both valid, then "$P \Rightarrow R$" is valid.

Using this rule, Rule 1 may be generalized as follows: If P_1 is valid, and if the implications

$$P_1 \Rightarrow P_2,$$
$$P_2 \Rightarrow P_3,$$
$$\vdots$$
$$P_{n-1} \Rightarrow P_n$$

are all valid, then P_n is valid.

3. *Rule of Contradiction.* A conclusion Q is valid if "Not Q" implies a contradiction—that is, a statement of the form "R and not R."

Proving the validity of Q by using Rule 3 is sometimes called proving Q by *reductio ad absurdum.* This type of proof is called an indirect proof. Any other type of proof is called direct.

Rule 3 may be used to show that a statement "$P \Rightarrow Q$" and its contrapositive, the statement "Not $Q \Rightarrow$ not P," are equivalent. That is, both are valid or both are invalid. Suppose that both the statements "$P \Rightarrow Q$" and "Not Q" are valid. We shall show that the statement "Not P" is valid also. In order to show that "Not P" is valid, we shall show that "Not (not P)" implies a contradiction. Now "Not (not P)" is the same as P; and, if P is valid, then Q must be valid also, since we assumed above that P implies Q. But we also assumed above that "Not Q" is valid. Thus, the assumption that P [or "Not (not P)"] is valid leads to the contradiction "Q and not Q." Hence, it must be that the conclusion "Not P" is valid. Thus, if $P \Rightarrow Q$" is valid, its contrapositive, "Not $Q \Rightarrow$ not P," is valid also. Similarly, if "Not $Q \Rightarrow$ not P" is valid, then "$P \Rightarrow Q$" is valid, for, if "Not Q" implies "Not P," then, by the reasoning above, "Not (not P)" implies "Not (not Q)." But "Not (not P)" is the same as P, and "Not (not Q)" is the same as Q.

Suppose that one wishes to prove that a statement "P" is equivalent to a statement "Q"; that is, "$P \Leftrightarrow Q$." Using the logical rules above, several procedures are available:

a) proving that both "$P \Rightarrow Q$" and "$Q \Rightarrow P$" are valid.

b) proving that both "$P \Rightarrow Q$" and "Not $P \Rightarrow$ not Q" are valid. As shown above, this last implication is equivalent to "$Q \Rightarrow P$."

c) proving that both "$P \longleftrightarrow R$" and "$Q \longleftrightarrow R$" are valid. This would mean that the two statements "$P \Rightarrow R$" and "$R \Rightarrow Q$" are valid, and hence, by Rule 2, that "$P \Rightarrow Q$" is valid. It would also mean that the two statements "$Q \Rightarrow R$" and "$R \Rightarrow P$" are valid, and hence, by Rule 2, that "$Q \Rightarrow P$" is valid.

Sometimes three or more statements are to be proved mutually necessary and sufficient conditions for each other. For example, suppose we must prove that the four statements "P," "Q," "R," and "S" are equivalent; that is, that "$P \longleftrightarrow Q$," "$P \longleftrightarrow R$," "$P \longleftrightarrow S$," "$Q \longleftrightarrow R$," "$Q \longleftrightarrow S$," and "$R \longleftrightarrow S$" are all valid. If the validity of all four assertions "$P \Rightarrow Q$," "$Q \Rightarrow R$," "$R \Rightarrow S$," and "$S \Rightarrow P$" can be proved, then the first three assertions, combined with Rule 2 used twice, show that "$P \Rightarrow S$" is valid. This, combined with the fourth assertion "$S \Rightarrow P$," proves the validity of "$P \longleftrightarrow S$." Indeed, repeated use of Rule 2 and the four assertions above will establish all six desired equivalences.

Given an apparently significant statement, one may not know whether or not it is valid. Often, one then alternates between trying to prove the statement and trying to disprove it. Usually, the simplest way to disprove a statement is by exhibiting a counterexample, that is, a special case in which the statement is not valid. For instance, consider the statement "All numbers are larger than 5." This statement can be disproved immediately by exhibiting the counterexample 4, since 4 is a number which is not larger than 5. To disprove a statement requires exhibiting only one special case in which the statement is not valid, for a statement, if valid, will be valid for every special case to which it is applicable.

Given a collection of axioms, there is, in general, no set procedure for constructing a proof; that is, it may be possible to construct more than one proof of a certain assertion, or the assertion may not be provable (or disprovable) from the collection of axioms. There are many mathematical conjectures which have never yet been proved, and the number of these increases every day. Some of these conjectures are provable, but no one yet has been able to prove them; some of the conjectures may not be provable from the axioms at all, but whether this is the case is not known. Furthermore, given a collection of axioms, there is, in general, no simple procedure showing whether an alleged proof really is a proof. Mathematical arguments exist which were accepted for many years (in some cases, even hundreds of years) before logical flaws were discovered in them. This situation, however, is the exception rather than the rule.

Usually, students studying abstract mathematics for the first time find themselves in considerable difficulty when they try constructing proofs of their own. This is only natural and should not be a source of discouragement. The difference between reading how to construct a proof and actually constructing one is very like the difference between reading how to drive a car and actually driving one. Instructions are helpful but can never take the place of experience. It is hoped that the many proofs and problems in these chapters will provide some of this experience.

A few pieces of advice might be helpful at this point:

1. Whenever in doubt as to how to begin a proof, try writing down all that is assumed and exactly what it is that you are trying to prove. Often, this will be of tremendous help in organizing your thoughts. Always keep in mind where it is that you are trying to go in your proof.

2. Sometimes it helps to work backwards. Start with the conclusion and try to work toward the hypothesis. If this can be done, often a reversal of your steps will give the desired result.

3. When using defined concepts, discard all preconceived notions concerning the meanings of these concepts, and use their exact definitions exclusively. Many words are used in mathematics with meanings very different from their everyday meanings—for example, real, imaginary, rational, irrational, group, field, tree, mob, and so on.

4. If you do not succeed with a certain line of attack, abandon it and try another one. Sometimes it is helpful to stop working on a proof for a few hours (or even days) and then to tackle it again, using a new approach.

5. If you think you have a proof, read it over carefully a few times, preferably with several hours between each reading. Often, an argument that seems convincing at first proves to be untenable upon reconsideration.

6. Check to see that every step in your proof can be defended on logical grounds, using only statements previously shown to be valid.

7. Check to see that you have not used any unnecessary steps in reaching your conclusion. A long, rambling discussion does not make a statement any more valid or your proof any more convincing. Aim for conciseness and clarity in all your arguments.

8. As you read the proofs in the following chapters and as you try to construct your own, continue to refer to this chapter. Many of the ideas introduced here will become more meaningful to you as your experience with abstract thinking increases.

EXERCISE

The following is a generalization of the rule of inference: If P_1 is valid, and if all the implications "$P_1 \Rightarrow P_2$," "$P_2 \Rightarrow P_3$," "$P_3 \Rightarrow P_4$" are valid, then P_4 is valid. Using Rules 1 and 2, prove that this generalization is valid.

2 / Theory of Sets

2-1. CONCEPT OF SET

The concept of set is basic to the study of every branch of mathematics. Intuitively, one might think of a set as a collection or aggregate. Many words, commonly used, describe sets in general: classes, assemblages, families; many describe sets of a particular kind: a class of students, a troop of boy scouts, a flock of sheep, a herd of cattle, a pride of lions, a school of fish, a litter of kittens.

In mathematics the word "set" is undefined. In attempting a definition, one would probably use words such as "collection," or "aggregate," or "assemblage." These words, however, do not really clarify the original notion "set," and, at best, lead to a chain of circular definitions.

A set is made up of objects called elements or members of that set. A set is said to be well defined if it can be determined whether or not a given object is a member of that set. We shall be working with well defined sets only. Some examples of well defined sets follow.

Examples
1. The set of all letters in the Greek alphabet.
2. The set of all books in your house.
3. The set consisting of this page, your kitchen sink, and my cat Phoebe.
4. The set consisting of all sets which consist of three distinct letters of the Greek alphabet.

In Example 4 the elements of the given set are sets themselves—namely, sets of three distinct letters of the Greek alphabet.

An axiomatic theory of sets can be developed in which the only undefined concepts are "set" and "is an element of." In this chapter, instead of presenting an axiomatic development, we shall give only an informal account of some of the most important ideas of set theory. In order to give examples of some of the concepts introduced, we shall use some of the elementary properties of the real numbers.

2-2. SUBSETS, VENN DIAGRAMS, AND THE EMPTY SET

Capital letters $A, B, C, \cdots$ will denote sets; small letters $a, b, c, \cdots$ will denote the elements of a set. The three dots mean "and so on."

The notation "$a \in A$" means that a is an element of A. If a is not an element of A, we write $a \notin A$. When possible, a set will be designated by exhibiting its elements in braces. For example, $\{1, 3, 5, 7, 9\}$ is the set of all odd positive integers less than 10; $\{1, 3, 5, \cdots\}$ is the set of all odd positive integers.

Two sets A and B are said to be equal if every element of A is an element of B and every element of B is an element of A; that is, A and B consist of exactly the same elements. This is denoted by $A = B$. Using the terminology of the preceding chapter, $A = B$ if for every element x, $x \in A$ if, and only if, $x \in B$. According to our definition, the sets $\{a, b, c\}$ and $\{c, b, a\}$ are equal; that is, $\{a, b, c\} = \{c, b, a\}$.

The set consisting of the single object a is not the same conceptually as the object a; that is, $\{a\} \neq a$.

A set A is said to be a subset of a set B whenever every element of A is an element of B. For example, the sets $\{a, b\}$, $\{a, c\}$, $\{b\}$, and $\{a, b, c\}$ are subsets of the set $\{a, b, c\}$. Can you find others? We indicate that A is a subset of B by writing $A \subseteq B$ or $B \supseteq A$. We read each of these statements as "A is contained in B," "A is included in B," "B contains A," or "B includes A."

A set A is said to be a proper subset of a set B if A is a subset of B and A does not equal B; that is, every element of A is an element of B, but B contains at least one element which is not in A. We indicate this by writing $A \subset B$ or $B \supset A$. We read each of these statements as "A is a proper subset of B." The sets $\{a, b\}$, $\{a, c\}$ and $\{b\}$ are proper subsets of $\{a, b, c\}$, while $\{a, b, c\}$ is not a proper subset of itself.

Using the above definitions, one may obtain the following three conclusions:

1. If $A \subset B$ and $B \subset C$, then $A \subset C$.

Proof: Let a be any element of A. $A \subset B$, by hypothesis. These two conditions together imply that $a \in B$. $B \subset C$, by hypothesis. The last two conditions together imply that $a \in C$. Therefore, any element in A is also in C. $Q.E.D.$[1]

2. If $A \subset B$, then $B \not\subset A$.

Proof: $A \subset B$, by hypothesis. Therefore, by the definition of "$\subset$," B contains an element x such that $x \notin A$. Assume that $B \subset A$. Then, by

---

[1] We sometimes indicate that the end of a proof has been reached by writing "$Q.E.D.$" This is an abbreviation for the Latin *quod erat demonstrandum*, meaning "which was to be demonstrated."

the definition of "$\subset$," every element of B is in A. These two conclusions are contradictory; hence the assumption that $B \subset A$ must be absurd. Therefore, $B \not\subset A$. (See Rule 3, Sec. 1-4.) *Q.E.D.*

3. $A = B$ if, and only if, $A \subseteq B$ and $B \subseteq A$.

Proof: If $A = B$, then, by definition, every element of A is an element of B and every element of B is an element of A; that is, $A \subseteq B$ and $B \subseteq A$. Conversely, if $A \subseteq B$ and $B \subseteq A$, then, by definition, every element of A is an element of B and every element of B is an element of A; that is, $A = B$. *Q.E.D.*

To visualize some of the concepts of set theory, we often use Venn diagrams, in which sets are represented pictorially as plane regions enclosed by curves. The points of the plane on and inside the boundary of the curve represent the elements of the given set; the points outside the boundary represent elements not belonging to the set. For example, Fig. 2-1 might represent sets A and B with $A \subset B$; Fig. 2-2 might represent sets A, B, and C with $A \subset B \subset C$.

Fig. 2-1. $A \subset B$.

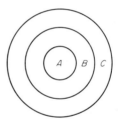

Fig. 2-2. $A \subset B \subset C$.

Since Venn diagrams concern particular sets only, one cannot use them to prove anything about sets in general. The diagrams are useful merely as thinking aids.

The notation $\{a \mid a \in A$ and a has property $p\}$ denotes the set of all elements a in A which have property p; that is, the subset of A consisting of those elements having property p. In this context the vertical line after a is read "such that."

Examples 1. $\{x \mid x$ is a real number and x is a positive integer$\}$ is the set of all numbers x such that x is real and x is a positive integer. Here, A is the set of all real numbers and the property p is the property of being a positive integer. The subset of the real numbers under consideration is the set of all positive integers.

2. $\{x \mid x$ is a real number and $0 \leq x \leq 1\}$ denotes the set of all real numbers between 0 and 1, inclusive. If the set A is the same throughout a discussion, we often omit "$x \in A$." Thus, if we are discussing real numbers only, the above set might be described as $\{x \mid 0 \leq x \leq 1\}$.
3. $\{x \mid x$ is a triangle and x has a right angle$\}$ denotes the set of all right triangles.

Suppose that A is the set of all cows in New York, and $B = \{a \mid a \in A$ and a is purple$\}$. As far as we know, this set B contains no elements whatever. In such a case we say that B is the empty set or null set. The empty set or set containing no elements will be denoted by the symbol ϕ, and, for logical reasons, is considered to be a subset of every set.

2-3. OPERATIONS ON SETS

The union or set-theoretic sum of two sets A and B is the set consisting of all elements which are either in A or in B; that is, the set consisting of all the elements of A together with all the elements of B. It is denoted by $A \cup B$, which is read "A union B." For example, let $A = \{a, b, c, d, e\}$; let $B = \{c, d, e, g\}$. Then $A \cup B = \{a, b, c, d, e, g\}$.

The definition of union implies:
1. $A \cup \phi = A$.
2. $A \cup A = A$ (idempotent law).
3. $A \subset A \cup B; B \subset A \cup B$.
4. $A \subset B \Longrightarrow A \cup B = B$.
5. $A \cup B = B \cup A$ (commutative law).

Proof of 4: Let a be any element of A. By hypothesis, $A \subset B$. These two conditions together imply that $a \in B$. Therefore, the set consisting of all elements either in A or in B; that is, $A \cup B$, consists of all elements in B.

Q.E.D.

The intersection or set-theoretic product of two sets A and B is the set consisting of all elements common to both A and B. It is denoted by $A \cap B$, which is read "A intersection B." For example, let $A = \{a, b, c, d, e\}$; let $B = \{c, d, e, g\}$. Then $A \cap B = \{c, d, e\}$.

The definition of intersection implies:
1. $A \cap \phi = \phi$.
2. $A \cap A = A$ (idempotent law).
3. $A \cap B \subset A; A \cap B \subset B$.
4. $A \subset B \Longrightarrow A \cap B = A$.
5. $A \cap B = B \cap A$ (commutative law).

Proof of 4: Let a be any element of A. By hypothesis, $A \subseteq B$. These two conditions together imply that $a \in B$. Therefore, $a \in A \cap B$ for all $a \in A$; that is, $A \subseteq A \cap B$. Now, by property 3 above, $A \cap B \subseteq A$. Since $A \subseteq A \cap B$ and $A \cap B \subseteq A$, it follows, from the definition of set equality, that $A \cap B = A$.   *Q.E.D.*

If A and B have no common elements, then $A \cap B = \phi$. In this case A and B are said to be disjoint.

The difference or set-theoretic difference of two sets A and B is the set consisting of all elements of A which are not in B. It is denoted by $A - B$, which is read "A minus B." For example, let $A = \{a, b, c, d, e\}$; let $B = \{c, d, e, g\}$. Then $A - B = \{a, b\}$, and $B - A = \{g\}$.

The definition of difference implies:

1. $A - \phi = A; \phi - A = \phi$.
2. $A - A = \phi$.
3. $A - B \subseteq A$.
4. $A \subseteq B \Rightarrow A - B = \phi$.
5. If $A \cap B = \phi$, then $A - B = A$ and $B - A = B$.
6. $A - B = B - A$ if, and only if, $A = B$.
7. $A - B = A - (A \cap B)$.

Proof of 6: If $A = B$, then $A - B = \phi = B - A$. Conversely, if $A - B = B - A$, then any element in A and not in B is also an element in B and not in A. But this is impossible unless $A - B = B - A = \phi$. But this means that every element of B is in A and every element of A is in B. Hence, by the definition of set equality, $A = B$.   *Q.E.D.*

Proof of 7: Let a be any element of $A - B$. Then $a \in A$ and $a \notin B$. Therefore, $a \notin A \cap B$. But $a \in A$ and $a \notin A \cap B$ means that $a \in A - (A \cap B)$. Conversely, if a is any element in $A - (A \cap B)$, then $a \in A$ and $a \notin A \cap B$. Therefore, $a \notin B$. But $a \in A$ and $a \notin B$ means that $a \in A - B$. Thus, every element in $A - B$ is also in $A - (A \cap B)$, and every element in $A - (A \cap B)$ is also in $A - B$. By the definition of set equality, this means that $A - B = A - (A \cap B)$. *Q.E.D.*

If $A \supseteq B$, then $A - B$ is called the complement of B in A. It is denoted by B'.

The definition of complement implies:

1. If $B = \phi$, then $B' = A$.
2. If $B = A$, then $B' = \phi$.
3. $B \cup B' = A$.
4. $B \cap B' = \phi$.
5. $(B')' = B$.

In Figs. 2-3, 2-4, 2-5, and 2-6, the shaded regions represent $A \cup B$, $A \cap B$, $A - B$, and B', respectively.

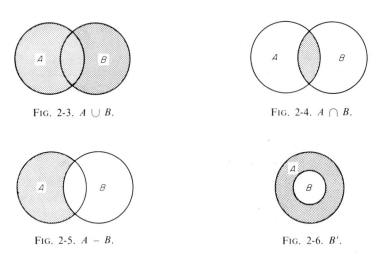

FIG. 2-3. $A \cup B$.   FIG. 2-4. $A \cap B$.

FIG. 2-5. $A - B$.   FIG. 2-6. B'.

A collection of sets is a set whose elements are themselves sets.

Examples   **1.** See Example 4 on page 11.

2. The set of lines in a plane through a given point is a set each element of which (that is, each line of which) is itself a set—namely, a set of points.

Precise definitions of finite and infinite sets are given on page 137. For the present, however, we may intuitively think of a set as being finite if there is a nonnegative integer n such that the set contains exactly n elements. Any set which is not finite is said to be infinite. The set in Example 1 above is finite; the set in Example 2 is infinite.

The notions of union and intersection can be extended to finite or infinite collections of sets. The union of all the sets in a collection F is the set consisting of all elements belonging to at least one of the sets of F. It is denoted by $\bigcup\limits_{A \in F} A$. If F is the collection of lines of Example 2 above, then the union of all the sets in the collection consists of all the points of the plane.

The intersection of all the sets in a collection F is the set consisting of all elements belonging to every one of the sets of F. It is denoted by $\bigcap\limits_{A \in F} A$. If F is the collection of lines of Example 2 above, then the intersection of all the sets in the collection is the point of intersection of all the lines.

One can show that the following associative laws hold for any sets $A_1, A_2,$ and A_3:

$$A_1 \cup (A_2 \cup A_3) = (A_1 \cup A_2) \cup A_3;$$
$$A_1 \cap (A_2 \cap A_3) = (A_1 \cap A_2) \cap A_3.$$

Using these results and mathematical induction (see page 44) one can show that there is no ambiguity in writing the expressions $A_1 \cup A_2 \cup \cdots \cup A_n$ and $A_1 \cap A_2 \cap \cdots \cap A_n$, in which there are no parentheses to indicate the order in which the sets are to be combined. Hence, if F is a finite collection—say $F = \{A_1, A_2, \cdots, A_n\}$—then $\bigcup\limits_{A \in F} A = A_1 \cup A_2 \cup \cdots \cup A_n$ and $\bigcap\limits_{A \in F} A = A_1 \cap A_2 \cap \cdots \cap A_n$.

In Figs. 2-7 and 2-8 the shaded regions represent $A_1 \cup A_2 \cup A_3$ and $A_1 \cap A_2 \cap A_3$, respectively, for a collection $F = \{A_1, A_2, A_3\}$.

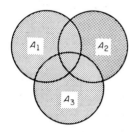

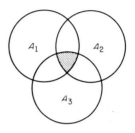

FIG. 2-7. $A_1 \cup A_2 \cup A_3$.   FIG. 2-8. $A_1 \cap A_2 \cap A_3$.

EXERCISES

1. Let $A = \{1, 2, 3, 4, 5, 6, 7\}$; let $B = \{1, 3, 5, 6\}$; let $C = \{2, 4, 6, 8, 10\}$; let $D = \{1, 2, 6, 7\}$. Find:

    a) $A \cap C \cap D$.

    b) $A - D$.

    c) $D - A$.

    d) $C \cup A - C \cap A$.

    e) $A - (B - C)$.

2. Consider the Venn diagram in Fig. 2-9. Determine the portion of the diagram that should be shaded in order to indicate the following sets:

    a) $A \cup B$.

    b) $A \cap C$.

    c) $(A \cup B) \cap C$.

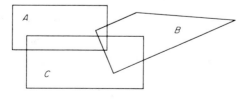

FIG. 2-9

d) $(A \cup C) \cup B$.

e) $(A \cap B) \cap C$.

f) $A \cap C - B$.

g) $(B \cap C) \cup (A \cap C)$.

h) $(A - B) \cup C$.

3. Prove that for any sets A, B, and C,

$$A \cap (B \cup C) = (A \cap B) \cup (A \cap C).$$

4. Prove that for any sets A, B, and C,

$$A - (B \cap C) = (A - B) \cup (A - C).$$

5. Prove that for any sets A and B, $A = (A - B) \cup (A \cap B)$.

6. Prove that for any sets A, B, and C,

$$A \cap (B - C) = B \cap (A - C)$$
$$= (A \cap B) - C$$
$$= (A \cap B) - (A \cap C).$$

7. Let B and C be subsets of A. Prove that $(B \cup C)' = B' \cap C'$, where the prime indicates the complement of the given set in A.

2-4. ORDERED PAIRS AND RELATIONS

Suppose that a and b are any two objects. If we wish to specify an order for a and b—say a first and b second—we write (a, b). "(a, b)" is called the ordered pair a, b. $(a, b) = (c, d)$ if and only if $a = c$ and $b = d$. Thus, $(a, b) \neq (b, a)$ unless $a = b$.

Examples 1. In referring to a certain date as $1/6$, one must indicate whether the month or day comes first. Does $1/6$ mean the sixth of January or the first of June?

2. In using the digits 2 and 7 to represent the cost of a certain item, one must indicate which digit comes first. Does the item cost 27 cents or 72 cents?

3. In writing the Cartesian coordinates (x, y) of a point in the plane, the order of the coordinates is important; the points $(2, 3)$ and $(3, 2)$ are not the same.

Given two sets A and B, the Cartesian product of A and B, denoted by $A \times B$, is the set consisting of all ordered pairs (a, b), where $a \in A$ and $b \in B$; that is, $A \times B = \{(a, b) \mid a \in A \text{ and } b \in B\}$.

Examples 1. Let $A = \{a, b, c\}$; let $B = \{b, d\}$. Then $A \times B = \{(a, b), (a, d), (b, b), (b, d), (c, b), (c, d)\}$; $B \times A = \{(b, a), (d, a), (b, b), (d, b), (b, c), (d, c)\}$; $A \times A = \{(a, a), (a, b), (a, c), (b, a), (b, b), (b, c), (c, a), (c, b), (c, c)\}$; $B \times B = \{(b, b), (b, d), (d, b), (d, d)\}$.

2. Let A be the set of all real numbers. Then $A \times A$, the set of all ordered pairs of real numbers, can be used to represent the set of all points in the plane. When a point of the plane is represented by an element of $A \times A$, we call that element the Cartesian coordinates of the point. This originally gave rise to the name "Cartesian product of two sets."

Given two sets A and B, a relation on $A \times B$ is a subset $\mathfrak{R}$ of $A \times B$; thus $\mathfrak{R} \subseteq A \times B$. The notation $a\mathfrak{R}b$ means $(a, b) \in \mathfrak{R}$. If $(a, b) \notin \mathfrak{R}$, we write $a\not\mathfrak{R}b$. $\overline{\mathfrak{R}}$ may be regarded as a relation on $A \times B$; it is the subset of $A \times B$ consisting of all pairs (a, b) of $A \times B$ such that $(a, b) \notin \mathfrak{R}$.

Examples   **1.** Let A be the set of all men; let B be the set of all women. Then $A \times B$ is the set of all ordered pairs—first a man, then a woman. a) The set of all married pairs—first a husband, then his wife—is a relation on $A \times B$. This relation is a proper subset of $A \times B$. b) The set of all ordered pairs—first a man, then a woman—such that the man is a brother of the woman is another relation on $A \times B$. This relation is also a proper subset of $A \times B$.

2. Let A be the set of all men. Then $A \times A$ is the set of all ordered pairs of men. a) The set of all ordered pairs of men such that the first member of the pair is the father of the second is a relation on $A \times A$. This relation is a proper subset of $A \times A$. b) The set of all ordered pairs of men such that the first member of the pair is taller than the second is another relation on $A \times A$ and is a proper subset of $A \times A$.

Additional examples of relations will be given in the following pages.

When the sets A and B are relatively small, relations on $A \times B$ may be represented pictorially. For example, suppose that $A = \{a, b, c, d\}$ and $B = \{b, e, f\}$. Three relations $\mathfrak{R}_1$, $\mathfrak{R}_2$, and $\mathfrak{R}_3$ are represented by Figs. 2-10, 2-11, and 2-12, respectively. The dots indicate which ordered pairs belong to the given relation. For example, a dot in row e and column c indicates that the ordered pair (c, e) is a pair in the given relation. The first two relations, $\mathfrak{R}_1$ and $\mathfrak{R}_2$, are proper subsets of $A \times B$; the third relation, $\mathfrak{R}_3$, is the set $A \times B$ itself. From the figures, one reads:

$$\mathfrak{R}_1 = \{(a, e), (b, b), (c, e), (c, f), (d, b)\}.$$

$$\mathfrak{R}_2 = \{(a, e), (b, f), (d, e)\}.$$

$$\mathfrak{R}_3 = \{(a, b), (a, e), (a, f), (b, b), (b, e), (b, f), (c, b), (c, e),$$
$$(c, f), (d, b), (d, e), (d, f)\}.$$

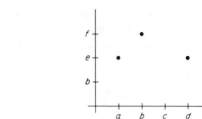

FIG. 2-10. $\mathcal{R}_1$.   FIG. 2-11. $\mathcal{R}_2$.

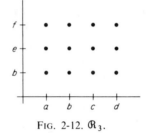

FIG. 2-12. $\mathcal{R}_3$.

The relation $\mathcal{R}_1$ is represented by Fig. 2-13.

Given a set A, the identity relation $\mathcal{E}$ on $A \times A$ is the subset of $A \times A$ defined as follows:

$$\mathcal{E} = \{(a, b) \mid a, b \in A \text{ and } a = b\},$$

or, equivalently,

$$\mathcal{E} = \{(a, a) \mid a \in A\}.$$

"$a\mathcal{E}b$" means $a = b$; "$a\cancel{\mathcal{E}}B$" means $a \neq b$. Figure 2-14 represents the identity relation $\mathcal{E}$ on the set $A \times A$, where $A = \{a, b, c\}$.

Given a relation $\mathcal{R}$ on $A \times B$, the inverse of $\mathcal{R}$, denoted by $\mathcal{R}^{-1}$, is the subset of $B \times A$ consisting of all ordered pairs (b, a) for which $a\mathcal{R}b$.

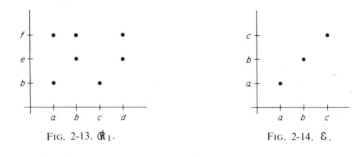

FIG. 2-13. $\mathcal{R}_1$.   FIG. 2-14. $\mathcal{E}$.

Thus, $\mathcal{R}^{-1}$ is a relation on $B \times A$; "$b\mathcal{R}^{-1}a$" means the same as "$a\mathcal{R}b$". The inverses of $\mathcal{R}_1$, $\mathcal{R}_2$, $\mathcal{R}_3$, and $\mathcal{R}_1$ (Figs. 2-10, 2-11, 2-12, and 2-13, respectively) are represented by Figs. 2-15, 2-16, 2-17, and 2-18, respectively. The inverse of $\mathcal{E}$ is $\mathcal{E}$ itself.

The domain of a relation $\mathcal{R}$ on $A \times B$ is the set of all elements $a \in A$ for which there exists at least one element $b \in B$ such that $a\mathcal{R}b$; that is, $\{a \mid a \in A \text{ and } a\mathcal{R}b \text{ for at least one } b \in B\}$. Equivalently, one might say that the domain of $\mathcal{R}$ is the set of all first elements appearing in the pairs (a, b) constituting $\mathcal{R}$. Thus, the domain of $\mathcal{R}$ is a subset of A — sometimes A itself.

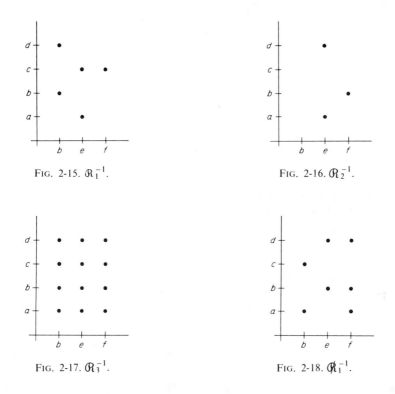

FIG. 2-15. $\mathcal{R}_1^{-1}$.

FIG. 2-16. $\mathcal{R}_2^{-1}$.

FIG. 2-17. $\mathcal{R}_3^{-1}$.

FIG. 2-18. $\mathcal{R}_1^{-1}$.

The range of a relation $\mathcal{R}$ on $A \times B$ is the set of all elements $b \in B$ for which there exists at least one element $a \in A$ such that $a\mathcal{R}b$; that is, $\{b \mid b \in B \text{ and } a\mathcal{R}b \text{ for at least one } a \in A\}$. Equivalently, one might say that the range of $\mathcal{R}$ is the set of all second elements appearing in the pairs (a, b) constituting $\mathcal{R}$. Thus, the range of $\mathcal{R}$ is a subset of B—sometimes B itself.

Examples

		Domain	Range
		Domain	Range
1.	1a, page 19	Set of all husbands	Set of all wives
2.	$\mathcal{R}_1$ (Fig. 2-10)	$\{a, b, c, d\}$	$\{b, e, f\}$
3.	$\mathcal{R}_2$ (Fig. 2-11)	$\{a, b, d\}$	$\{e, f\}$
4.	$\mathcal{R}_3$ (Fig. 2-12)	$\{a, b, c, d\}$	$\{b, e, f\}$
5.	$\mathcal{R}_1^{-1}$ (Fig. 2-15)	$\{b, e, f\}$	$\{a, b, c, d\}$
6.	$\mathcal{R}_2^{-1}$ (Fig. 2-16)	$\{e, f\}$	$\{a, b, d\}$

EXERCISES

1. Let A be the set $\{a, b, c, d, e\}$. Give the domains and ranges of each of the following relations on $A \times A$:

    a) $\mathcal{R}_1 = \{(a, b), (b, c)\}$.

    b) $\mathcal{R}_2 = \{(c, d), (d, e), (c, e)\}$.

    c) $\mathcal{R}_3 = \{(a, b), (b, a)\}$.

    d) $\mathcal{R}_4 = \{(a, b), (b, c), (d, e)\}$.

    e) $\mathcal{R}_5 = \mathcal{E}$ (the identity relation).

    f) $\mathcal{R}_6 = \{(a, b), (a, c), (a, d), (a, e), (b, c), (b, d),$
          $(b, e), (c, d), (c, e), (d, e)\}$.

    g) $\mathcal{R}_7 = \{(a, d), (b, c), (b, d), (c, d)\}$.

2. Consider the following relations on $R \times R$, where R is the set of all real numbers:

    a) $\mathcal{R}_1 = \{(x, y) \mid x^2 + y^2 = 1\}$.

    b) $\mathcal{R}_2 = \{(x, y) \mid y = \sin x\}$.

    c) $\mathcal{R}_3 = \{(x, y) \mid x = \sin y\}$.

    d) $\mathcal{R}_4 = \{(x, y) \mid x^3 + y = 0\}$.

    e) $\mathcal{R}_5 = \{(x, y) \mid x^2 - y^4 = 0, \ y \geq 0\}$.

Give the largest possible domains and ranges (in the set of real numbers) for each of the given relations.

2-5. FUNCTIONS

Let A and B be two sets. A function or mapping from A to B is a relation $\mathcal{F}$ on $A \times B$ such that for every element a in the domain of $\mathcal{F}$ there is exactly one element $b \in B$ satisfying $a\mathcal{F}b$. Equivalently, $\mathcal{F}$ is a function if, whenever $a\mathcal{F}b_1$ and $a\mathcal{F}b_2$ ($a \in A$; $b_1, b_2 \in B$), then $b_1 = b_2$.

Examples   1. The relation "is the husband of " (1a, page 19) is a function in a monogamous society, since there every husband has exactly one wife.

           2. The relation "is the brother of a woman" (1b, page 19) is not a function since a man may have more than one sister.

3. The relation "is a father of a son" (2a, page 19) is not a function, since a father may have several sons. The inverse relation "is a son of a father" is a function, since every son has exactly one father.

4. $\mathcal{R}_1$ (Fig. 2-10) is not a function since there is a pair of elements e and f in B and an element c in A such that $c\mathcal{R}_1 e$, $c\mathcal{R}_1 f$, and $e \neq f$.

5. $\mathcal{R}_2$ (Fig. 2-11) is a function.

6. Let A be the set of all real numbers. The relation $\mathcal{R}$ on $A \times A$ consisting of $\{(x,y) \mid x \in A$ and $y = x^2\}$ is a function. Its graph is shown in Fig. 2-19. The inverse relation $\mathcal{R}^{-1}$ (Fig. 2-20) consisting of $\{(y,x) \mid x \in A$ and $y = x^2\}$ is not a function since for each nonzero y in the domain $\{y \mid 0 \leq y < \infty\}$ there exist two real numbers x_1 and x_2 in the range $\{x \mid -\infty < x < \infty\}$ such that $y\mathcal{R}^{-1}x_1$, $y\mathcal{R}^{-1}x_2$, and $x_1 \neq x_2$.

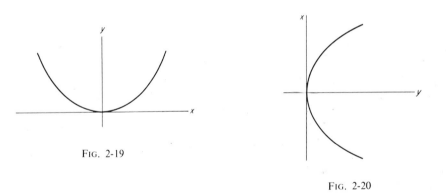

FIG. 2-19

FIG. 2-20

If $\mathcal{F}$ is a function from A to B such that the range of $\mathcal{F}$ is B, then $\mathcal{F}$ is said to be a function from A *onto* B; in this case, for every $b \in B$ there is an $a \in A$ such that $a\mathcal{R}b$. If the range of $\mathcal{F}$ is B or a proper subset of B, then $\mathcal{F}$ is said to be a function from A *into* B; in this case there may be an element $b \in B$ such that for all $a \in A$, $a\mathcal{F}b$. Notice that every "onto" function is also "into," but not every "into" function is "onto."

Examples   **1.** The function $\mathcal{E}$ (Fig. 2-14) is onto (as well as into).

2. $\mathcal{R}_2$ (Fig. 2-11) is into, but not onto.

3. The function shown in Fig. 2-19 is into, but not onto, since its range is $\{y \mid 0 \leq y < \infty\}$ and not $\{y \mid -\infty < y < \infty\}$.

Let a be an element in the domain of a function $\mathfrak{F}$ from A to B. We denote by "$\mathfrak{F}(a)$" the unique element $b \in B$ such that $a\mathfrak{F}b$.

Examples   1. For the function $\mathfrak{R}_2$ (Fig. 2-11), $\mathfrak{R}_2(a) = e$; $\mathfrak{R}_2(b) = f$; $\mathfrak{R}_2(d) = e$.

2. For the function "is a son of" (Example 3, page 23), for every man a, "$\mathfrak{R}(a)$" denotes his father.

Two functions $\mathfrak{F}_1$ and $\mathfrak{F}_2$ are said to be equal whenever the domain of $\mathfrak{F}_1$ equals the domain of $\mathfrak{F}_2$, and, for each element a in the common domain, $\mathfrak{F}_1(a) = \mathfrak{F}_2(a)$.

Let $\mathfrak{F}$ be a function from a set A to a set B; let $\mathfrak{G}$ be a function from a set B to a set C. Then $\mathfrak{F}$ composed with $\mathfrak{G}$, denoted by $\mathfrak{G} \circ \mathfrak{F}$, is the function from A to C defined as follows:

$$\mathfrak{G} \circ \mathfrak{F} = \{(x, \mathfrak{G}(\mathfrak{F}(x))) \mid x \in A\}.$$

For example, let $A = \{1, 2, 3\}$; $B = \{1, 2, 3, 4\}$; $C = \{1, 2, 3, 4, 5\}$. Let $\mathfrak{F}$ be the function from A to B: $\{(1, 2), (2, 1), (3, 4)\}$. Let $\mathfrak{G}$ be the function from B to C: $\{(1, 5), (2, 1), (3, 5), (4, 2)\}$. Then $\mathfrak{G} \circ \mathfrak{F} = \{(1, 1), (2, 5), (3, 2)\}$.

Let A and B be sets and $\mathfrak{F}$ a function from A to B. Then $\mathfrak{F}$ is a 1:1 correspondence between A and B if, and only if, a) the domain of $\mathfrak{F}$ is A, b) the range of $\mathfrak{F}$ is B (that is, $\mathfrak{F}$ is onto), and c) whenever $a_1 \neq a_2$, then $\mathfrak{F}(a_1) \neq \mathfrak{F}(a_2)$; that is, $\mathfrak{F}^{-1}$ is a function.

Examples   1. The relation "is the husband of" (1a, page 19) is (in a monogamous society) a 1:1 correspondence between the set of all husbands and the set of all wives: the domain is the set of all husbands; the range is the set of all wives; the inverse relation "is the wife of" is also a function.

2. $\mathfrak{R}_2$ (Fig. 2-11) is a function but not a 1:1 correspondence, since none of the three requirements for a 1:1 correspondence is satisfied.

3. $\mathfrak{F} = \{(x, y) \mid x \text{ is real and } y = x^2\}$ (Fig. 2-19) is not a 1:1 correspondence between the set of all real numbers and itself, since $\mathfrak{F}^{-1}$ is not a function. Can you find other reasons?

4. The identity relation $\mathcal{E}$ (Fig. 2-14) is a 1:1 correspondence.

5. The relation, illustrated in Fig. 2-21, on the set $A \times A$, where $A = \{a_1, a_2, a_3\}$, is a 1:1 correspondence.

6. If all the chairs in a classroom are occupied by students and no student in the room is standing, then there is a 1:1 correspondence between the set of all students in the room and the set of all chairs in the room, providing that no chair contains more than one student and no student occupies more than one chair.

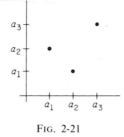

FIG. 2-21

7. Let A be the set of all positive integers; that is, $A = \{1, 2, 3, \cdots\}$. Let B be the set of all positive integers which are multiples of 5; that is, $B = \{5, 10, 15, \cdots\}$. Then the correspondence $1 \leftrightarrow 5$, $2 \leftrightarrow 10$, $3 \leftrightarrow 15$, $\cdots$ is a 1:1 correspondence between A and B.

Notice that two finite sets A and B must have the same number of elements in order for there to be a 1:1 correspondence between them, for each element of A must be paired with exactly one element of B and each element of B with exactly one element of A. In the case of two infinite sets A and B, we define "A has the same number of elements as B" to mean "there is a 1:1 correspondence between A and B." (See page 134.)

If A_1, A_2, and A_3 are three sets (not necessarily distinct), a function $\mathcal{F}$ from $A_1 \times A_2$ to A_3 is called a binary operation or simply an operation.

Examples   **1.** Let R be the set of all real numbers. Then addition is a function or binary operation from $R \times R$ to R. This function consists of all ordered pairs $((r_1, r_2), r_1 + r_2)$ such that $r_1, r_2 \in R$; the first element of the pair is the pair (r_1, r_2) and the second element of the pair is the real number $r_1 + r_2$. Similarly, multiplication is a binary operation pairing $(r_1, r_2) \in R \times R$ with $r_1 \cdot r_2 \in R$ (that is, with the product of r_1 and r_2 in R).

2. Let R be the set of all real numbers and let C be the set of all complex numbers. Let $\mathcal{F} = \{((a, b), c) \mid (a, b) \in R \times R,\ c \in C,$ and $c = a + b\sqrt{-1}\}$. Then $\mathcal{F}$ is a function and, moreover, a binary operation with domain $R \times R$ and range C.

A set is said to be closed with respect to the binary operation $*$ if for any two elements a, b in the set, $a * b$ is also in the set. For example, the set $\{1, 2, 3, \cdots\}$, considered as a subset of the set of all real numbers, is closed with respect to addition. It is not closed with respect to division.

EXERCISES

1. Which of the relations in Exercise 2 of Sec. 2-4 are functions? Give reasons.

2. In Examples 1 and 2 on page 25, certain binary operations are considered. Are their inverses functions? Why?

3. Let S' be the set of all subsets of a given set S. Thus, $S' = \{A, B, C, \cdots\}$, where $A \subseteq S, B \subseteq S, \cdots$. Show that union and intersection are binary operations from $S' \times S'$ to S'.

4. a) If $\mathcal{F}(x) = x^2$ for all real x, and $\mathcal{G}(x) = 2x$ for all real x, find $\mathcal{G} \circ \mathcal{F}$ and $\mathcal{F} \circ \mathcal{G}$. b) If $\mathcal{F}(x) = |x|$ for all real x, and $\mathcal{G}(x) = x^2 + 1$ for all real x, find $\mathcal{G} \circ \mathcal{F}$ and $\mathcal{F} \circ \mathcal{G}$.

5. If $\mathcal{F}$ is a 1:1 correspondence between sets A and B, and if $\mathcal{G}$ is a 1:1 correspondence between sets B and C, show that $\mathcal{G} \circ \mathcal{F}$ is a 1:1 correspondence between A and C. Also show that $(\mathcal{G} \circ \mathcal{F})^{-1} = \mathcal{F}^{-1} \circ \mathcal{G}^{-1}$.

6. A function $\mathcal{F}$ from S to S is said to have period n if $\mathcal{F}^n = \mathcal{E}$, but $\mathcal{F}^k \neq \mathcal{E}$ for $0 < k < n$. Prove that a periodic function is a 1:1 correspondence. ($\mathcal{F}^k$ means $\mathcal{F} \circ \mathcal{F} \circ \cdots \circ \mathcal{F}$, k times.)

7. Prove that a function $\mathcal{F}$ from A to B is a 1:1 correspondence between A and B if, and only if, there is a function $\mathcal{G}$ from B to A such that $\mathcal{G} \circ \mathcal{F}$ is the identity function on A and $\mathcal{F} \circ \mathcal{G}$ is the identity function on B.

2-6. EQUIVALENCE RELATIONS

An equivalence relation on a set S is a subset $\mathcal{R}$ of $S \times S$ (that is, a relation on $S \times S$) with the following properties:

1. $a\mathcal{R}a$ for all $a \in S$. That is, $\mathcal{R}$ is reflexive.
2. $a\mathcal{R}b \Rightarrow b\mathcal{R}a$ for all $a, b \in S$. That is, $\mathcal{R}$ is symmetric.
3. $a\mathcal{R}b$ and $b\mathcal{R}c \Rightarrow a\mathcal{R}c$ for all $a, b, c \in S$. That is, $\mathcal{R}$ is transitive.

As before, "$a\mathcal{R}b$" means "$(a, b) \in \mathcal{R}$" (see page 19). In the case of equivalence relations, we read "$a\mathcal{R}b$" as "a is equivalent to b."

Examples   1. Let S be the set of all real numbers. Then equality is an equivalence relation. It is the relation $\mathcal{R}$ defined by: $a\mathcal{R}b$ if, and only if, $a = b$ for $a, b \in S$. Note that $a = a$; if $a = b$, then $b = a$; if $a = b$ and $b = c$, then $a = c$. That is, all the requirements for an equivalence relation are satisfied.

              2. Let S be a certain set of persons. The relation "has the same age as" is an equivalence relation: a person has the same age as himself; if a has the same age as b, then b has the same age as a; if a has the same age as b, and b has the same age as c, then a has the same age as c. Figure

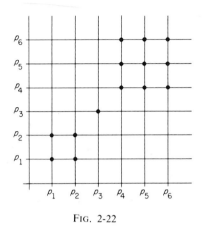

FIG. 2-22

2-22 illustrates this equivalence relation on a particular set S of six persons: p_1, p_2, p_3, p_4, p_5, and p_6. We observe from the figure: $(p_i, p_i) \in \mathcal{R}$ for $i = 1, 2, 3, 4, 5, 6$ ($\mathcal{R}$ reflexive); $(p_1, p_2) \in \mathcal{R}$ and $(p_2, p_1) \in \mathcal{R}$, $(p_4, p_5) \in \mathcal{R}$ and $(p_5, p_4) \in \mathcal{R}$, etc. ($\mathcal{R}$ symmetric); $(p_4, p_5) \in \mathcal{R}$, $(p_5, p_6) \in \mathcal{R}$, and $(p_4, p_6) \in \mathcal{R}$, etc. ($\mathcal{R}$ transitive).

3. Let S be the set of all lines in the euclidean plane. Then, since a line may be considered as parallel to itself, parallelism is an equivalence relation. Perpendicularity is not an equivalence relation, since perpendicularity is neither reflexive nor transitive.

4. Let S be the set of all integers. Then the relation $\mathcal{R}$ defined by $a\mathcal{R}b$ if, and only if, $(a - b)$ is divisible by 3 [that is, $(a - b)$ divided by 3 is an integer] is an equivalence relation. $(a - a) = 0$ is divisible by 3; if $(a - b)$ is divisible by 3, then $(b - a)$ is divisible by 3; if both $(a - b)$ and $(b - c)$ are divisible by 3, then $(a - b) + (b - c)$ is divisible by 3—but $(a - b) + (b - c) = (a - c)$. Figure 2-23 represents a subset of this equivalence relation where the only ordered pairs indicated are those involving the first 10 positive integers.

A partition of a set S is a collection of disjoint nonempty subsets of S such that every element of S is in one of the subsets of the collection. Thus, the union of all the sets of a partition is S itself, since the sets constituting a partition are subsets of S and every element of S is in one of the subsets. Also, the intersection of any two sets of a partition is the empty set, since the subsets of a partition are disjoint.

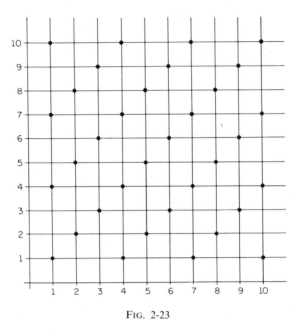

FIG. 2-23

Examples   Let $S = \{a, b, c, d, e, f\}$.
1. $[\{a, b, c\}, \{d, e, f\}]$ is a partition of S, since the subsets $\{a, b, c\}$ and $\{d, e, f\}$ are disjoint and their union is S.
2. $[\{a, c, e\}, \{d\}, \{b, f\}]$ is a partition of S, since the subsets $\{a, c, e\}$, $\{d\}$, and $\{b, f\}$ are disjoint and their union is S.
3. $[\{a\}, \{b, c, d, e, f\}]$ is a partion of S.
4. $[\{a\}, \{b\}, \{c\}, \{d\}, \{e\}, \{f\}]$ is a partition of S.

Let $\Re$ be an equivalence relation on a set S. For every element $x \in S$, define a subset $\Re_x$ of S as follows:

$$\Re_x = \{y \mid y \in S \text{ and } y \Re x\}.$$

$\Re_x$ is called the equivalence class of x; it consists of all elements $y \in S$ such that y is equivalent to x.

Examples   1. For the equivalence relation of Example 1, page 26, there are an infinite number of equivalence classes, each class consisting of exactly one real number.
2. For the equivalence relation of Example 2, page 26, each equivalence class consists of all persons of S having the same age. In particular, for the equivalence relation represented by Fig. 2-22, there are three equivalence classes—namely $\{p_1, p_2\}$, $\{p_3\}$, and $\{p_4, p_5, p_6\}$.

3. For the equivalence relation of Example 3, page 27, there are an infinite number of equivalence classes, each class consisting of all lines parallel to a given line.

4. For the equivalence relation of Example 4, page 27, there are three equivalence classes, namely, $\{\cdots, -6, -3, 0, 3, 6, \cdots\}$, $\{\cdots, -5, -2, 1, 4, 7, \cdots\}$, and $\{\cdots, -4, -1, 2, 5, 8, \cdots\}$.

We shall now prove two lemmas which we shall use to prove (Theorem 1) that the set of all equivalence classes of a set S forms a partition of S.

LEMMA 1. Let $\mathcal{R}$ be an equivalence relation on a set S. Then $a\mathcal{R}b \longleftrightarrow \mathcal{R}_a = \mathcal{R}_b$.

Proof: Suppose that $a\mathcal{R}b$. We must show that any element $c \in \mathcal{R}_a$ is also in $\mathcal{R}_b$ and, conversely, that any element $c \in \mathcal{R}_b$ is also in $\mathcal{R}_a$. Suppose that c is any element in $\mathcal{R}_a$. Then, by the definition of $\mathcal{R}_a$, $c\mathcal{R}a$. But $c\mathcal{R}a$ and $a\mathcal{R}b$ (hypothesis) $\Longrightarrow c\mathcal{R}b$, since $\mathcal{R}$ is transitive. Therefore, $c \in \mathcal{R}_b$, by the definition of $\mathcal{R}_b$. Conversely, suppose that c is any element in $\mathcal{R}_b$. Then $c\mathcal{R}b$, by the definition of $\mathcal{R}_b$. $a\mathcal{R}b$ (hypothesis) $\Longrightarrow b\mathcal{R}a$, since $\mathcal{R}$ is symmetric. $c\mathcal{R}b$ and $b\mathcal{R}a \Longrightarrow c\mathcal{R}a$, since $\mathcal{R}$ is transitive. Therefore, $c \in \mathcal{R}_a$, by the definition of $\mathcal{R}_a$. Thus, we have shown that $a\mathcal{R}b \Longrightarrow \mathcal{R}_a = \mathcal{R}_b$.

Now we must prove the converse—namely $\mathcal{R}_a = \mathcal{R}_b \Longrightarrow a\mathcal{R}b$. $b\mathcal{R}b$, since $\mathcal{R}$ is reflexive. Therefore, $b \in \mathcal{R}_b$, by the definition of $\mathcal{R}_b$. Since $\mathcal{R}_a = \mathcal{R}_b$ (hypothesis), $b \in \mathcal{R}_a$. Therefore, $b\mathcal{R}a$, by the definition of $\mathcal{R}_a$. But $b\mathcal{R}a \Longrightarrow a\mathcal{R}b$, since $\mathcal{R}$ is symmetric. Thus, $\mathcal{R}_a = \mathcal{R}_b \Longrightarrow a\mathcal{R}b$.

$$Q.E.D.$$

LEMMA 2. Let $\mathcal{R}$ be an equivalence relation on a set S. If $\mathcal{R}_a$ and $\mathcal{R}_b$ contain a common element c, then $\mathcal{R}_a = \mathcal{R}_b$. (That is, if $\mathcal{R}_a \neq \mathcal{R}_b$, then $\mathcal{R}_a$ and $\mathcal{R}_b$ cannot overlap.)

Proof: $c \in \mathcal{R}_a \Longrightarrow c\mathcal{R}a$, by the definition of $\mathcal{R}_a$. $c\mathcal{R}a \Longrightarrow a\mathcal{R}c$, since $\mathcal{R}$ is symmetric. $c \in \mathcal{R}_b \Longrightarrow c\mathcal{R}b$, by the definition of $\mathcal{R}_b$. $a\mathcal{R}c$ and $c\mathcal{R}b \Longrightarrow a\mathcal{R}b$, since $\mathcal{R}$ is transitive. But $a\mathcal{R}b \Longrightarrow \mathcal{R}_a = \mathcal{R}_b$, by Lemma 1. $Q.E.D.$

THEOREM 1. Let $\mathcal{R}$ be an equivalence relation on a set S. The set of all distinct equivalence classes $\mathcal{R}_x$ of S forms a partition of S.

Proof: Every element x of S is in one of the equivalence classes—namely in $\mathcal{R}_x$, since $x\mathcal{R}x$ by the reflexivity of $\mathcal{R}$. Since $\mathcal{R}_x$ contains x, any equivalence class $\mathcal{R}_x$ is nonempty. Distinct equivalence classes $\mathcal{R}_x$ of S are disjoint, since, by Lemma 2, if two classes contain a common element, then they consist of precisely the same elements and hence are not distinct.

Thus, the set of all distinct equivalence classes $\mathfrak{R}_x$ of S satisfies the conditions for a partition of S. $Q.E.D.$

THEOREM 2.   Let P be a partition of a set S. Define a relation $\mathfrak{R}$ as follows: For elements $a, b \in S$, $a\mathfrak{R}b$ if, and only if, there is a set $S_0 \in P$ such that $a \in S_0$ and $b \in S_0$. Then $\mathfrak{R}$ is an equivalence relation on S, and the partition of S induced by $\mathfrak{R}$ (see Theorem 1) is the given partition P.

Proof: First we show that $\mathfrak{R}$ is an equivalence relation on S: $a\mathfrak{R}a$ since a is in the same set of P as a. $a\mathfrak{R}b \Longrightarrow b\mathfrak{R}a$ since, if a and b are in the same set of P, then b and a are in the same set of P. $a\mathfrak{R}b$ and $b\mathfrak{R}c \Longrightarrow a\mathfrak{R}c$ since, if a and b are in a set S_0 of P, and if b and c are in a set S_0' of P, then $S_0 \cap S_0' \neq \phi$ since $S_0 \cap S_0'$ contains b. The sets constituting a partition are disjoint; hence, since S_0 and S_0' have an element in common, they must be one and the same set; that is, $S_0 = S_0'$. Thus, a and c are in the same set S_0 of P, which means that $a\mathfrak{R}c$.

Now we must show that the partition of S induced by $\mathfrak{R}$ is the original partition P. We do this by showing that any equivalence class $\mathfrak{R}_x$ is a set of P and any set of P is an equivalence class $\mathfrak{R}_x$. By the definition of $\mathfrak{R}$, $\mathfrak{R}_x$ consists of all elements y of S such that x and y are in the same set of the partition P. Therefore, $\mathfrak{R}_x$ is a set of the partition P. Conversely, let S_0 be a set of the partition P. Then S_0 contains an element x_0 of S. x_0 together with all the other elements (if any) of S_0 constitute the equivalence class $\mathfrak{R}_{x_0}$; that is, S_0 is one of the equivalence classes $\mathfrak{R}_x$.
                                                                        $Q.E.D.$

EXERCISES

1. Let $A = \{a, b\}$. Find the following:
    a) All relations on $A \times A$.
    b) All symmetric relations on $A \times A$.
    c) All relations on $A \times A$ which are symmetric and reflexive.
2. Which of the following are equivalence relations?
    a) a and b are sisters.
    b) a and b are cousins.
    c) a and b have the same weight and height.
    d) a and b have the same weight or height.
3. Let A be the set $\{a, b, c, d, e\}$. Consider the following relation $\mathfrak{R}$ on $A \times A$:

$$\mathfrak{R} = \{(a, b), (a, d), (d, b), (c, e), (b, d), (b, a), (e, c), (d, a)\} \cup \mathcal{E},$$

where $\mathcal{E}$ is the identity relation. Prove that $\mathfrak{R}$ is an equivalence relation. List the equivalence classes into which A is partitioned by $\mathfrak{R}$.

4. Prove that an equivalence relation $\mathcal{R}$ on a set S is a function if, and only if, $\mathcal{R}$ is the identity relation $\mathcal{E}$.

2-7. ORDER RELATIONS

A partial ordering of a set S (or an order relation on S) is a subset $\mathcal{R}$ of $S \times S$ (that is, a relation on $S \times S$) with the following properties:

1. $a\cancel{\mathcal{R}}a$ for all $a \in S$; that is, $\mathcal{R}$ is irreflexive.
2. $a\mathcal{R}b \Rightarrow b\cancel{\mathcal{R}}a$ for all $a, b \in S$; that is, $\mathcal{R}$ is asymmetric.
3. $a\mathcal{R}b$ and $b\mathcal{R}c \Rightarrow a\mathcal{R}c$ for all $a, b, c \in S$; that is, $\mathcal{R}$ is transitive.

It is convenient, but not necessary, to have asymmetry in the definition of partial ordering; asymmetry is a consequence of irreflexivity and transitivity. This can be seen as follows: Suppose that a relation $\mathcal{R}$, which is irreflexive and transitive, is also symmetric. Then $a\mathcal{R}b \Rightarrow b\mathcal{R}a$, since $\mathcal{R}$ is symmetric. $a\mathcal{R}b$ and $b\mathcal{R}a \Rightarrow a\mathcal{R}a$, since $\mathcal{R}$ is transitive. But $a\mathcal{R}a$ is impossible, since $\mathcal{R}$ is irreflexive. Hence the assumption that an irreflexive, transitive relation can be symmetric leads to a contradiction.

Some authors define an order relation $\mathcal{R}$ on a set S as a relation on $S \times S$ which is reflexive, asymmetric, and transitive. Hence, in reading other texts, it is important to observe which definition is being used and to interpret the statements in these texts accordingly. In this book we shall consistently use our given definition; that is, we shall always consider an order relation to be irreflexive.

A partially ordered set S is a set S together with an order relation $\mathcal{R}$ on S. Such a set is said to be partially ordered by $\mathcal{R}$. The expression "partial ordering" is used, since there may be elements $x, y \in S$ for which $x \neq y$, $x\cancel{\mathcal{R}}y$, and $y\cancel{\mathcal{R}}x$.

A linearly ordered set S is a partially ordered set in which for every pair of distinct elements $x, y \in S$ either $x\mathcal{R}y$ or $y\mathcal{R}x$. The relation $\mathcal{R}$ is called a linear ordering of S; S is said to be linearly ordered by $\mathcal{R}$.

Examples   1. The set of all real numbers is linearly ordered by the relation "less than," denoted by $<$. This relation $<$ is the subset of the set of all ordered pairs (x, y) of real numbers in which x is less than y; that is, $x < y$. Thus, $< = \{(x, y) \mid x$ and y are real and $x < y\}$. $<$ is a partial ordering of the real numbers because for any real numbers x, y, z: $x \not< x$; $x < y \Rightarrow y \not< x$; $x < y$ and $y < z \Rightarrow x < z$. Moreover, $<$ is a linear ordering of the real numbers because for any two distinct real numbers x and y either $x < y$ or $y < x$. In Fig. 2-24 the shaded region represents pairs (x, y) belonging to the relation $<$; points on or below the line $y = x$ represent pairs not belonging to $<$.

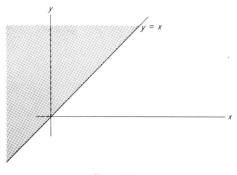

FIG. 2-24

2. Let S be the set of all integers. The relation "divides,"
denoted by "$\mathfrak{D}$," is the subset of the set of all ordered
pairs (x, y) of integers in which x divides y; that is, y
divided by x is an integer. "x divides y" is denoted by
$x \mid y$. Thus, $\mathfrak{D} = \{(x, y) \mid x$ and y are integers and $x \mid y\}$.
The relation $\mathfrak{D} - \mathcal{E}$, where $\mathcal{E}$ is the identity relation on S,
is the set $\{(x, y) \mid x$ and y are integers, $x \neq y$, and $x \mid y\}$.
$\mathfrak{D} - \mathcal{E}$ is a partial ordering of S because for any integers
x, y, z: $(x, x) \notin \mathfrak{D} - \mathcal{E}$, by the definition of $\mathfrak{D} - \mathcal{E}$; if
$x \neq y$, then $x \mid y \Rightarrow y \nmid x$, where "$\nmid$" means "does not
divide"; if $x \neq y$ and $x \mid y$ (thus, $x < y$) and if $y \neq z$ and
$y \mid z$ (thus, $y < z$), then $x \neq z$ and $x \mid z$. $\mathfrak{D} \mathrel{\llcorner} \mathcal{E}$ is not a
linear ordering of S because there are pairs of integers
(x, y) such that $x \nmid y$ and $y \nmid x$. For example, $(2, 3)$ is such
a pair. In Fig. 2-25 a subset of the relation $\mathfrak{D} - \mathcal{E}$ is
indicated—namely, the subset involving the integers -4,
$-3, -2, -1, 0, 1, 2, 3$, and 4.

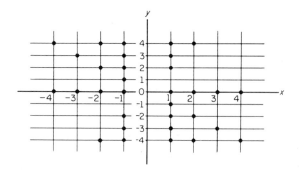

FIG. 2-25

3. The set S of all subsets of a given set T is partially or dered by the relation "is a proper subset of," denoted by $\mathcal{P}$. This relation $\mathcal{P}$ is the subset of the set of all ordered pairs (X, Y) of subsets of T in which X is a proper subset of Y. Thus, $\mathcal{P} = \{(X, Y) \mid X, Y \in S \text{ and } X \subset Y\}$, or $\mathcal{P} = \{(X, Y) \mid X, Y \subseteq T \text{ and } X \subset Y\}$. $\mathcal{P}$ is a partial ordering of S because for any subsets X, Y, Z of T: $X \not\subset X$; if $X \subset Y$, then $Y \not\subset X$; if $X \subset Y$ and $Y \subset Z$, then $X \subset Z$. In general, $\mathcal{P}$ is not a linear ordering of S since if a and b are any two distinct elements of T, then $\{a\} \not\subset \{b\}$ and $\{b\} \not\subset \{a\}$. If the set T contains, at most, one element, then the set of all subsets of T is linearly ordered by $\mathcal{P}$.

4. Let S be the set of all points in the configuration

Define a relation $\mathcal{R}$ on S as follows: For $x, y \in S$, $x\mathcal{R}y$ if, and only if, one can proceed from point x to point y by moving upward only in the configuration. $\mathcal{R}$ is a partial ordering of S, but not a linear ordering, since for points z_1 and z_2 on different branches of the fork—for example,

z_2, $z_1\not\mathcal{R}z_2$ and $z_2\not\mathcal{R}z_1$.

THEOREM 3. If a set S is partially or linearly ordered by a relation $\mathcal{R}$, then S is partially or linearly ordered by $\mathcal{R}^{-1}$.

Proof: $(x, x) \notin \mathcal{R}^{-1}$ since $(x, x) \notin \mathcal{R}$. Suppose that (x, y) and (y, z) are both in $\mathcal{R}^{-1}$. Then (z, y) and (y, x) are both in $\mathcal{R}$. Therefore, since $\mathcal{R}$ is transitive, $(z, x) \in \mathcal{R}$. But then $(x, z) \in \mathcal{R}^{-1}$ and hence $\mathcal{R}^{-1}$ is transitive. Since $\mathcal{R}^{-1}$ is irreflexive and transitive, $\mathcal{R}^{-1}$ is a partial ordering of S (see page 31). If $\mathcal{R}$ is a linear ordering of S, then for every pair of distinct elements $x, y \in S$, either $x\mathcal{R}y$ or $y\mathcal{R}x$. But then, for every pair of distinct elements $x, y \in S$, either $y\mathcal{R}^{-1}x$ or $x\mathcal{R}^{-1}y$. Hence, if $\mathcal{R}$ is a linear ordering of S, then $\mathcal{R}^{-1}$ is also. Q.E.D.

Let S be a set partially ordered by a relation $\mathcal{R}$, and let A be a subset of S. An element $x \in S$ is said to be an upper bound of A if for each $a \in A$ either $a = x$ or $a\mathcal{R}x$. (Of course, for a particular element a, we cannot have both $a = x$ and $a\mathcal{R}x$, since any order relation is irreflexive.) An element $x \in S$ is said to be the least upper bound (lub) of A if x is an upper bound of A and $x\mathcal{R}x'$ for all upper bounds x' of A such that $x' \neq x$.

Similarly, an element $y \in S$ is said to be a lower bound of A if for each $a \in A$ either $a = y$ or $y\Re a$. y is said to be the greatest lower bound (glb) of A if y is a lower bound of A and $y'\Re y$ for all lower bounds y' of A such that $y' \neq y$.

Examples
1. Let S be the set of real numbers ordered by the relation "less than" (Example 1, page 31). Then S has no upper or lower bounds. The subset $A = \{x \mid x \in S$ and $5 \leq x < \infty\}$ has no upper bound. All real numbers which are less than or equal to 5 are lower bounds of A; 5 is the greatest lower bound. For the subset $B = \{x \mid x \in S$ and $0 < x \leq 1\}$, the greatest lower bound is 0; the least upper bound is 1. All real numbers less than or equal to zero are lower bounds; all real numbers greater than or equal to 1 are upper bounds.

2. Let S be the set of all integers ordered by the relation $\mathfrak{D} - \mathfrak{E}$ (Example 2, page 32). For the subset $A = \{2, 3, 5\}$, 1 is the greatest lower bound; 30 is the least upper bound. -1 is the only other lower bound; all integral multiples of 30 are upper bounds.

3. Let S be the set of all subsets of a given set T ordered by the relation $\mathcal{P}$ (Example 3, page 33). Then the greatest lower bound of $\{A, B\}$, where $A, B \in S$, is $A \cap B$, since $A \cap B \subseteq A, A \cap B \subseteq B$, and $A \cap B$ is the "largest" subset common to both A and B. The least upper bound of $\{A, B\}$ is $A \cup B$, since $A \subseteq A \cup B, B \subseteq A \cup B$, and $A \cup B$ is the "smallest" subset containing both A and B. A lower bound of $\{A, B\}$ is any subset of $A \cap B$; an upper bound is any set containing $A \cup B$.

4. Let S and R be defined as in Example 4, page 33. Let $A = \{x_1, x_2, x_3\}$, where the points x_1, x_2, x_3, and x_4 are arranged as follows: . Then the least upper bound of A is x_4; all points above and including x_4 are upper bounds of A. A has no lower bounds and hence no greatest lower bound.

5. Let $S = \{x \mid x$ is a real number and $0 \leq x < 1$ or $1 < x \leq 6\}$ be ordered by the relation "less than." Then the subset $A = \{x \mid x$ is a real number and $0 \leq x < 1\}$ has as upper bounds every element of the set $\{x \mid x$ is a real number and $1 < x \leq 6\}$, but A has no least upper bound.

A partially ordered set S is said to be well ordered if every nonempty subset A of S has a greatest lower bound in A.

Examples

1. The real numbers are not well ordered by the relation "less than" (Example 1, page 31). The subset $A = \{x \mid x$ is real and $0 < x \le 1\}$ has a greatest lower bound, namely 0, but $0 \notin A$.

2. The set of all integers is not well ordered by the relation $\mathcal{D} - \mathcal{E}$ (Example 2, page 32). The subset $A = \{2, 3, 5\}$ has a greatest lower bound, namely 1, but $1 \notin A$.

3. The set of all subsets of a given set T is not well ordered by the relation $\mathcal{P}$ (Example 3, page 33). The subset $\{A, B\}$ of S has a greatest lower bound, namely $A \cap B$, but, in general, $A \cap B \ne A$ or B.

4. The positive integers are well ordered by the relation "less than"; the set of all integers greater than any particular integer is well ordered by "less than."

5. The set of all integers is not well ordered by "less than," since, for example, the subset $\{\cdots, -3, -2, -1, 0\}$ does not have a greatest lower bound.

6. Any linearly ordered finite set is well ordered.

THEOREM 4. If a set S is well ordered by a relation $\mathcal{R}$, then S is linearly ordered by $\mathcal{R}$.

Proof: Suppose that S is not linearly ordered by $\mathcal{R}$. Then S contains two distinct elements x and y such that $x\mathcal{R}y$ and $y\mathcal{R}x$. Therefore, the subset of S consisting of x and y, that is, $\{x, y\}$, does not contain a greatest lower bound. Hence S is not well ordered. Thus, if S is well ordered, S must be linearly ordered. (See the discussion on the contrapositive of a statement, page 8.) $Q.E.D.$

EXERCISES

1. Which of the relations in Exercise 1 of Sec. 2-4 are order relations on $A \times A$? Which of the order relations are a linear ordering of A? Give reasons.

2. The following questions refer to relation $\mathcal{R}_7$ of Exercise 1 of Sec. 2-4:
   a) Is A well ordered by $\mathcal{R}_7$; why?
   b) Find the least upper bounds, if any, of the subsets: i) $\{a, b, c\}$; ii) $\{a\}$; iii) $\{c, d\}$.

3. Prove that if a least upper bound exists, it is unique.

2-8. ISOMORPHIC SYSTEMS

An algebraic system consists of one or more nonempty sets $S_1, S_2, \cdots, S_k$ together with a number of operations (possibly none) $\mathcal{O}_1, \mathcal{O}_2, \cdots, \mathcal{O}_m$ and a number of relations (possibly none) $\mathcal{R}_1, \mathcal{R}_2, \cdots, \mathcal{R}_n$. We denote such a system by $[S_1, \cdots, S_k; \mathcal{O}_1, \cdots, \mathcal{O}_m; \mathcal{R}_1, \cdots, \mathcal{R}_n]$.

Examples   1. $[S; \mu]$ is an algebraic system, where $S = \{1, 2, 3\}$ and the binary operation μ is defined by the table

μ	1	2	3
1	2	3	1
2	3	1	2
3	1	2	3

  2. $[S; +; <]$ is an algebraic system, where S is the set of all real numbers, $+$ is ordinary addition, and $<$ is the order relation "less than."

Consider two algebraic systems each of which consists of a set, two binary operations, and a relation. Let us denote the first system by $[S; +, \cdot; \mathcal{R}]$ and the second system by $[\overline{S}; \overline{+}, \overline{\cdot}; \overline{\mathcal{R}}]$, where S and $\overline{S}$ are sets; $+, \cdot, \overline{+}, \overline{\cdot}$ are binary operations; and $\mathcal{R}$ and $\overline{\mathcal{R}}$ are relations. The two systems are said to be isomorphic if there is a 1:1 correspondence ψ between the elements of S and the elements of $\overline{S}$ such that for all $a, b \in S$ 1) $\psi(a + b) = \psi(a) \overline{+} \psi(b)$; 2) $\psi(a \cdot b) = \psi(a) \overline{\cdot} \psi(b)$; and 3) $a \mathcal{R} b \longleftrightarrow \psi(a) \overline{\mathcal{R}} \psi(b)$. Such a correspondence ψ is called an *isomorphism* between the two systems. Using the notation "$x \leftrightarrow \overline{x}$" to indicate that an element $x \in S$ corresponds under ψ to the element $\overline{x} \in \overline{S}$, parts 1 and 2 may be restated as $a \leftrightarrow \psi(a)$ and $b \leftrightarrow \psi(b)$ imply that $a + b \leftrightarrow \psi(a) \overline{+} \psi(b)$ and $a \cdot b \leftrightarrow \psi(a) \overline{\cdot} \psi(b)$.

Sometimes we say that the correspondence ψ preserves the operations and relations. Loosely speaking, two systems are isomorphic when they are indistinguishable abstractly; that is, when the only difference between them is in the notation used for their elements, operations, and relations. In other words, the structures of the two systems are so similar that one system may be regarded simply as a relabeling of the other. For systems containing more than one set, or containing a greater or smaller number of operations and relations, the definition of isomorphism given above can be extended or modified accordingly in conformity with conditions 1, 2, and 3.

Examples 1. Consider the following two systems:

a) $[S_1; \mu]$, where $S_1 = \{1, 2, 3\}$ and the binary operation μ is defined by the table:

μ	1	2	3
1	2	3	1
2	3	1	2
3	1	2	3

b) $[S_2; \nu]$, where $S_2 = \{a, b, c\}$ and the binary operation ν is defined by the table:

ν	a	b	c
a	b	c	a
b	c	a	b
c	a	b	c

These two systems are isomorphic, since there is a 1:1 correspondence ψ between S_1 and S_2, namely, $\psi(1) = a$; $\psi(2) = b$; $\psi(3) = c$; and $\psi(1 \; \mu \; 2) = \psi(3) = c = a \; \nu \; b = \psi(1) \; \nu \; \psi(2)$; $\psi(2 \; \mu \; 3) = \psi(2) = b = b \; \nu \; c = \psi(2) \; \nu \; \psi(3)$; etc.

2. Let S be the set of all real numbers; let S' be the set of positive-real numbers; let $<$ be the order relation "less than"; let $+$ be ordinary addition; let $\cdot$ be ordinary multiplication. Then $[S; +; <]$ and $[S'; \cdot; <]$ are isomorphic since there is a 1:1 correspondence ψ between S and S', namely, $\psi(x) = 10^x$ for $x \in S$, where $\psi(x + y) = 10^{x+y} = 10^x \cdot 10^y = \psi(x) \cdot \psi(y)$ and $x < y \iff 10^x < 10^y$; that is, $x < y \iff \psi(x) < \psi(y)$.

3. Consider the following three systems:

a) $[S; \mu]$, where $S = \{a, b, c, d\}$ and the binary operation μ is defined by the table:

μ	a	b	c	d
a	a	b	c	d
b	b	c	d	a
c	c	d	a	b
d	d	a	b	c

b) $[T; \nu]$, where $T = \{1, 2, 3, 4\}$ and the binary operation ν is defined by the table:

ν	1	2	3	4
1	1	2	3	4
2	2	1	4	3
3	3	4	1	2
4	4	3	2	1

c) $[U; \eta]$, where $U = \{p, q, r, s\}$ and the binary operation η is defined by the table:

η	p	q	r	s
p	r	s	p	q
q	s	r	q	p
r	p	q	r	s
s	q	p	s	r

The first two systems are not isomorphic: For the 1:1 correspondence $\psi(a) = 1$; $\psi(b) = 2$; $\psi(c) = 3$; and $\psi(d) = 4$, we have $\psi(b \, \mu \, b) = \psi(c) = 3 \neq 1 = 2 \, \nu \, 2 = \psi(b) \, \nu \, \psi(b)$. For the 1:1 correspondence $\psi(a) = 2$; $\psi(b) = 3$; $\psi(c) = 1$; and $\psi(d) = 4$, we have $\psi(a \, \mu \, b) = \psi(b) = 3 \neq 4 = 2 \, \nu \, 3 = \psi(a) \, \nu \, \psi(b)$. Similarly, one can show that for any 1:1 correspondence between the first two sets S and T, the operation μ is not preserved under the correspondence. The second and third systems are isomorphic; the isomorphism is $\psi(1) = r$; $\psi(2) = p$; $\psi(3) = q$; and $\psi(4) = s$. Notice that $\psi(2 \, \nu \, 3) = \psi(4) = s = p \, \eta \, q = \psi(2) \, \eta \, \psi(3)$, etc.

It is easy to show that the relation of being isomorphic to is an equivalence relation on a given set of algebraic systems. Hence, since the first two systems in the above example are not isomorphic, it follows that the first and third systems are also not isomorphic. Otherwise, if the first and third systems were isomorphic, this isomorphism composed (see page 24) with the isomorphism of the second and third systems would be an isomorphism of the first and second.

EXERCISES

1. Let I be the set of all positive integers; that is, $I = \{1, 2, 3, \cdots\}$. Let $\bar{I} = \{5, 10, 15, \cdots\}$. Consider the systems $S = [I; +, \cdot; <]$ and $\bar{S} = [\bar{I}; +, \cdot; <]$, where "$+$", "$\cdot$", and "$<$" denote ordinary addition, ordinary multiplication, and the relation "less than," respectively. Show that S is isomorphic to $\bar{S}$.

2. Suppose that there is an isomorphism between $[S_1; \mathcal{O}_1]$ and $[S_2; \mathcal{O}_2]$, where S_1 and S_2 are sets and $\mathcal{O}_1$ and $\mathcal{O}_2$ are order relations. Prove that if S_1 is well ordered by $\mathcal{O}_1$, then S_2 is well ordered by $\mathcal{O}_2$.

3 / The Positive Integers

3-1. AXIOMS FOR THE POSITIVE INTEGERS

In the preceding chapters we discussed certain basic mathematical concepts. To illustrate these concepts, we used examples involving properties of the integers or of the real numbers. None of these examples played an essential role in the development of the concepts discussed; they served merely as illustrations.

In this chapter we shall develop an axiomatic theory of the positive integers $1, 2, 3, \cdots$. This means that we shall assume no previous knowledge concerning the positive integers but shall deduce from our axioms, by logical means, any of the properties of the positive integers which we wish to consider.

Many possible sets of axioms might be chosen for any axiomatic theory. In the axiom set which we have chosen, there are three undefined concepts: positive integer, addition $(+)$, and multiplication $(\cdot)$, where addition and multiplication are binary operations.

DEFINITION 1. The set of positive integers is a set **I**, closed[1] with respect to two binary operations, called addition $(+)$ and multiplication $(\cdot)$, and satisfying the following axioms:

Axiom 1. Addition and multiplication are associative: For all elements a, b, c in **I**, $a + (b + c) = (a + b) + c$; and $a(bc) = (ab)c$. (We often use the notation "ab" in place of "$a \cdot b$.")

Axiom 2. Addition and multiplication are commutative: For all elements a, b in **I**, $a + b = b + a$; and $ab = ba$.

Axiom 3. Multiplication is distributive over addition: For all elements a, b, c in **I**, $a(b + c) = ab + ac$.

[1]See page 25.

Axiom 4. There is an element in **I**, denoted by "1," such that $1a = a$ for every element a in **I**. (Such an element 1 is called a unit element or a multiplicative identity.)

Axiom 5. The cancellation laws of addition and multiplication hold: For all elements a, b, c in **I**, if $a + b = a + c$, then $b = c$; if $ab = ac$, then $b = c$.

Axiom 6. For any two elements a, b in **I**, exactly one of the following alternatives holds: $a = b$; there is an element x in **I** such that $a + x = b$; there is an element y in **I** such that $a = b + y$.

Axiom 7. Any subset H of **I** which has the following two properties is all of **I**: a) $1 \in H$, and b) whenever $x \in H$, then $x + 1 \in H$.

It can be shown that some of these axioms (2, 5, and the associativity of multiplication in 1) are redundant, since they can be proved from the remaining axioms. They are listed, however, to simplify the proofs of the theorems which will follow.

3-2. CONSEQUENCES OF AXIOMS 1 THROUGH 6

In this section we shall deduce some elementary consequences of the first six axioms.

Axiom 4 asserts the existence of a multiplicative identity; that is, an element 1 with the property that $1a = a$ for all elements a in **I**. Nothing is said, however, about whether there are other positive integers with this same property. Theorem 1 asserts that there are not; that is, that the element 1 is the only such positive integer.

THEOREM 1. The element 1 is unique; that is, if there is an element $1'$ in **I** such that $1'a = a$ for all a in **I**, then $1' = 1$.

Proof: $1'a = a$, by hypothesis; hence, $1'a = 1a$, by Axiom 4. Therefore, $a1' = a1$, by Axiom 2, and $1' = 1$, by Axiom 5. *Q.E.D.*

Axiom 6 asserts that if $a \neq b$, then there is an element x such that $a + x = b$ or an element y such that $a = b + y$. Again, nothing is said about the uniqueness of these elements x and y. Theorem 2, however, asserts that x and y are unique.

THEOREM 2. The elements x and y of Axiom 6 are unique.

Proof: Suppose that $a + x = b$ and $a + x' = b$. Then, by substitution, $a + x = a + x'$. Therefore, by Axiom 5, $x = x'$. A similar argument establishes the uniqueness of y. *Q.E.D.*

The notion of order is introduced by means of Axiom 6, according to the following definition.

DEFINITION 2.   If a and b are elements in $\mathbf{I}$, then a is said to be less than b (or, equivalently, b is said to be greater than a) if, and only if, there is an element x in $\mathbf{I}$ such that $a + x = b$.

We denote "a is less than b" by $a < b$ or $b > a$. If $a = b$ or $a < b$, we write $a \leq b$ or $b \geq a$. In proving Theorem 6 we show that "less than" is indeed an order relation. (See Sec. 2-7.)

THEOREM 3.   For any two elements a, b in $\mathbf{I}$, exactly one of the following alternatives holds: $a = b, a < b$, or $b < a$.

Proof: This theorem merely restates Axiom 6 in terms of the symbol "$<$."

THEOREM 4.   For any two elements a, b in $\mathbf{I}$, $a < a + b$.

Proof: There is an element x in $\mathbf{I}$, namely $x = b$, such that $a + x = a + b$. Therefore, by Definition 2, $a < a + b$.   *Q.E.D.*

We shall denote "$1 + 1$" by "2," "$2 + 1$" by "3," "$3 + 1$" by "4," and so on.

THEOREM 5.   a) $1 \neq 2$.
                b) $2 \neq 3$.
                c) $1 \neq 3$.
                d) $2 + 2 = 4$.

Proof: a) By our notation, $1 + 1 = 2$. Therefore, by Definition 2, $1 < 2$. Hence, by Theorem 3, $1 \neq 2$.

b) By our notation, $2 + 1 = 3$. Therefore, by Definition 2, $2 < 3$. Hence, by Theorem 3, $2 \neq 3$.

c) By our notation and Axiom 2, $1 + 2 = 3$. Therefore, by Definition 2, $1 < 3$. Hence, by Theorem 3, $1 \neq 3$.

d) By our notation and substitution, $2 + 2 = 2 + (1 + 1)$. Therefore, by Axiom 1, $2 + 2 = (2 + 1) + 1$. Or, by our notation, $2 + 2 = 3 + 1$. Using our notation again, $2 + 2 = 4$.   *Q.E.D.*

THEOREM 6.   "Less than" is an order relation on $\mathbf{I}$.

Proof: For any element a in $\mathbf{I}$, $a = a$. Therefore, by Theorem 3, $a \not< a$. If $a < b$, then, by Theorem 3, $b \not< a$. Next we must show that if $a < b$ and $b < c$, then $a < c$. Now if $a < b$, then, by Definition 2, there is an element x in $\mathbf{I}$ such that $a + x = b$. If $b < c$, then, by Definition 2, there is an element y in $\mathbf{I}$ such that $b + y = c$. Substituting $(a + x)$ for b in the last equation gives $(a + x) + y = c$. Applying Axiom 1 to the left side of the above equation, we have $a + (x + y) = c$. But, by Definition 2, this means that $a < c$.   *Q.E.D.*

COROLLARY.   The positive integers are linearly ordered by "less than."

Proof: This is an immediate consequence of Theorems 3 and 6.

THEOREM 7.   For any elements a, b, c in $\mathbf{I}$, $a < b$ if, and only if, $a + c < b + c$.

Proof: If $a < b$, then, by Definition 2, there is an element x in $\mathbf{I}$ such that $a + x = b$. Adding c to both sides of this equation, we have $(a + x) + c = b + c$. Applying Axiom 1 to the left side of the above equation, we have $a + (x + c) = b + c$. By Axiom 2, this equation may be replaced by $a + (c + x) = b + c$. Using Axiom 1 again, we have $(a + c) + x = b + c$. But, by Definition 2, this means that $a + c < b + c$.

Conversely, suppose that $a + c < b + c$. Then, by Definition 2, there is an element x in $\mathbf{I}$ such that $(a + c) + x = b + c$. Applying Axiom 2 to both sides of the above equation, we have $(c + a) + x = c + b$. By Axiom 1, this equation may be replaced by $c + (a + x) = c + b$. But, by Axiom 5, this means that $a + x = b$. Hence, by Definition 2, $a < b$.   *Q.E.D.*

THEOREM 8.   For any elements a, b, c in $\mathbf{I}$, $a < b$ if, and only if, $ac < bc$.

Proof: If $a < b$, then, by Definition 2, there is an element x in $\mathbf{I}$ such that $a + x = b$. Multiplying both sides of this equation by c, we have $(a + x)c = bc$. Therefore, by Axioms 2 (used twice) and 3, we have $ac + xc = bc$. But, by Definition 2, this means that $ac < bc$.

Conversely, suppose that $ac < bc$. By Theorem 3, either $a = b$, $a < b$, or $b < a$. If $a = b$, then $ac = bc$; by Theorem 3, this is contrary to the hypothesis. If $b < a$, then, by the first half of the proof of this theorem, $bc < ac$. But, by Theorem 3, this is contrary to the hypothesis. Therefore, the only remaining alternative is $a < b$.   *Q.E.D.*

THEOREM 9.   For any elements a, b, c, d in $\mathbf{I}$, if $a < b$ and $c < d$, then a) $a + c < b + d$, and b) $ac < bd$.

Proof: a) By hypothesis, $a < b$. Therefore, by Theorem 7, $a + c < b + c$. By hypothesis, $c < d$. Therefore, by Theorem 7, $c + b < d + b$. Using Axiom 2, this last inequality may be replaced by $b + c < b + d$. Therefore, since $a + c < b + c$ and since $b + c < b + d$, it follows from Theorem 6 that $a + c < b + d$.

b) By hypothesis, $a < b$. Therefore, by Theorem 8, $ac < bc$. By hypothesis, $c < d$. Therefore, by Theorem 8, $cb < db$. Using Axiom 2, this last inequality may be replaced by $bc < bd$. Therefore, since $ac < bc$ and since $bc < bd$, it follows from Theorem 6 that $ac < bd$.   *Q.E.D.*

EXERCISES

1. Finish the proof of Theorem 2 (page 41); that is, prove that y is unique.

2. Prove that if $a + c = b + c$, then $a = b$.
3. Prove that if $a > b$ and $b > c$, then $a > c$.
4. Prove that $(a + b) + c = (c + b) + a$.
5. Prove that $a + a = 2a$. (HINT: Use Axioms 3 and 4.)
6. Prove that $(a + b)(c + d) = ac + ad + bc + bd$.
7. Prove that $(a + b)(a + b) = a^2 + 2ab + b^2$.
8. Prove each of the following:
    a) $2 + 3 = 5$.
    b) $2 \cdot 3 = 6$.
    c) $2 \cdot 4 = 8$.
9. Prove that for any positive integer a, if $1 < a$, then $a < a^2 < a^3$.
10. Let a, b, c, and d be elements of $\mathbf{I}$. Prove that if $a + b = c + d$ and $a < c$, then $d < b$.
11. Prove that there is no positive integer x such that $2x = 1$.

3-3. CONSEQUENCES OF AXIOMS 1 THROUGH 7

Now we shall investigate some consequences of Axiom 7, which states that any subset H of $\mathbf{I}$ with the following two properties is the set $\mathbf{I}$ itself: a) $1 \in H$, and b) whenever $x \in H$, then $x + 1 \in H$. According to this axiom, the positive integers are of the form 1, $1 + 1$, $(1 + 1) + 1$, $((1 + 1) + 1) + 1, \cdots$. We shall denote these integers by "1," "2," "3," "4," $\cdots$.

Axiom 7 will be used in proving Theorem 10, sometimes called the first principle of finite induction. This theorem will be seen to be extremely useful in proving statements involving all the positive integers.

THEOREM 10. (First Principle of Finite Induction). Suppose that a statement P_n is associated with every positive integer n. If the statement P_1 is valid, and if $P_n \Rightarrow P_{n+1}$ for all positive integers n, then the statements P_n are all valid.

Proof: The set of positive integers n for which P_n is valid satisfies the hypothesis of Axiom 7. Hence the conclusion of Axiom 7 must hold. Thus, the set of positive integers n for which P_n is valid is the entire set of positive integers. *Q.E.D.*

Suppose that we have a statement P_1 which is valid, and suppose that $P_1 \Rightarrow P_2$. Then, by Rule 1, Sec. 1-4, P_2 is also valid. Now if, in addition, $P_2 \Rightarrow P_3$, then, by Rule 1, P_3 is valid. Moreover, if $P_3 \Rightarrow P_4$, then, by Rule 1 again, P_4 is valid; and so on. Indeed, according to Theorem 10, as long as $P_n \Rightarrow P_{n+1}$ for all positive integers n, then all the statements P_n will be valid (providing that P_1 is).

We shall now show how Theorem 10 may be used in proving certain statements involving all the positive integers. A proof using Theorem 10 is called a proof by mathematical induction. For purposes of illustration, we shall use, in the following two examples, some of the properties of the positive integers with which we were acquainted before our present axiomatic study.

Examples 1. Suppose we wish to prove that for all positive integers n,

$1 + 2 + 3 + \cdots + n = \dfrac{n(n + 1)}{2}$. We let P_n be the state-

ment "$1 + 2 + 3 + \cdots + n = \dfrac{n(n + 1)}{2}$." Thus, a state-

ment "P_n" is associated with every positive integer n. Then

P_1 is the statement "$1 = \dfrac{1(1 + 1)}{2}$," which is valid. Now

we must show that $P_n \implies P_{n+1}$, where P_{n+1} is the statement

"$1 + 2 + 3 + \cdots + n + (n + 1)$

$$= \frac{(n + 1)((n + 1) + 1)}{2},"$$

the right side of which equals $\dfrac{(n + 1)(n + 2)}{2}$. But, by P_n,

the sum of the first n terms on the left may be replaced by

$\dfrac{n(n + 1)}{2}$; that is,

$$1 + 2 + 3 + \cdots + n + (n + 1) = \frac{n(n + 1)}{2} + (n + 1).$$

Moreover,

$$\frac{n(n + 1)}{2} + (n + 1) = \frac{n(n + 1) + 2(n + 1)}{2}$$

$$= \frac{(n + 1)(n + 2)}{2}.$$

Therefore,

$$1 + 2 + 3 + \cdots + n + (n + 1) = \frac{(n + 1)(n + 2)}{2}.$$

Thus, by using P_n, we have established P_{n+1}; that is, we have shown that $P_n \implies P_{n+1}$. Now the entire hypothesis of Theorem 10 is satisfied; hence the conclusion of Theorem 10 must hold—namely, that our statements P_n are valid for all positive integers n.

2. Suppose we wish to prove that a set of n elements has exactly 2^n subsets. We let P_n be the statement "A set of

n elements has exactly 2^n subsets." Thus, a statement "P_n" is associated with every positive integer n. Then P_1 is the statement "A set of 1 element has exactly 2^1 (that is, 2) subsets." P_1 is valid, since a set consisting of a single element, say the set $\{a\}$, has exactly two subsets, namely, ϕ and $\{a\}$. Now we must show that $P_n \Rightarrow P_{n+1}$, where P_{n+1} is the statement "A set of $(n + 1)$ elements has exactly 2^{n+1} subsets." Suppose that S is a set of $(n + 1)$ elements. Then, by P_n, exactly 2^n subsets of S can be formed using any n elements of S (one of these subsets being ϕ). By adjoining the remaining $(n + 1)^{st}$ element to each of these 2^n subsets, we obtain 2^n additional subsets of S. These 2^n subsets together with the original 2^n subsets constitute all of the subsets of S. Thus, we have altogether $2^n + 2^n$ subsets. But $2^n + 2^n = 2 \cdot 2^n = 2^{n+1}$. Thus, we have shown that $P_n \Rightarrow P_{n+1}$. Now the entire hypothesis of Theorem 10 is satisfied; hence the conclusion of Theorem 10 must hold—namely, that our statements P_n are valid for all positive integers n.

Notice that in constructing a proof by mathematical induction it is absolutely essential that we do both of the following two things:

1. We must show that P_1 is valid.
2. We must show that $P_n \Rightarrow P_{n+1}$ for all positive integers n. Even if $P_n \Rightarrow P_{n+1}$ for all positive integers n, unless P_1 is valid we cannot conclude anything about the validity of $P_2, P_3, P_4, \cdots$. For example, the statement

$$P_n: \text{``}1 + 2 + 3 + \cdots + n = \frac{n^2 + n + 1}{2}\text{''}$$ is not valid for $n = 1$, since

$1 \neq \dfrac{1^2 + 1 + 1}{2} = \dfrac{3}{2}$; that is, P_1 is not valid. P_2 is not valid, since

$1 + 2 \neq \dfrac{2^2 + 2 + 1}{2} = \dfrac{7}{2}$. But we can show that $P_n \Rightarrow P_{n+1}$, where P_{n+1} is the statement

$$\text{``}1 + 2 + 3 + \cdots + n + (n + 1) = \frac{(n + 1)^2 + (n + 1) + 1}{2}\text{.''}$$

For, by P_n, the sum of the first n terms on the left may be replaced by $\dfrac{n^2 + n + 1}{2}$; that is, $1 + 2 + 3 + \cdots + n + (n + 1) = \dfrac{n^2 + n + 1}{2} + (n + 1)$. Moreover, $\dfrac{n^2 + n + 1}{2} + (n + 1) = \dfrac{n^2 + n + 1 + 2(n + 1)}{2} = \dfrac{(n + 1)^2 + (n + 1) + 1}{2}$. Thus, by using P_n, we have established P_{n+1}; that is, we have shown that $P_n \Rightarrow P_{n+1}$. Nevertheless, P_n is not valid for

any positive integer n; indeed, in Example 1 (page 45) we proved that
$1 + 2 + 3 + \cdots + n = \dfrac{n(n + 1)}{2}$.

Similarly, consider the statement P_n: "If n is a positive integer, then the only positive integers x which divide $N = n^2 - n + 11$ are N and 1." (We say that x divides N is there is an integer y such that $x \cdot y = N$.) P_1 is valid, since the only positive integers which divide $1^2 - 1 + 11 = 11$ are 1 and 11. P_2 is valid, since the only positive integers which divide $2^2 - 2 + 11 = 13$ are 1 and 13. Similarly, it can be shown that P_3, $P_4, \cdots$, and P_{10} are all valid. Nevertheless, we cannot conclude that P_n is valid for all n. Indeed P_{11} is not valid, since 1, 11, and 121 all divide $11^2 - 11 + 11 = 121$.

We shall now return to our axiomatic study of the positive integers, obtaining further results by using the first principle of finite induction.

DEFINITION 3. For any elements x and m in **I**, a) $x^1 = x$; and b) $x^{m+1} = x^m \cdot x^1$.

THEOREM 11. For any elements x, m, n in **I**, $x^m \cdot x^n = x^{m+n}$.

Proof: Let P_n be the statement "$x^m \cdot x^n = x^{m+n}$ for a fixed m in **I**." Then P_1 is the statement "$x^m \cdot x^1 = x^{m+1}$." By Definition 3b, P_1 is valid. Now we must show that $P_n \Rightarrow P_{n+1}$, where P_{n+1} is the statement "$x^m \cdot x^{n+1} = x^{m+(n+1)}$." By Definition 3b, $x^m \cdot x^{n+1} = x^m(x^n \cdot x^1)$. Using Axiom 1, this equation may be replaced by $x^m \cdot x^{n+1} = (x^m \cdot x^n)x^1$. Applying P_n to the right side of this equation, we have $x^m \cdot x^{n+1} = x^{m+n} \cdot x^1$. By Definition 3b, this equation may be replaced by $x^m \cdot x^{n+1} = x^{(m+n)+1}$. Finally, by Axiom 1, we have $x^m \cdot x^{n+1} = x^{m+(n+1)}$. Thus, we have shown that $P_n \Rightarrow P_{n+1}$. Now, since the hypothesis of Theorem 10 is satisfied, the conclusion of Theorem 10 must hold—namely, that our statements P_n are valid for all positive integers n. *Q.E.D.*

Our next theorem states that the unit element 1 is the smallest positive integer.

THEOREM 12. For all elements n in **I**, $1 \leq n$.

Proof: Let P_n be the statement "$1 \leq n$." Then P_1 is the statement "$1 \leq 1$." Since $1 = 1$, P_1 is valid. Now we must show that $P_n \Rightarrow P_{n+1}$, where P_{n+1} is the statement "$1 \leq n + 1$." According to P_n, either $1 = n$ or $1 < n$. If $1 = n$, then, by substituting n for 1, we have $1 + 1 = n + 1$. Hence, by Definition 2, $1 < n + 1$. If $1 < n$, then, by Theorem 7, $1 + 1 < n + 1$. Therefore, by Definition 2, there is a positive integer x such that $(1 + 1) + x = n + 1$. By Axiom 1, this equation may be replaced by $1 + (1 + x) = n + 1$. But, by Definition 2, this means that $1 < n + 1$.

Hence $P_n \Rightarrow P_{n+1}$. Thus, by Theorem 10, our statements P_n are valid for all positive integers n.   *Q.E.D.*

THEOREM 13.   For any elements a, b in $\mathbf{I}$, a) if $a < b + 1$, then $a < b$ or $a = b$; and b) if $a < b$, then $a + 1 \leq b$.

Proof: a) If $a < b + 1$, then, by Definition 2, there is an x in $\mathbf{I}$ such that $a + x = b + 1$. By Theorem 12, either $1 = x$ or $1 < x$. If $1 = x$, then, by substitution, $a + 1 = b + 1$. Therefore, by Axiom 2, $1 + a = 1 + b$, and, by Axiom 5, $a = b$. If $1 < x$, then, by Definition 2, there is a y in $\mathbf{I}$ such that $1 + y = x$. Substituting $(1 + y)$ for x in the first equation of the proof, we have $a + (1 + y) = b + 1$. Therefore, by Axiom 2, $a + (y + 1) = 1 + b$, and, by Axiom 1, $(a + y) + 1 = 1 + b$. Using Axiom 2 again, we have $1 + (a + y) = 1 + b$. Hence, by Axiom 5, $a + y = b$. Therefore, by Definition 2, $a < b$.

b) If $a < b$, then, by Theorem 7, $a + 1 < b + 1$. Therefore, by Theorem 13a, $a + 1 < b$ or $a + 1 = b$; that is, by our notation, $a + 1 \leq b$.
                    Q.E.D.

COROLLARY.   If b is a positive integer, then there is no positive integer a such that $b < a < b + 1$.

Proof: Suppose that there is a positive integer a such that $b < a < b + 1$. Then, by Theorem 13a, either $a < b$ or $a = b$. But, by Theorem 3, this is contrary to the hypothesis that $b < a$. Hence our assumption leads to a contradiction (see Rule 3, Sec. 1-4) and must be invalid.   *Q.E.D.*

THEOREM 14.   The positive integers are well ordered[2] by the relation "less than."

Proof: Let P_n be the statement "Any subset S of $\mathbf{I}$ which has a positive integer a such that $a \leq n$ has a positive integer m such that $m \leq x$ for all x in S; that is, has a smallest positive integer m."

Then P_1 is the statement "Any subset S of $\mathbf{I}$ which has a positive integer a such that $a \leq 1$ has a smallest positive integer m."

Now by Theorems 3 and 12, 1 is the only element a of $\mathbf{I}$ such that $a \leq 1$. Therefore, any subset S of $\mathbf{I}$ which has a positive integer a such that $a \leq 1$ must contain 1. By Theorem 12, $1 \leq x$ for all x in $\mathbf{I}$ and, in particular, for all x in $S \subseteq \mathbf{I}$. Therefore, P_1 is valid.

Now we must show that $P_n \Rightarrow P_{n+1}$, where P_{n+1} is the statement "Any subset S of $\mathbf{I}$ which has a positive integer a such that $a \leq n + 1$ has a smallest positive integer m." Now suppose that S is a subset of $\mathbf{I}$ containing a positive integer a such that $a \leq n + 1$. Then, by our notation, either $a < n + 1$ or $a = n + 1$. If $a < n + 1$, then, by Theorem 13a,

[2] See Sec. 2-7.

$a \leq n$. Hence, by P_n, S has a smallest positive integer m. If $a = n + 1$, and if for all x in S, $n + 1 \leq x$ (that is, for no x in S does it hold that $x < n + 1$), then $n + 1$ is the smallest element of S. If $a = n + 1$, and if there is an element a' in S such that $a' < n + 1$, then, by Theorem 13a, $a' \leq n$. Hence, by P_n again, S has a smallest element m.   *Q.E.D.*

THEOREM 15 (Second Principle of Finite Induction). Suppose that a statement P_n is associated with every positive integer n and that P_1 is valid. If for each m, the validity of the statements P_k for all $k < m$ implies the validity of the statement P_m, then the statements P_n are valid for all n.

Proof: Let S be the set of positive integers for which P_n is not valid. If S is nonempty, then, by Theorem 14, S has a smallest positive integer m. Since m is the smallest integer for which P_n is not valid, it follows that for all $k < m$, P_k is valid. By the hypothesis, this implies that P_m is valid. But this contradicts the statement above that P_m is not valid. Hence our assumption that S is nonempty leads to a contradiction (see Rule 3, Sec. 1-4) and must be invalid.   *Q.E.D.*

Notice that if $m = 1$, then the set of all positive integers k such that $k < 1$ is empty. Therefore, in using the second principle of finite induction, one must explicitly prove P_1. One cannot simply say that P_k is valid for all $k < 1$ (which is true vacuously) and therefore that P_1 is valid.

EXERCISES

1. Prove that $1 + 3 + 5 + \cdots + (2n - 1) = n^2$.

2. Prove that $1^3 + 2^3 + \cdots + n^3 = \left[\dfrac{n(n + 1)}{2}\right]^2$.

3. Prove that $\dfrac{1}{1 \cdot 2} + \dfrac{1}{2 \cdot 3} + \dfrac{1}{3 \cdot 4} + \cdots + \dfrac{1}{n(n + 1)} = \dfrac{n}{n + 1}$.

4. Use induction to prove that $n(n + 1)(n + 2)$ is divisible by 6.

5. Use induction to prove that $1^n = 1$, where 1 is the unit element for the positive integers, and 1^n is defined to be $1 \cdot 1 \cdot \cdots \cdot 1$, n times.

6. Prove that for any elements a, m, n in **I**, $(a^m)^n = a^{mn}$.

3-4. THE "WELL ORDERING PRINCIPLE" AND AXIOM 7

The "well ordering principle" of Theorem 14 is equivalent to Axiom 7 in the following sense: According to Theorem 14, the seven axioms for the positive integers imply the well ordering principle; in addition, it can be shown that the first six axioms for the positive integers together with the well ordering principle imply Axiom 7. We shall establish this last result in proving Theorem 17. First, however, we must prove that (Theorem 16) the first six axioms for the positive integers together with the well ordering principle imply that for all elements n in $\mathbf{I}$, $1 \leq n$. You will recall that Theorem 12 states that for all elements n in $\mathbf{I}$, $1 \leq n$. We proved Theorem 12, however, by using Axiom 7. Now we must establish this same result again, using well ordering instead, for, we need this result to prove that well ordering, together with the first six axioms, implies Axiom 7.

THEOREM 16. The first six axioms for the positive integers together with the well ordering principle imply that for all elements n in $\mathbf{I}$, $1 \leq n$.

Proof: Let S be the set of all positive integers n such that $n < 1$. If S is nonempty, then, by the well ordering principle, S has a smallest integer m; moreover, since m is in S, it follows that $m < 1$. By Theorem 8[3] and Axiom 4, since $m < 1$, $m \cdot m < 1 \cdot m = m$. Now, since "less than" is an order relation, by Theorem 6, $m \cdot m < m$ and $m < 1 \Rightarrow m \cdot m < 1$. Thus, we have obtained an integer $m \cdot m$ in S which is smaller than m, where m is the smallest integer in S. Hence the assumption that S is nonempty leads to a contradiction (see Rule 3, Sec. 1-4) and must be invalid.   *Q.E.D.*

THEOREM 17. The first six axioms for the positive integers together with the well ordering principle imply Axiom 7.

Proof: Suppose that H is a set of positive integers such that a) $1 \in H$, and b) whenever $x \in H$, then $x + 1 \in H$. We must show that $H = \mathbf{I}$. To do this, let H' consist of those elements of $\mathbf{I}$ which are not in H. Suppose that H' is not empty. Then, by the well ordering principle, H' contains a smallest element h. $1 \notin H'$, since $1 \in H$. Therefore, by Theorem 16, $1 < h$. By Definition 2, there must then be an element a in $\mathbf{I}$ such that $1 + a = h$. By Axiom 2, this equation can be replaced by $a + 1 = h$. Hence, by Definition 2, $a < h$. This means that $a \in H$, since h is the smallest element in H'. By the hypothesis, $a \in H \Rightarrow a + 1 \in H$. But this is impossible, since $a + 1 = h \in H'$, and H and H' are disjoint. Thus, the assumption that H' is not empty leads to a contradiction. (See Rule 3, Sec. 1-4.) Therefore, all elements of $\mathbf{I}$ must be in H.   *Q.E.D.*

It can be shown that any two algebraic systems satisfying the axioms for the positive integers are isomorphic. We shall not do this, however.

---

[3] We can use Theorem 8 in this proof, since the proofs of all theorems before Theorem 10 depend only upon the first six axioms for $\mathbf{I}$.

4 / The Integers

4-1. AXIOMS FOR THE INTEGERS

In this chapter we shall develop an axiomatic theory of the integers $\cdots, -2, -1, 0, 1, 2, \cdots$. We shall assume no previous knowledge of the integers but shall deduce from our axioms, by logical means, any of the properties of the integers which we wish to consider. In the axiom set which we shall use, there are three undefined concepts: integer, addition $(+)$, and multiplication $(\cdot)$, where addition and multiplication are binary operations.

DEFINITION 1. The set of integers is a set **J**, closed[1] with respect to two binary operations, called addition $(+)$ and multiplication $(\cdot)$, and satisfying the following axioms:

Axiom 1. Addition and multiplication are associative: For all elements a, b, c in **J**, $a + (b + c) = (a + b) + c$; and $a(bc) = (ab)c$. (We often use the notation "ab" in place of "$a \cdot b$.")

Axiom 2. Addition and multiplication are commutative: For all elements a, b in **J**, $a + b = b + a$; and $ab = ba$.

Axiom 3. Multiplication is distributive over addition: For all elements a, b, c in **J**, $a(b + c) = ab + ac$.

Axiom 4. There is an element in **J**, denoted by "0," such that $a + 0 = a$ for every element a in **J**. (Such an element 0 is called a zero element or an additive identity.)

Axiom 5. There is an element in **J**, denoted by "1," such that $1a = a$ for every element a in **J**, and $1 \neq 0$. (Such an element 1 is called a unit element or a multiplicative identity.)

Axiom 6. For each element a in **J**, there is an element in **J**, denoted by

[1] See page 25.

51

"$-a$," such that $a + (-a) = 0$. [We shall show (Theorem 4) that this element $(-a)$ is unique. $(-a)$ is called the negative of a or the additive inverse of a.]

Axiom 7. The cancellation law of multiplication holds: For all elements a, b, c in **J** such that $a \neq 0$, if $ab = ac$, then $b = c$.

Axiom 8. There is a subset P of **J**, called the set of positive elements, satisfying the following requirements:

        a) If $a, b \in P$, then $a + b \in P$.
        b) If $a, b \in P$, then $ab \in P$.

        c) For any element a in **J**, exactly one of the following alternatives holds: $a \in P$, $a = 0$, or $-a \in P$. (We shall show later how these positive elements may be identified with the positive integers of Chapter 3.)

Axiom 9. The set P is well ordered by the relation "less than," where "less than" is defined in Definition 2 below. [We shall show (Theorem 12) that "less than" is indeed an order relation.]

DEFINITION 2. If a and b are elements in **J**, then a is said to be less than b (or, equivalently, b is said to be greater than a) if, and only if, there is an element x in P such that $a + x = b$.

We denote "a is less than b" by $a < b$ or $b > a$. If $a = b$ or $a < b$, we write $a \leq b$ or $b \geq a$.

DEFINITION 3. An integral domain is a set D, closed with respect to two binary operations, called addition ($+$) and multiplication ($\cdot$), and satisfying Axioms 1 through 7 for the integers **J**.

Examples
1. The integers **J**.
2. The rational numbers (Chapter 5).
3. The real numbers (Chapter 6).
4. The complex numbers (Chapter 6).
5. The set $\{a + b\sqrt{5} \mid a, b \in J\}$ (Chapter 6).
6. The positive integers **I** (Chapter 3) do not form an integral domain; Axioms 4 and 6 are not satisfied.

DEFINITION 4. An ordered integral domain is a set D, closed with respect to two binary operations, called addition ($+$) and multiplication ($\cdot$), and satisfying Axioms 1 through 8 for the integers **J**.

Examples
1. The integers **J**.
2. The rational numbers (Chapter 5).
3. The real numbers (Chapter 6).
4. The complex numbers (Chapter 6) do not form an ordered

integral domain. This is a consequence of Theorem 19 and the fact that $i^2 = -1$.

In view of Definitions 1 and 4, the set of integers **J** might be defined to be an ordered integral domain in which the positive elements are well ordered by the relation "less than."

In Chapter 7 we shall show that a 1:1 correspondence does not exist between the integers and the real numbers. Hence two integral domains, or even two ordered integral domains, need not be isomorphic. It can be shown, however (but we shall not do this), that any two ordered integral domains in which the positive elements are well ordered by the relation "less than" are isomorphic. We describe this situation by saying that the integers are uniquely characterized "up to isomorphism" by Axioms 1 through 9 of Definition 1.

At this point you might well be wondering how the positive integers of Chapter 3 are related to the set of integers **J**. In Sec. 4-2 we shall show that, starting with the set **I** of positive integers, we can construct a set of elements satisfying the axioms for **J**; moreover, the set of positive elements (Axiom 8) so constructed is isomorphic to the set **I**.

EXERCISE

Show that the system consisting of the set $S = \{0, 1\}$, with addition and multiplication defined as below, is an integral domain.

+	0	1		·	0	1
0	0	1		0	0	0
1	1	0		1	0	1

4-2. CONSTRUCTION OF THE INTEGERS FROM THE POSITIVE INTEGERS

In this section we shall prove the following theorem:

THEOREM 1. There exists a set J of elements satisfying the axioms for the set **J** of integers. J contains a subset P' which is isomorphic to the set **I** of positive integers.

Since any two algebraic systems satisfying the axioms for **J** are isomorphic (Sec. 4-1), the set of elements J which we shall construct is, in fact, the set of integers **J**. Briefly, then, Theorem 1 asserts that if the set **I** exists, then the set **J** exists also. In order to prove Theorem 1, we first prove a series of lemmas.

Consider the set of all ordered pairs (m, n), where m and n are in $\mathbf{I}$; that is, consider the set $\mathbf{I} \times \mathbf{I}$. Define a relation $\sim$ on $(\mathbf{I} \times \mathbf{I}) \times (\mathbf{I} \times \mathbf{I})$ (Sec. 2-4) as follows: $(m, n) \sim (r, s)$ if, and only if, $m + s = n + r$; that is, $((m, n), (r, s)) \in \sim$ if, and only if, $m + s = n + r$.

LEMMA 1. $\sim$ is an equivalence relation on $\mathbf{I} \times \mathbf{I}$.

Proof: Let (m, n), (r, s), and (i, j) be any elements of $\mathbf{I} \times \mathbf{I}$. By the definition of $\sim$, $(m, n) \sim (m, n)$, since, by Axiom 2 for $\mathbf{I}$, $m + n = n + m$. Therefore, $\sim$ is reflexive. By the definition of $\sim$, $(m, n) \sim (r, s) \Rightarrow$ $m + s = n + r$. But by Axiom 2 for $\mathbf{I}$, $m + s = n + r \Rightarrow r + n = s + m$. By the definition of $\sim$, $r + n = s + m \Rightarrow (r, s) \sim (m, n)$. Therefore, $(m, n) \sim (r, s) \Rightarrow (r, s) \sim (m, n)$ (see Rule 2, Sec. 1-4), and $\sim$ is symmetric. By the definition of $\sim$, $(m, n) \sim (r, s) \Rightarrow m + s = n + r$. By the definition of $\sim$, $(r, s) \sim (i, j) \Rightarrow r + j = s + i$. Adding the two equalities above, we have $(m + s) + (r + j) = (n + r) + (s + i)$. Therefore, by Axioms 1, 2, and 5 for $\mathbf{I}$, $m + j = n + i$. But, by the definition of $\sim$, this last equation implies that $(m, n) \sim (i, j)$. Therefore, $(m, n) \sim (r, s)$ and $(r, s) \sim (i, j) \Rightarrow (m, n) \sim (i, j)$, and $\sim$ is transitive.　　　Q.E.D.

We now use the equivalence relation $\sim$ to partition the set $\mathbf{I} \times \mathbf{I}$ into disjoint equivalence classes (Chapter 2, Theorem 1). We denote this set of equivalence classes by J; we denote the class containing the pair (m, n) by $(m, n)\tilde{}$; that is, $(m, n)\tilde{} = \{(x, y) \mid (x, y) \sim (m, n)\}$.

By now you are probably wondering where this equivalence relation $\sim$ came from. The equivalence relation $\sim$ was motivated by the notion of "subtraction" in the following way: Intuitively, we are thinking of representing an element in J as a "difference" of two positive integers m and n. For example, $7 - 2$ might represent an element in J; $2 - 7$ might represent another. But, expressions like $m - n$ do not, in general, make sense in our axiomatic theory of the positive integers $\mathbf{I}$; ordered pairs (m, n) do make sense. Now, if we were able to represent an element in J by $7 - 2$, we would also want to represent that same element by $8 - 3$ or $9 - 4$, and so on. Hence we want the pairs $(7, 2)$, $(8, 3)$, $(9, 4)$, $\cdots$ to be equivalent. But, by our definition of the equivalence relation $\sim$, $(7, 2) \sim$ $(8, 3)$, since $7 + 3 = 2 + 8$ (or $7 - 2 = 8 - 3$). Likewise, $(7, 2) \sim (9, 4)$, since $7 + 4 = 2 + 9$ (or $7 - 2 = 9 - 4$), and so on. Thus, we think of the set of ordered pairs equivalent to $(7, 2)$ under $\sim$, that is, the equivalence class $(7, 2)\tilde{}$, as an element in J. This element can also be represented by $(8, 3)\tilde{}$, $(9, 4)\tilde{}$, and so on. The set of all equivalence classes $(m, n)\tilde{}$, where m and n are in $\mathbf{I}$, constitutes J.

Now that we have our set of elements J, we must define binary operations, addition $(+)$ and multiplication $(\cdot)$, on J. For addition $(+)$, we proceed as follows:

Let a and b be any two elements in J. (Thus, a and b are equivalence classes of ordered pairs of positive integers, where $\sim$ is the equivalence relation.) Choose any element (m, n) in a and any element (r, s) in b. We define $a + b$ as follows: $a + b = (m + r, n + s)^{\sim}$.

We must show that the definition of $a + b$ is unambiguous; that is, we must show that for any other pair (m', n') in a and any other pair (r', s') in b, the equivalence class $(m' + r', n' + s')^{\sim}$ is identical with the equivalence class $(m + r, n + s)^{\sim}$. To show this, we must prove Lemma 2.

LEMMA 2. If $(m, n) \sim (m', n')$ and if $(r, s) \sim (r', s')$, then $(m + r, n + s) \sim (m' + r', n' + s')$.

Proof: By hypothesis and the definition of $\sim$, $m + n' = n + m'$ and $r + s' = s + r'$. Therefore, by adding the two equalities above and using Axioms 1 and 2 for **I**, $(m + r) + (n' + s') = (n + s) + (m' + r')$. By the definition of $\sim$, this last result implies that $(m + r, n + s) \sim (m' + r', n' + s')$. $\hspace{2cm}$ Q.E.D.

Thus, we have shown that our definition of $a + b$ is unambiguous; it does not depend on the particular elements of a and b which are chosen to form $a + b$. We say, in such a case, that the sum $a + b$ is well defined.

The definition of $a + b$ was also motivated by the motion of "subtraction." If we think of $(m, n)^{\sim}$ as $m - n$ and of $(r, s)^{\sim}$ as $r - s$, then $(m, n)^{\sim} + (r, s)^{\sim} = (m - n) + (r - s) = (m + r) - (n + s) = (m + r, n + s)^{\sim}$.

Example. $(7, 4)^{\sim} + (3, 2)^{\sim} = (7 + 3, 4 + 2)^{\sim} = (10, 6)^{\sim}$. Interpreting $(m, n)^{\sim}$ as $m - n$, this illustrates that $3 + 1 = 4$.

We next define multiplication ($\cdot$) on J. Let a and b be any two elements in J. Choose any element (m, n) in a and any element (r, s) in b. We define $a \cdot b$ as follows: $a \cdot b = (mr + ns, nr + ms)^{\sim}$. To show that $a \cdot b$ is well defined, we must prove Lemma 3.

LEMMA 3. If $(m, n) \sim (m', n')$ and if $(r, s) \sim (r', s')$, then $(mr + ns, nr + ms) \sim (m'r' + n's', n'r' + m's')$.

Proof:

1. $m + n' = n + m'$ and $r + s' = s + r'$, by hypothesis and the definition of $\sim$.

2. $(mr + ns) + (n'r + m's) = (m + n')r + (n + m')s$, by repeated use of Axioms 1, 2, and 3 for **I**.

3. $(m + n')r + (n + m')s = (n + m')r + (m + n')s$, by line 1.

4. $(n + m')r + (m + n')s = (nr + ms) + (m'r + n's)$, by repeated use of Axioms 1, 2, and 3 for **I**.

5. Therefore, $(mr + ns) + (n'r + m's) = (nr + ms) + (m'r + n's)$, by substitution.

6. Hence $(mr + ns, nr + ms) \sim (m'r + n's, n'r + m's)$, by the definition of $\sim$.

7. $(m'r + n's) + (n'r' + m's') = m'(r + s') + n'(s + r')$, by repeated use of Axioms 1, 2, and 3 for **I**.

8. $m'(r + s') + n'(s + r') = m'(s + r') + n'(r + s')$, by line 1.

9. $m'(s + r') + n'(r + s') = (n'r + m's) + (m'r' + n's')$, by repeated use of Axioms 1, 2, and 3 for **I**.

10. Therefore, $(m'r + n's) + (n'r' + m's') = (n'r + m's) + (m'r' + n's')$, by substitution.

11. Hence $(m'r + n's, n'r + m's) \sim (m'r' + n's', n'r' + m's')$, by the definition of $\sim$.

12. Therefore, $(mr + ns, nr + ms) \sim (m'r' + n's', n'r' + m's')$, by lines 6 and 11 and since $\sim$ is an equivalence relation.   *Q.E.D.*

The definition of $a \cdot b$ was also motivated by the notion of "subtraction." If we think of $(m, n)\tilde{}$ as $m - n$ and of $(r, s)\tilde{}$ as $r - s$, then $(m, n)\tilde{} \cdot (r, s)\tilde{} = (m - n)(r - s) = (mr + ns) - (nr + ms) = (mr + ns, nr + ms)\tilde{}$.

Example. $(3, 2)\tilde{} \cdot (7, 4)\tilde{} = (3 \cdot 7 + 2 \cdot 4, 2 \cdot 7 + 3 \cdot 4)\tilde{} = (29, 26)\tilde{} = (4, 1)\tilde{}$. Interpreting $(m, n)\tilde{}$ as $m - n$, this illustrates that $1 \cdot 3 = 3$.

We next define a relation "less than" on $J \times J$. Let a and b be any two elements in J. Choose any element (m, n) in a and any element (r, s) in b. Then a is said to be less than b, denoted by "$a\mathcal{L}b$," if, and only if, $m + s < n + r$; that is, $a\mathcal{L}b \Longleftrightarrow m + s < n + r$. This relation "less than" will be used in showing that a certain subset of J satisfies Axiom 9 for **J**. To show that "less than" is well defined, we must prove Lemma 4.

LEMMA 4.   If $(m, n) \sim (m', n')$, if $(r, s) \sim (r', s')$, and if $m + s < n + r$, then $m' + s' < n' + r'$.

Proof: By hypothesis and the definition of $\sim$, $n + m' = m + n'$, $r + s' = s + r'$, and $m + s < n + r$. Adding the first two equations, we have $(n + m') + (r + s') = (m + n') + (s + r')$. Applying Theorem 7, Chapter 3, to this equation and the inequality above, we have

$$(m + s) + [(n + m') + (r + s')] < (n + r) + [(m + n') + (s + r')].$$

By repeated use of Axioms 1 and 2 for **I**, this last inequality may be expressed as $(m' + s') + [(m + n) + (r + s)] < (n' + r') + [(m + n) + (r + s)]$. But by Theorem 7, Chapter 3, this means that $m' + s' < n' + r'$.
     Q.E.D.

LEMMA 5. "Less than" is an order relation on J.

Proof: Let a be any element in J and choose any element (m, n) in a. If $a\mathcal{L}a$, then, by the definition of "less than" and by Axiom 2 for **I**, $m + n < m + n$. But this is impossible by Theorem 3, Chapter 3, since $m + n = m + n$. Thus, the assumption $a\mathcal{L}a$ leads to a contradiction and must be invalid. Therefore, $a\cancel{\mathcal{L}}a$.

Let a and b be any two elements in J. Choose any element (m, n) in a and any element (r, s) in b. If $a\mathcal{L}b$, then, by the definition of "less than," $m + s < n + r$. If $b\mathcal{L}a$, then, by the definition of "less than" and Axiom 2 for **I**, $n + r < m + s$. But by Theorem 3, Chapter 3, the two inequalities above are mutually exclusive. Thus, the assumption that $a\mathcal{L}b$ and $b\mathcal{L}a$ leads to a contradiction and must be invalid. Therefore, if $a\mathcal{L}b$, then $b\cancel{\mathcal{L}}a$.

Let a, b, and c be any three elements in J. Choose any element (m, n) in a, any element (r, s) in b, and any element (i, j) in c. Suppose that $a\mathcal{L}b$ and $b\mathcal{L}c$. Then, by the definition of "less than," $m + s < n + r$ and $r + j < s + i$. Therefore, by Theorem 9a, Chapter 3, and by repeated use of Axioms 1 and 2 for **I**, $(m + j) + (r + s) < (n + i) + (r + s)$. But by Theorem 7, Chapter 3, this means that $(m + j) < (n + i)$. By the definition of "less than," this last inequality implies that $a\mathcal{L}c$. Therefore, if $a\mathcal{L}b$ and $b\mathcal{L}c$, then $a\mathcal{L}c$. *Q.E.D.*

The definition of "less than" on $J \times J$ was motivated by the notion of "subtraction" and the usual notion of "less than." If we think of $(m, n)^\sim$ as $m - n$ and of $(r, s)^\sim$ as $r - s$, then $(m, n)^\sim \mathcal{L}(r, s)^\sim$ if, and only if, $m - n < r - s$. But then, $m + s < n + r$.

Example. $(3, 2)^\sim \mathcal{L}(7, 4)^\sim \iff 3 + 4 < 2 + 7$; that is, $7 < 9$. Interpreting $(m, n)^\sim$ as $m - n$, this illustrates that $1 < 3$.

Now we must show that the set J, together with the operations addition ($+$) and multiplication ($\cdot$) and the order relation "less than," satisfies all the axioms for the set **J** of integers.

LEMMA 6. J satisfies Axiom 1 for **J**; that is, for all elements a, b, c in J, $a + (b + c) = (a + b) + c$ and $a \cdot (b \cdot c) = (a \cdot b) \cdot c$.

Proof: Let (m, n) be any element in a, let (r, s) be any element in b, and let (i, j) be any element in c.

By the definition of addition in J, $a + (b + c) = (m + (r + i), n + (s + j))^\sim$. Therefore, by Axiom 1 for **I**, $a + (b + c) = ((m + r) + i, (n + s) + j)^\sim$. But the right side of this equation equals $(a + b) + c$.

By the definition of multiplication in J, $a \cdot (b \cdot c) = (m(ri + sj) + n(si + rj), n(ri + sj) + m(si + rj))^\sim$. Therefore, by Axioms 1, 2, and 3 for **I**,

$a \cdot (b \cdot c) = ((mr + ns)i + (nr + ms)j, (nr + ms)i + (mr + ns)j)\tilde{}.$

But the right side of this equation equals $(a \cdot b) \cdot c.$ *Q.E.D.*

LEMMA 7. J satisfies Axiom 2 for J; that is, for all elements a, b in J, $a + b = b + a$ and $a \cdot b = b \cdot a$.

Proof: Let (m, n) be any element in a and let (r, s) be any element in b. By the definition of addition in J, $a + b = (m + r, n + s)\tilde{}$. Therefore, by Axiom 2 for **I**, $a + b = (r + m, s + n)\tilde{}$. But the right side of this equation equals $b + a$.

By the definition of multiplication in J, $a \cdot b = (mr + ns, nr + ms)\tilde{}$. Therefore, by Axiom 2 for **I**, $a \cdot b = (rm + sn, sm + rn)\tilde{}$. But the right side of this equation equals $b \cdot a$.   *Q.E.D.*

LEMMA 8. J satisfies Axiom 3 for J; that is, for all elements a, b, c in J, $a \cdot (b + c) = a \cdot b + a \cdot c$.

Proof: Let (m, n) be any element in a; let (r, s) be any element in b, and let (i, j) be any element in c.

By the definition of addition in J, $b + c = (r + i, s + j)\tilde{}$, and, by the definition of multiplication in J, $a \cdot (b + c) = (m(r + i) + n(s + j), n(r + i) + m(s + j))\tilde{}$. Therefore, by Axioms 1, 2, and 3 for **I**,

$a \cdot (b + c) = ((mr + ns) + (mi + nj), (nr + ms) + (ni + mj))\tilde{}.$

But the right side of this equation equals $(mr + ns, nr + ms)\tilde{} + (mi + nj, ni + mj)\tilde{}$, and this last expression equals $a \cdot b + a \cdot c$.   *Q.E.D.*

For any two positive integers m and n, $(m, m) \sim (n, n)$, since $m + n = m + n$. We shall denote by $0'$ the equivalence class of all such pairs (m, m), where m is in **I**; that is, $0' = (m, m)\tilde{}$.

LEMMA 9. J satisfies Axiom 4 for J; that is, there is an element $0'$ in J such that $a + 0' = a$ for every element a in J.

Proof: Let $0' = (m, m)\tilde{}$ and let $a = (r, s)\tilde{}$.

By the definition of addition in J, $a + 0' = (r + m, s + m)\tilde{}$.

By the definition of $\sim$ and by Axioms 1 and 2 for **I**, $(r + m, s + m) \sim (r, s)$, since $(r + m) + s = (s + m) + r$. Therefore, $(r + m, s + m)\tilde{} = (r, s)\tilde{}$. Hence, by substitution, $a + 0' = a$.   *Q.E.D.*

For any two positive integers m and n, $(m + 1, m) \sim (n + 1, n)$, where 1 is the unit element of **I**, since, by Axioms 1 and 2 for **I**, $(m + 1) + n = m + (n + 1)$. We shall denote by $1'$ the equivalence class of all such pairs $(m + 1, m)$, where m is in **I**; that is, $1' = (m + 1, m)\tilde{}$.

LEMMA 10. J satisfies Axiom 5 for J; that is, there is an element $1'$ in J such that $1' \cdot a = a$ for every element a in J and $1' \neq 0'$.

Proof: Let $1' = (m + 1, m)^\sim$ and let $a = (r, s)^\sim$.

By the definition of multiplication in J, $1' \cdot a = ((m + 1)r + ms, mr + (m + 1)s)^\sim$.

By the definition of $\sim$ and by Axioms 1, 2, 3, and 4 for **I**,

$$((m + 1)r + ms, mr + (m + 1)s) \sim (r, s),$$

since $[(m + 1)r + ms] + s = [mr + (m + 1)s] + r$. Therefore,

$$((m + 1)r + ms, mr + (m + 1)s)^\sim = (r, s)^\sim.$$

Hence, by substitution, $1' \cdot a = a$.

Suppose that $1' = 0'$. Then it would follow that $(m + 1, m) \sim (m, m)$, where m is in **I**. By the definition of $\sim$, this would mean that $(m + 1) + m = (m + m)$. By Axioms 1 and 2 for **I**, we may replace this equation by $(m + m) + 1 = (m + m)$. But, by Theorems 3 and 4 of Chapter 3, this equation cannot hold. Thus, the assumption that $1' = 0'$ leads to a contradiction and hence must be invalid. Therefore, $1' \neq 0'$. *Q.E.D.*

Let a be any element in J and let (m, n) be any element in a. We shall denote by $(-a)$ the equivalence class $(n, m)^\sim$. To show that $(-a)$ is well defined, we must prove Lemma 11.

LEMMA 11. If $(m, n) \sim (m', n')$, then $(n, m) \sim (n', m')$.

Proof: By hypothesis, $(m, n) \sim (m', n')$. Therefore, by the definition of $\sim$, $m + n' = n + m'$. Using the definition of $\sim$ again, this last equation implies that $(n, m) \sim (n', m')$. *Q.E.D.*

LEMMA 12. J satisfies Axiom 6 for **J**; that is, for each element a in J, there is an element $(-a)$ in J such that $a + (-a) = 0'$.

Proof: Let $a = (m, n)^\sim$ and let $(-a) = (n, m)^\sim$.

By the definition of addition in J, $a + (-a) = (m + n, n + m)^\sim$. Therefore, by Axiom 2 for **I**, $a + (-a) = (m + n, m + n)^\sim$. But, by the definition of $0'$ (page 58), $(m + n, m + n)^\sim = 0'$. Hence, by substitution, $a + (-a) = 0'$. *Q.E.D.*

LEMMA 13. J satisfies Axiom 7 for **J**; that is, for all elements a, b, c in J such that $a \neq 0'$, if $a \cdot b = a \cdot c$, then $b = c$.

Proof: Let (m, n) be any element in a, let (r, s) be any element in b, and let (i, j) be any element in c.

By the definition of multiplication in J, $a \cdot b = (mr + ns, nr + ms)^\sim$ and $a \cdot c = (mi + nj, ni + mj)^\sim$.

By hypothesis, $a \cdot b = a \cdot c$; therefore, $(mr + ns, nr + ms) \sim (mi + nj, ni + mj)$. By the definition of $\sim$, this means that $(mr + ns) + (ni + mj) = (nr + ms) + (mi + nj)$. By Axioms 1, 2, and 3 for **I**, this equation may be replaced by $m(r + j) + n(s + i) = m(s + i) + n(r + j)$.

By hypothesis, $a \neq 0'$; therefore, $m \neq n$. Hence, by Axiom 6 for **I**, either there is an x in **I** such that $m + x = n$ or there is a y in **I** such that $m = n + y$. Without loss of generality, we can assume that there is an x in **I** such that $m + x = n$. (A similar argument holds if the other alternative is taken.) By substituting $(m + x)$ for n in the equation $m(r + j) + n(s + i) = m(s + i) + n(r + j)$ obtained above, and by using Axioms 2 and 3 for **I**, we have $m(r + j) + [m(s + i) + x(s + i)] = m(s + i) + [m(r + j) + x(r + j)]$. By Axioms 1 and 2 for **I**, this equation may be replaced by

$$[m(r + j) + m(s + i)] + x(s + i) = [m(r + j) + m(s + i)] + x(r + j).$$

By Axiom 5 for **I**, this means that $x(s + i) = x(r + j)$. Applying Axiom 5 for **I** to this last equation, we have $s + i = r + j$. By the definition of $\sim$, this implies that $(r, s) \sim (i, j)$. But this means that $b = c$.   *Q.E.D.*

By Axiom 6 for **I**, any ordered pair (m, n) in $\mathbf{I} \times \mathbf{I}$ can be represented in exactly one of the following three forms: (m, m), $(m, m + x)$, or $(n + y, n)$, where x and y are in **I**.

LEMMA 14. An ordered pair in any one of the above three forms is not equivalent, under $\sim$, to an ordered pair in any other of the forms. For x and y fixed, an ordered pair in any one of the above three forms is equivalent, under $\sim$, to an ordered pair in the same form.

Proof: Suppose that $(m, m) \sim (m, m + x)$. Then, by the definition of $\sim$, $m + (m + x) = m + m$. By Axiom 1 for **I**, this equation may be replaced by $(m + m) + x = m + m$. But by Theorems 3 and 4 of Chapter 3, this equation cannot hold. Thus, the assumption that $(m, m) \sim (m, m + x)$ leads to a contradiction and hence must be invalid.

Similarly, we can show that $(m, m) \not\sim (n + y, n)$ and $(m, m + x) \not\sim (n + y, n)$. (See Exercise 1, page 62.)

It was shown, on page 58, that for any two positive integers m and n, $(m, m) \sim (n, n)$. For any positive integers m, r, and x, $(m, m + x) \sim (r, r + x)$, since, by the definition of $\sim$ and by Axioms 1 and 2 for **I**, $m + (r + x) = (m + x) + r$.

Similarly, we can show that for any positive integers n, s, and y, $(n + y, n) \sim (s + y, s)$. (See Exercise 1, page 62.)   *Q.E.D.*

Pairs of the form (m, m) are elements of $0'$. (See page 58.) We shall denote by P' the set of all equivalence classes of the form $(n + y, n)^\sim$, where n and y are in **I**; that is, $P' = \{(n + y, n)^\sim \mid n, y \in \mathbf{I}\}$.

LEMMA 15. For any element a in J, $a \in P' \Longleftrightarrow 0' \mathcal{L} a$.

Proof: Suppose that $a \in P'$. Let (m, m) be any element in $0'$ and let $(n + y, n)$ be any element in a. By Theorem 4, Chapter 3, $(m + n) <$

$(m + n) + y$. By Axiom 1 for **I**, this inequality may be replaced by $(m + n) < m + (n + y)$. By the definition of "less than" in J, this last inequality implies that $0'\mathcal{L}a$.

Conversely, suppose that $0'\mathcal{L}a$. Let (m, m) be any element in $0'$ and let (r, s) be any element in a. By the definition of "less than" in J, since $0'\mathcal{L}a$, it follows that $m + s < m + r$. By Axiom 2 for **I**, this inequality may be replaced by $s + m < r + m$. By Theorem 7, Chapter 3, this means that $s < r$. By Definition 2, Chapter 3, since $s < r$, there is an element y in **I** such that $s + y = r$. Therefore, by substitution, $a = (s + y, s)\tilde{}$. But then, by the definition of P', $a \in P'$.   *Q.E.D.*

LEMMA 16. J satisfies Axiom 8 for **J**; that is, there is a subset P' of J satisfying the following requirements:

 a) If $a, b \in P'$, then $a + b \in P'$.
 b) If $a, b \in P'$, then $a \cdot b \in P'$.
 c) For any element a in J, exactly one of the following alternatives holds: $a \in P', a = 0'$, or $-a \in P'$.

Proof: Let a and b be any two elements in P'. Choose any element $(m + x, m)$ in a and any element $(n + y, n)$ in b. Then, by the definition of addition in J, $a + b = ((m + x) + (n + y), m + n)\tilde{}$. Therefore, by Axioms 1 and 2 for **I**, $a + b = ((m + n) + (x + y), m + n)\tilde{}$. Hence, by the definition of P', $a + b \in P'$.

By the definition of multiplication in J, $a \cdot b = ((m + x)(n + y) + mn, m(n + y) + (m + x)n)\tilde{}$. Therefore, by Axioms 1, 2, and 3 for **I**, $a \cdot b = ([[(m + x)n + m(n + y)] + xy, [(m + x)n + m(n + y)]])\tilde{}$. Hence, by the definition of P', $a \cdot b \in P'$.

By Axiom 6 for **I** and by Lemma 14, any element $a = (m, n)\tilde{}$ in J can be represented in exactly one of the following three forms: $(m, m)\tilde{}$, $(m, m + x)\tilde{}$, or $(n + y, n)\tilde{}$, where m, n, x, and y are in **I**. If a is of the first form, then $a = 0'$. If a is of the second form, then $(-a)$ is of the form $(m + x, m)\tilde{}$. (See page 59.) But then $(-a) \in P'$. If a is of the third form, then $a \in P'$.   *Q.E.D.*

LEMMA 17.   There is an isomorphism between **I** and P'; that is, there is a 1:1 correspondence ψ between **I** and P' such that for all elements x and y in **I**, $\psi(x + y) = \psi(x) + \psi(y)$; $\psi(x \cdot y) = \psi(x) \cdot (y)$; and $x < y$ if, and only if, $\psi(x) < \psi(y)$.

Proof: We first show that there is a 1:1 correspondence ψ between **I** and P'. By Lemma 14, $(n + x, n) \sim (n' + x, n')$ for any elements n, n', and x in **I**. Let $\psi(x) = (n + x, n)\tilde{}$. Then ψ is a function from **I** to P'. The domain of ψ is **I**; the range of ψ is P'. If $\psi(x) = \psi(y)$, then $(n + x, n) \sim (n + y, n)$. By the definition of $\sim$, this means that $(n + x) + n =$

$n + (n + y)$. But, by Axioms 1, 2, and 5 for **I**, this, in turn, means that $x = y$. Thus, ψ is a 1:1 correspondence between **I** and P'. (See Sec. 2-5.)

By the definition of ψ, $\psi(x + y) = (n + (x + y), n)\tilde{\ }$; $\psi(x) = (n + x, n)\tilde{\ }$; and $\psi(y) = (n + y, n)\tilde{\ }$. By the definition of addition in J, $\psi(x) + \psi(y) = ((n + x) + (n + y), n + n)\tilde{\ }$. Therefore, by Axioms 1 and 2 for **I**, $\psi(x) + \psi(y) = ((n + n) + (x + y), n + n)\tilde{\ }$. But, by Lemma 14, $((n + n) + (x + y), n + n)\tilde{\ } = (n + (x + y), n)\tilde{\ }$. Therefore, by substitution, $\psi(x + y) = \psi(x) + \psi(y)$.

By the definition of ψ, $\psi(x \cdot y) = (n + x \cdot y, n)\tilde{\ }$; $\psi(x) = (n + x, n)\tilde{\ }$; and $\psi(y) = (n + y, n)\tilde{\ }$. By the definition of multiplication in J,

$$\psi(x) \cdot \psi(y) = ((n + x)(n + y) + n \cdot n, n(n + y) + (n + x)n)\tilde{\ }.$$

Therefore, by Axioms 1, 2, and 3 for **I**,

$$\psi(x) \cdot \psi(y) = ([(n + x)n + n(n + y)] + x \cdot y,$$
$$[(n + x)n + n(n + y)])\tilde{\ }.$$

But, by Lemma 14, this last equivalence class is the same as the equivalence class $(n + x \cdot y, n)\tilde{\ }$. Therefore, by substitution, $\psi(x \cdot y) = \psi(x) \cdot \psi(y)$.

By Axioms 1 and 2 for **I** and by Theorem 7, Chapter 3, if $x < y$, then $(n + x) + n < n + (n + y)$. By the definition of "less than" in J, this last inequality implies that $(n + x, n)\tilde{\ } \mathcal{L} (n + y, n)\tilde{\ }$; that is, that $\psi(x)\mathcal{L}\psi(y)$. Conversely, if $\psi(x)\mathcal{L}\psi(y)$, then $x < y$. (See Exercise 2, page 63.)   *Q.E.D.*

LEMMA 18. J satisfies Axiom 9 for **J**; that is, the set P' is well ordered by the relation "less than" in J.

Proof: By Lemma 17, there is an isomorphism ψ between **I** and P' which is order preserving; that is, for x and y in **I**, $x < y \Longleftrightarrow \psi(x)\mathcal{L}\psi(y)$. By Theorem 14, Chapter 3, the set **I** is well ordered by the relation "less than" defined for the positive integers. Therefore, by Exercise 2 (page 39), P' is well ordered by the relation "less than" defined for J.   *Q.E.D.*

Proof of Theorem 1 *(page 53)*:   By Lemmas 6, 7, 8, 9, 10, 12, 13, 16, and 18, the set J of equivalence classes $(m, n)\tilde{\ }$, where m and n are in **I**, together with the operations of addition and multiplication and the relation "less than" all defined on J, satisfies the nine axioms for the set **J** of integers. By Lemma 17, the subset P' of J is isomorphic to the set **I** of positive integers.   *Q.E.D.*

EXERCISES

1. Complete the proof of Lemma 14; that is, prove that if m, n, x, y, r, and s are any elements of **I**, then:

     a) $(m, m) \not\sim (n + y, n)$.

b) $(m, m + x) \not\sim (n + y, n)$.

c) $(n + y, n) \sim (s + y, s)$.

2. Complete the proof of Lemma 17; that is, prove that if $\psi(x) \mathcal{L} \psi(y)$, then $x < y$.

4-3.   CONSEQUENCES OF AXIOMS 1 THROUGH 7

In this section we shall derive some elementary consequences of the first seven axioms for the integers **J**. Since these seven axioms characterize integral domains, all the results of this section are valid for any integral domain whatever. We shall denote the elements of **J** by the letters $a, b, c, \cdots$ rather than by the equivalence classes $(m, n)\tilde{\ }$ of Sec. 4-2. (See Exercises 1, 2, and 3, page 65.)

Axiom 5 asserts the existence of a unit element; that is, an element 1 with the property that $1a = a$ for all elements a in **J**. Just as in the case of the positive integers (Theorem 1, Chapter 3), it can be shown that the unit element 1 is unique. The proof we shall give is identical with the proof given for the positive integers.

THEOREM 2.   The element 1 is unique; that is, if there is an element $1'$ in **J** such that $1'a = a$ for all a in **J**, then $1' = 1$.

Proof: $1'a = a$, by hypothesis. $1'a = 1a$, by Axiom 5. Therefore, $a1' = a1$, by Axiom 2, and $1' = 1$, by Axiom 7.   *Q.E.D.*

Axiom 4 asserts the existence of a zero element; that is, an element 0 with the property that $a + 0 = a$ for all elements a in **J**. Our next theorem states that the zero element is unique.

THEOREM 3.   The element 0 is unique; that is, if there is an element $0'$ in **J** such that $a + 0' = a$ for all a in **J**, then $0' = 0$.

Proof: $0 + 0' = 0$, by hypothesis. $0' + 0 = 0'$, by Axiom 4. But $0 + 0' = 0' + 0$, by Axiom 2. Therefore, $0 = 0'$, by substitution.   *Q.E.D.*

Axiom 6 asserts the existence of an additive inverse; that is, for each element a in **J** an element $(-a)$ such that $a + (-a) = 0$. We shall now establish the uniqueness of $(-a)$.

THEOREM 4.   For each element a in **J**, the element $(-a)$ is unique; that is, if there is an element a' in **J** such that $a + a' = 0$, then $a' = (-a)$.

Proof: By hypothesis, $a + a' = 0$. Therefore, by Axiom 4 and by substitution, $(-a) = (-a) + 0 = (-a) + (a + a')$. Hence, by Axiom 1, $(-a) = [(-a) + a] + a'$. Using Axiom 2 twice, we have $(-a) = a' + [a + (-a)]$. By substitution and by Axiom 4, this becomes $(-a) = a' + 0 = a'$. *Q.E.D.*

COROLLARY. $(-(-a)) = a.$

Proof: By Axioms 2 and 6, $(-a) + a = 0$. Therefore, by Theorem 4, $a = (-(-a))$.   *Q.E.D.*

THEOREM 5.   The cancellation law for addition holds: For all elements a, b, c in **J**, if $a + b = a + c$, then $b = c$.

Proof: By hypothesis, $a + b = a + c$. Adding $(-a)$ to both sides of this equation, we have $(-a) + (a + b) = (-a) + (a + c)$. Therefore, by Axiom 1, $((-a) + a) + b = ((-a) + a) + c$. By Axioms 2 and 6, this equation may be replaced by $0 + b = 0 + c$. Hence, by Axioms 2 and 4, $b = c$.   *Q.E.D.*

Theorem 4 is a special case of the following theorem.

THEOREM 6.   Let a and b be any two elements in **J**. Then there is exactly one element x in **J** such that $a + x = b$.

Proof: Let $x = (-a) + b$. Then, by substitution, $a + x = a + ((-a) + b)$. Therefore, by Axiom 1, $a + x = (a + (-a)) + b$. By Axioms 6, 2, and 4, $a + x = 0 + b = b + 0 = b$. If there is an element x' in **J** such that $a + x' = b$, then, by substitution, $a + x = a + x'$. But then, by Theorem 5, $x = x'$.   *Q.E.D.*

THEOREM 7.   For every element a in **J**, $a \cdot 0 = 0$.

Proof: By Axiom 4, $a + 0 = a$. Multiplying both sides of this equation by a, we have $a(a + 0) = a \cdot a$. Therefore, by Axiom 3, $a \cdot a + a \cdot 0 = a \cdot a$. Using Axiom 4 again, we have $a \cdot a + a \cdot 0 = a \cdot a + 0$. Therefore, by Theorem 5, $a \cdot 0 = 0$.   *Q.E.D.*

THEOREM 8.   For any elements a and b in **J**, $(-a)b = -(ab)$.

Proof: By Axioms 2 and 3, $ab + (-a)b = ba + b(-a) = b(a + (-a))$. Therefore, by Axiom 6, $ab + (-a)b = b \cdot 0$. Hence, by Theorem 7, $ab + (-a)b = 0$. But, by Theorem 4, this means that $(-a)b = -(ab)$.   *Q.E.D.*

COROLLARY. $(-1)a = -a$ for all a in **J**.

Proof: By Theorem 8, $(-1)a = -(1 \cdot a)$. By Axiom 5, $1 \cdot a = a$. Therefore, by substitution, $(-1)a = -a$.   *Q.E.D.*

THEOREM 9.   For any elements a and b in **J**, $(-a)(-b) = ab$.

Proof: By Theorem 8, $(-a)(-b) = -(a(-b))$. Therefore, by Axiom 2, $(-a)(-b) = -((-b)a)$. Using Theorem 8 again, we have $(-a)(-b) = -(-(ba))$. But, by the corollary to Theorem 4, $-(-(ba)) = ba$. Therefore, by substitution and by Axiom 2, $(-a)(-b) = ba = ab$.   *Q.E.D.*

COROLLARY. $(-1)(-1) = 1.$

Proof: By Theorem 9, $(-1)(-1) = 1 \cdot 1$. By Axiom 5, $1 \cdot 1 = 1$. *Q.E.D.*

We shall denote $a + (-b)$ by $a - b$. It can be shown that $a(b - c) = ab - ac$; $a - (b + c) = (a - b) - c$; $-(a + b) = (-a) + (-b)$; $-(b - a) = a - b$; and $(-a)b = a(-b)$. (See Exercises 4 and 5, page 66.)

THEOREM 10. Let a and b be elements in **J**. If $ab = 0$, then either $a = 0$ or $b = 0$.

Proof: Either $a = 0$ or $a \neq 0$. If $a = 0$, there is nothing more to prove. Suppose that $a \neq 0$. By Theorem 7, $a \cdot 0 = 0$. Therefore, by the hypothesis and by substitution, $ab = a \cdot 0$. But, by Axiom 7, this means that $b = 0$. *Q.E.D.*

THEOREM 11. Let S be a set of elements satisfying the first six axioms for **J**. Suppose also that for any two elements a and b in S, if $ab = 0$, then either $a = 0$ or $b = 0$. Then S satisfies Axiom 7 for **J**.

Proof: Assume that a, b, and c are elements in S such that $ab = ac$ and $a \neq 0$. We must show that $b = c$. By Axiom 6, $ab + (-(ab)) = 0$. Therefore, by substitution, $ab + (-(ac)) = 0$. By Theorem 8 and Exercise 5C (page 66), this last equation can be replaced by $ab + a(-c) = 0$. Therefore, by Axiom 3, $a(b + (-c)) = 0$. By hypothesis, since $a \neq 0$, it follows that $b + (-c) = 0$. Adding c to both sides of this equation, we have $(b + (-c)) + c = 0 + c$. By Axioms 1 and 2 (used twice), this equation can be replaced by $b + (c + (-c)) = c + 0$. Now, by Axioms 6 and 4 (used twice), we have $b = c$. *Q.E.D.*

DEFINITION 5. A nonzero element a is called a zero divisor if there is a nonzero element b such that $ab = 0$.

Theorem 10 thus asserts that in an integral domain there are no zero divisors. Theorem 11 asserts that any set of elements satisfying the first six axioms for **J** and having no zero divisors is an integral domain; that is, the set satisfies the first seven axioms for **J**. Examples of algebraic systems containing zero divisors are given in Sec. 4-9.

EXERCISES

1. Prove Theorem 2, using the equivalence classes and definitions of Sec. 4-2; that is, prove that if $i, j, r, s,$ and m are any elements of **I**, and if $(r, s)\tilde{} \cdot (i, j)\tilde{} = (i, j)\tilde{}$, then $(r, s) \sim (m + 1, m)$.

2. Prove Theorem 3, using the equivalence classes and definitions of Sec. 4-2; that is, prove that if $i, j, r, s,$ and m are any elements of **I**, and if $(i, j)\tilde{} + (r, s)\tilde{} = (i, j)\tilde{}$, then $(r, s) \sim (m, m)$.

3. Prove Theorem 4, using the equivalence classes and definitions of Sec. 4-2; that is, prove that if $i, j, r, s,$ and m are any elements of $\mathbf{I}$, and if $(i, j)\tilde{} + (r, s)\tilde{} = (m, m)\tilde{}$, then $(r, s) \sim (j, i)$.

4. Prove that for any elements a, b, and c of an integral domain:
   a) $a(b - c) = ab - ac$.
   b) $a - (b + c) = (a - b) - c$.

5. Prove that for any elements a and b of an integral domain:
   a) $-(a + b) = (-a) + (-b)$.
   b) $-(b - a) = a - b$.
   c) $(-a)b = a(-b)$.

4-4.   CONSEQUENCES OF AXIOMS 1 THROUGH 8

In this section we shall derive some elementary consequences of the first eight axioms for the integers $\mathbf{J}$. Since these eight axioms characterize ordered integral domains, all the results of this section are valid for any ordered integral domain whatever.

THEOREM 12.   "Less than" (Definition 2, page 52) is an order relation on $\mathbf{J}$.

Proof: By Axiom 4 and Theorem 6, for any element a in $\mathbf{J}$, the equation $a + x = a$ has a unique solution, namely, $x = 0$. By Axiom 8c, $0 \notin P$. Therefore, by Definition 2, $a \not< a$.

Let a and b be any elements in $\mathbf{J}$. Then, by Definition 2, if $a < b$, there is an element x in P such that $a + x = b$. If $b < a$, there is an element y in P such that $b + y = a$. Substituting $(b + y)$ for a in the first equation, we have $(b + y) + x = b$. Therefore, by Axiom 1, $b + (y + x) = b$. By Axiom 8a, since x and y are in P, $x + y$ is in P also. But then, by Definition 2, $b < b$. This, however, contradicts the result established above—namely, that for all elements a in $\mathbf{J}$, $a \not< a$. Thus, the assumption that $a < b$ and $b < a$ leads to a contradiction and hence must be invalid. Therefore, if $a < b$, then $b \not< a$.

Let a, b, and c be any elements in $\mathbf{J}$. Then, by Definition 2, if $a < b$, there is an element x in P such that $a + x = b$. If $b < c$, there is an element y in P such that $b + y = c$. Substituting $(a + x)$ for b in the second equation, we have $(a + x) + y = c$. Therefore, by Axiom 1, $a + (x + y) = c$. By Axiom 8a, since x and y are in P, $x + y$ is in P also. Therefore, by Definition 2, $a < c$. Hence, if $a < b$ and $b < c$, then $a < c$.

Q.E.D.

THEOREM 13.   The integers $\mathbf{J}$ are linearly ordered by "less than."

Proof: We must show that for any two elements a and b in $\mathbf{J}$ exactly one holds: $a < b$; $a = b$; or $b < a$.

Now, by Axiom 8c, exactly one holds: $a - b \in P$, $a - b = 0$, or $-(a - b) \in P$. Suppose that $a - b = x \in P$. Adding b to both sides of this equation, we have $(a - b) + b = x + b$. By our notation and Axiom 1, this equation may be replaced by $a + ((-b) + b) = x + b$. Therefore, by Axioms 2, 6, and 4, $a = b + x$. But, by Definition 2, this means that $b < a$.

Suppose that $a - b = 0$. Adding b to both sides of this equation, we have $(a - b) + b = 0 + b$. By our notation and Axioms 1, 2, 6, and 4, this means that $a = b$.

If $-(a - b) = x \in P$, then, by Exercise 5b (page 66), $b - a = x$. Therefore, by the same argument as that used in the first part of this proof, $b = a + x$. Hence, by Definition 2, $a < b$. Thus, at least one of the following—$a < b$, $a = b$, $b < a$—holds. Since, by Theorem 12, "less than" is an order relation on **J**, at most one of the above holds. Hence exactly one holds. *Q.E.D.*

THEOREM 14. $a \in P$ if, and only if, $0 < a$.

Proof: Suppose that $a \in P$. By Axioms 2 and 4, $0 + a = a$. Therefore, by Definition 2, $0 < a$. Conversely, suppose that $0 < a$. Then, by Definition 2, there is an element x in P such that $0 + x = a$. But, by Axioms 2 and 4, $0 + a = a$. Therefore, by Theorem 6, $x = a$. Hence, by substitution, since $x \in P$, it follows that $a \in P$. *Q.E.D.*

In Axiom 8, the subset P of **J** was defined to be the set of positive elements. According to Theorem 14, an element a is positive if, and only if, $0 < a$. We shall now define "negative element."

DEFINITION 6. A negative element or negative integer is an element a in **J** such that $a < 0$.

COROLLARY. For any element a in **J**, exactly one holds: a is positive; a is negative; or $a = 0$.

Proof: This is a direct consequence of Theorems 13 and 14 and the definitions of "positive element" and "negative element."

THEOREM 15. Let a and b be any elements in **J**. Then $a < b$ if, and only if, $-b < -a$.

Proof: Suppose that $a < b$. Then, by Definition 2, there is an element x in P such that $a + x = b$. Therefore, by substitution and Theorem 6, $-(a + x) = -b$. Hence, by Exercise 5a (page 66), $(-a) + (-x) = -b$. Adding x to both sides of this equation, we have $((-a) + (-x)) + x = (-b) + x$. Therefore, by Axioms 1, 2, 6, and 4, $-a = (-b) + x$. But then, by Definition 2, $-b < -a$.

Conversely, suppose that $-b < -a$. Then, by Definition 2, there is an element x in P such that $(-b) + x = (-a)$. Adding $(-x)$ to both sides of this equation, we have $((-b) + x) + (-x) = (-a) + (-x)$. Therefore, by Axioms 1, 6, and 4, $(-b) = (-a) + (-x)$. Hence, by Exercise 5a (page 66), $(-b) = -(a + x)$. By substitution, Axiom 2, and Theorem 6, this means that $b = a + x$. But, by Definition 2, this means that $a < b$.

Q.E.D.

COROLLARY 1. For all a in **J**, $0 < a$ if, and only if, $-a < 0$.

Proof: By Theorem 15, $0 < a$ if, and only if, $-a < -0$. By Axiom 4, $0 + 0 = 0$. Therefore, by Axiom 6 and Theorem 4, $0 = -0$. Hence by substitution, $0 < a$ if, and only if, $-a < 0$. *Q.E.D.*

COROLLARY 2. For all a in **J**, $a < 0$ if, and only if, $0 < -a$.

Proof: By Theorem 15, $a < 0$ if, and only if $-0 < -a$. By the same argument as that used in the proof of Corollary 1, $-0 = 0$. Therefore, by substitution, $a < 0$ if, and only if, $0 < -a$. *Q.E.D.*

THEOREM 16. Let a, b, and c be any elements in **J**. Then $a < b$ if, and only if, $a + c < b + c$.

Proof: A proof may be given similar to the proof of Theorem 7, Chapter 3 (Exercise 1, page 71).

THEOREM 17. Let a, b, and c be any elements in **J** such that $0 < c$. Then $a < b$ if, and only if, $ac < bc$.

Proof: A proof may be given similar to the proof of Theorem 8, Chapter 3 (Exercise 2, page 71).

COROLLARY 1. If $0 < a$ and $0 < b$, then $0 < ab$.

Proof: Exercise 3, page 71.

Corollary 1 asserts that the product of two positive integers is positive. This assertion may be proved by using Theorem 14 instead of Theorem 17 (Exercise 3, page 71).

COROLLARY 2. If $0 < a$ and $b < 0$, then $ab < 0$.

Proof: Exercise 4, page 71.

Corollary 2 asserts that the product of a positive integer and a negative integer is negative.

COROLLARY 3. If $a < 0$ and $b < 0$, then $0 < ab$.

Proof: By hypothesis, $b < 0$. Therefore, by Corollary 2 of Theorem 15, $0 < (-b)$. By Theorem 17, since $a < 0$ (hypothesis), and since $0 < (-b)$, we have $a(-b) < 0(-b)$. But, by Exercise 5c (page 66), and Theorem 8, $a(-b) = (-a)b = -(ab)$. By Axiom 2 and Theorem 7, $0(-b) = 0$. Therefore, by substitution, $-(ab) < 0$. By Corollary 1 of Theorem 15, this means that $0 < ab$. *Q.E.D.*

Corollary 3 asserts that the product of two negative integers is positive.

COROLLARY 4. For any elements a, b, c in **J** such that $c < 0$; $a < b$ if, and only if, $bc < ac$.

Proof: Exercise 5, page 71.

THEOREM 18. For any elements a, b, c, d in **J**, if $a < b$ and $c < d$, then $a + c < b + d$.

Proof: A proof may be given similar to the proof of Theorem 9a, Chapter 3 (Exercise 6, page 71).

COROLLARY 1. If $0 < a$ and $0 < b$, then $0 < a + b$.

Proof: Exercise 7, page 71.

Corollary 1 asserts that the sum of two positive integers is positive. This assertion may be proved using Theorem 14 instead of Theorem 18 (Exercise 7, page 71).

COROLLARY 2. If $a < 0$ and $b < 0$, then $a + b < 0$.

Proof: Exercise 8, page 71.

Corollary 2 asserts that the sum of two negative integers is negative.

THEOREM 19. In any ordered integral domain, if $x \neq 0$, then $x^2 \in P$, where $x^2 = x \cdot x$.

Proof: By Axiom 8c, if $x \neq 0$, then $x \in P$ or $(-x) \in P$. By Theorem 9, $x^2 = (-x)^2$. Therefore, by Axiom 8b, $x^2 \in P$. *Q.E.D.*

COROLLARY 1. The complex numbers[2] do not form an ordered integral domain.

Proof: Suppose that there is a subset P of the complex numbers satisfying Axiom 8. Then, by Theorem 19 and Axiom 5, $1^2 = 1 \in P$. By Axiom 8c, since $1 \in P$, $(-1) \notin P$. But $i^2 = -1$; therefore, by Theorem 19, $-1 \in P$. Thus, the assumption that there is a subset P of the complex numbers satisfying Axiom 8 leads to a contradiction and hence must be invalid. *Q.E.D.*

[2] A rigorous development of the complex numbers will be discussed in Chapter 6. In proving this corollary, we shall use only the equation $i^2 = -1$. (See page 2.)

COROLLARY 2. $1 > 0$.

Proof: By Theorem 19, $1 \cdot 1 \in P$. By Axiom 5, $1 \cdot 1 = 1$. Therefore, by substitution, $1 \in P$. Hence, by Theorem 14, $1 > 0$. $\hspace{2cm}$ *Q.E.D.*

DEFINITION 7. The absolute value of an integer a, denoted by "$|a|$," is defined as follows:

$$|a| = \begin{cases} a \text{ if } a \geq 0; \\ -a \text{ if } a < 0. \end{cases}$$

For example, $|1| = 1$; $|-1| = 1$; $|0| = 0$.

COROLLARY 1. For all a in **J**, $|a| \geq 0$.

Proof: By Theorem 13, exactly one holds: $a = 0$, $a > 0$, or $a < 0$. If $a = 0$, then, by Definition 7, $|a| = 0$. If $a > 0$, then, by Definition 7, $|a| = a$. Hence, by substitution, $|a| > 0$.

$\hspace{1em}$ If $a < 0$, then, by Definition 7, $|a| = -a$. But, by Corollary 2 of Theorem 15, since $a < 0$, it follows that $-a > 0$. Hence, by substitution, $|a| > 0$. $\hspace{2cm}$ *Q.E.D.*

COROLLARY 2. For all elements a and b in **J**, $|ab| = |a| \cdot |b|$.

Proof: This assertion can be proved by considering all possible cases: a or $b = 0$; $a < 0$ and $b < 0$; $a > 0$ and $b > 0$; $a < 0$ and $b > 0$; and $a > 0$ and $b < 0$. For example, suppose that $a > 0$ and $b < 0$. Then, by Definition 7, $|a| = a$ and $|b| = -b$. Therefore, by substitution, $|a| \cdot |b| = a(-b)$. But, by Exercise 5c (page 66) and Theorem 8, $a(-b) = (-a)b = -(ab)$. Therefore, by substitution, $|a| \cdot |b| = -(ab)$. By Corollary 2 of Theorem 17, since $a > 0$ and $b < 0$ (hypothesis), it follows that $ab < 0$. Hence, by Definition 7, $|ab| = -(ab)$. Therefore, by substitution, $|ab| = |a| \cdot |b|$.

$\hspace{1em}$ The proofs of the other cases are left as an exercise (Exercise 13, page 71). $\hspace{2cm}$ *Q.E.D.*

COROLLARY 3. For all elements a and b in **J**, $|a| \leq b$ if, and only if, $-b \leq a \leq b$.

Proof: Suppose that $|a| \leq b$. By Definition 7, if $a \geq 0$, then $|a| = a$. Therefore, by substitution, $a \leq b$. By Definition 7, if $a < 0$, then $|a| = -a$. Therefore, by substitution, $-a \leq b$. But, by Theorem 15 and the corollary of Theorem 4, this means that $-b \leq -(-a) = a$. Combining the results from our two possibilities ($a \geq 0$ and $a < 0$), if $|a| \leq b$, then $-b \leq a \leq b$.

$\hspace{1em}$ Conversely, suppose that $-b \leq a \leq b$. If $|a| = a$, then, by substitution, $|a| \leq b$. If $|a| = -a$, we must show that $-a \leq b$. By hypothesis, $-b \leq a$. Therefore, by Theorem 15 and the corollary of Theorem 4, $-a \leq -(-b) = b$. $\hspace{2cm}$ *Q.E.D.*

Our next inequality, $|a + b| \leq |a| + |b|$, is often called the triangle inequality. This is because, in the complex number system, $|a + b|$, $|a|$, and $|b|$ may be interpreted as the lengths of the sides of a triangle.

COROLLARY 4. For all elements a and b in **J**, $|a + b| \leq |a| + |b|$.

Proof: By Exercise 12 (page 71), $-|a| \leq a \leq |a|$ and $-|b| \leq b \leq |b|$. Therefore, by Theorem 18, $-|a| + (-|b|) \leq a + b \leq |a| + |b|$. Applying Exercise 5a (page 66), we have $-(|a| + |b|) \leq a + b \leq |a| + |b|$. Hence, by Corollary 3, $|a + b| \leq |a| + |b|$.

$$Q.E.D.$$

EXERCISES

1. Prove Theorem 16, giving all reasons for every step in your proof.

2. Prove Theorem 17, giving all reasons for every step in your proof.

3. Give two proofs of Corollary 1 of Theorem 17, one proof using Theorem 17 and the other using Theorem 14.

4. Prove Corollary 2 of Theorem 17.

5. Prove Corollary 4 of Theorem 17.

6. Prove Theorem 18, giving all reasons for every step in your proof.

7. Give two proofs of Corollary 1 of Theorem 18, one proof using Theorem 18 and the other using Theorem 14.

8. Prove Corollary 2 of Theorem 18.

9. $-5 < 1$ and $-6 < 1$, but $(-5)(-6) = 30 \not< 1(1) = 1$. Hence, to have a multiplication theorem analogous to Theorem 18, a certain restriction must be placed on at least one of the integers $a, b, c,$ or d. Place a restriction on a so that a statement analogous to Theorem 18 will be valid. Prove this statement valid, giving all reasons for every step in your proof.

10. Give a proof of Theorem 19 different from the one given in the text.

11. Prove that if $a, b, x,$ and y are elements of an ordered integral domain, then $a - b < a - c$ if, and only if, $c < b$.

12. Prove that for all elements a in **J**, $-|a| \leq a \leq |a|$.

13. Complete the proof of Corollary 2 of Definition 7 (page 70).

14. Prove that if a and b are elements in **J**, then:

   a) $|a|^2 = |a^2|$.

   b) $|a - b| \leq |a| + |b|$.

15. Prove that for all elements a and b in **J** such that $b \geq 0$; $|a| \geq b$ if, and only if, $a \geq b$ or $-a \leq -b$.

4-5. CONSEQUENCES OF AXIOMS 1 THROUGH 9

In the remaining sections of this chapter, we shall derive consequences of all nine axioms for the integers **J**.

THEOREM 20.   There is no integer n such that $0 < n < 1$.

Proof: A proof may be given similar to the proof of Theorem 16, Chapter 3 (Exercise 1, page 76).

THEOREM 21.   Any subset H of P which has the following two properties is all of P: a) $1 \in H$, and b) whenever $x \in H$, then $x + 1 \in H$.

Proof: A proof may be given similar to the proof of Theorem 17, Chapter 3 (Exercise 2, page 76).

As in Chapter 3 on the positive integers, we denote $1 + 1$ by $2, 2 + 1$ by $3, 3 + 1$ by $4, \cdots$.

THEOREM 22.   The first and second principles of finite induction hold.

Proof: A proof may be given similar to the proofs of Theorems 10 and 15, Chapter 3 (Exercise 3, page 76).

In Sec. 4-1 we stated (but did not prove) that any two algebraic systems satisfying the axioms for **J** are isomorphic. Thus, the set P of Axiom 8 is isomorphic to the set P' of Theorem 1. By Lemma 17, P' is isomorphic to the set **I** of positive integers. Therefore, since the composition of two isomorphisms is an isomorphism, P is isomorphic to **I**. Because of this isomorphism, any property of the set **I** is a property of the set P as well; in particular, P has the properties asserted by Theorems 20, 21, and 22 simply because **I** has these properties.

THEOREM 23.   For any elements a and b in **J**, a) if $a < b + 1$, then $a < b$ or $a = b$; and b) if $a < b$, then $a + 1 \leq b$.

Proof: A proof may be given similar to the proof of Theorem 13, Chapter 3 (Exercise 4, page 76).

COROLLARY.   Let b be any element of **J**. Then there is no integer a such that $b < a < b + 1$.

Proof: A proof may be given similar to the proof of the Corollary of Theorem 13, Chapter 3. Another proof may be given by using Theorem 20 (Exercise 5, page 76).

THEOREM 24 (The Division Algorithm).   Let a and b be any integers in **J** with $b \neq 0$. Then there are unique integers q and r such that $a = bq + r$ and $0 \leq r < |b|$ (q being called the quotient and r the remainder).

Proof: Let $S = \{a - |b|x \,|\, x \in \mathbf{J}\}$. We first show that S contains a nonnegative integer. Suppose that $a \geq 0$. By notation, Theorems 7 and 8 and Axiom 4, $a - |b| \cdot 0 = a + (-|b| \cdot 0) = a + [(-|b|) \cdot 0] = a + 0 = a$. Therefore, $a - |b| \cdot 0$ is a nonnegative integer in S. Suppose that $a < 0$. Then, by Corollary 2 of Theorem 15, $-a > 0$. By hypothesis, Corollary 1 of Definition 7, and Theorem 20, $|b| \geq 1$. Therefore, by Theorem 17 and Axiom 5, $|b|(-a) \geq 1(-a) = -a$. Hence, by Exercise 6 (page 76), $a + |b|(-a)$ is a nonnegative integer in S.

Let S^* be the following subset of S:

$$S^* = \{y \,|\, y \in S \text{ and } y \geq 0\}.$$

By Axiom 9, S^* contains a smallest element r. Therefore, there is an integer z such that $r = a - |b|z$, $r \geq 0$. We now show that $r < |b|$. Suppose that $r \geq |b|$. By substitution, Axioms 2 and 5, Exercise 4b (page 66), Axiom 3, Theorem 8, and notation, $r - |b| = (a - |b|z) - |b| = (a - |b|z) - |b|1 = a - (|b|z + |b|1) = a - |b|(z + 1)$. Since $r - |b|$ has the form $a - |b|x$ and since $r \geq |b|$ (assumption), it follows, from our notation and Axiom 6, that $r - |b| \in S^*$. Now, by Definitions 2 and 7 and by Axioms 1, 2, 6, and 4, $r - |b| < r$. But this means that $r - |b|$ is an element of S^* which is less than the smallest element r of S^*. Thus, the assumption that $r \geq |b|$ leads to a contradiction and hence must be invalid. Therefore, $r < |b|$.

We next prove that z and r are unique. Suppose that $a = |b|z_1 + r_1 = |b|z_2 + r_2$, where $0 \leq r_1 < |b|$ and $0 \leq r_2 < |b|$. (Show how $r_1 = a - |b|z_1$ and $r_2 = a - |b|z_2$ lead to the above equations.) Without loss of generality, we may assume that $r_1 \leq r_2$. By Exercise 7 (page 76), $0 \leq r_2 - r_1 < |b|$. Therefore, by Axioms 1, 2, 6, and 4 and by substitution, $|b|z_1 - |b|z_2 = r_2 - r_1 < |b|$. Hence, by Exercise 4a (page 66), $|b|(z_1 - z_2) = r_2 - r_1 < |b|$.

Suppose that $z_1 \neq z_2$. Then, by Theorem 13, either $z_1 < z_2$ or $z_2 < z_1$. If $z_2 < z_1$, then, by Theorem 16, Axiom 6, Theorem 20, and notation, $z_1 - z_2 \geq 1$. Therefore, by hypothesis, Definition 7, Theorem 17, and Axioms 2 and 5, $|b|(z_1 - z_2) \geq |b| \cdot 1 = |b|$. But this contradicts the inequality above, that $|b|(z_1 - z_2) < |b|$. If $z_1 < z_2$, then (give all reasons) $|b|(z_1 - z_2) < 0$. But this contradicts the result above, that $|b|(z_1 - z_2) = r_2 - r_1 \geq 0$. Thus, the assumption that $z_1 \neq z_2$ leads to contradictions and hence must be invalid. Therefore, $z_1 = z_2$.

Since $z_1 = z_2$, it follows that (give all reasons) $z_1 - z_2 = 0$. Substituting 0 for $z_1 - z_2$ in the equation $|b|(z_1 - z_2) = r_2 - r_1$, we have, by Theorem 7, $0 = r_2 - r_1$. Hence (give all reasons) $r_1 = r_2$. Thus, we have shown that there are unique integers z and r such that $a = |b|z + r$.

If $b > 0$, then, by Definition 7, $|b| = b$. In this case, take q as z.

If $b < 0$, then, by Definition 7, $|b| = -b$. Since, by Exercise 5c (page 66), $-b(z) = b(-z)$, in this case we take q as $-z$. In either case, there are unique integers q and r such that $a = bq + r$.   *Q.E.D.*

Examples   1. If $a = 10$ and $b = 2$, then $q = 5$ and $r = 0$.
2. If $a = 10$ and $b = 3$, then $q = 3$ and $r = 1$.
3. If $a = 10$ and $b = 13$, then $q = 0$ and $r = 10$.
4. If $a = 10$ and $b = -3$, then $q = -3$ and $r = 1$.
5. If $a = 10$ and $b = -13$, then $q = 0$ and $r = 10$.
6. If $a = -10$ and $b = 3$, then $q = -4$ and $r = 2$.
7. If $a = -10$ and $b = 13$, then $q = -1$ and $r = 3$.
8. If $a = -10$ and $b = -3$, then $q = 4$ and $r = 2$.

Notice that, in each of the above examples, $0 \leq r < |b|$.

We shall use the following two lemmas in the proof of Theorem 25.

LEMMA 19.   In the equation $a = bq + r$, where $0 \leq r < b$, if $a \geq 0$ and $b > 0$, then $q \geq 0$.

Proof: By Theorem 13, exactly one holds: $a < b$, $a = b$, or $a > b$. If $a < b$, then $a = b \cdot 0 + a$; therefore, $q = 0$. If $a = b$, then $a = b \cdot 1 + 0$; therefore, $q = 1$.

Suppose that $a > b$. Then, by Definition 2 (page 52), there is an element x in P such that $a = b + x$. Substituting for a in the equation $a = bq + r$ and using the inequality $0 \leq r < b$, we have $b + x < bq + b$. Therefore, by Axiom 2 and Theorem 16, $x < bq$. Since x and b are both positive, q must be positive also. (Give all reasons.)   *Q.E.D.*

LEMMA 20.   In the equation $a = bq + r$, where $0 \leq r < b$, if $a > 0$ and $b > 1$, then $a > q$.

Proof: By Lemma 19, $q \geq 0$. (Why can we use Lemma 19?) If $q = 0$, there is nothing more to prove. Suppose that $q > 0$. By hypothesis, $a = bq + r$ and $r \geq 0$. Therefore, by Definition 2 (page 52), $bq \leq a$. If $a \leq q$, then, by Theorem 12 and Axiom 5, $bq \leq q = 1q$. Since $q > 0$ (assumption), it follows, from Theorem 17 and Axioms 2 and 7, that $b \leq 1$. But this contradicts the hypothesis that $b > 1$. Thus, the assumption that $a \leq q$ leads to a contradiction and hence must be invalid. Therefore, $a > q$.   *Q.E.D.*

DEFINITION 8.   For any elements x in J and m in P:
   a) $x^1 = x$;
   b) $x^{m+1} = x^m \cdot x^1$.

THEOREM 25.   Let a be any positive integer; let b be an integer greater than 1. Then, for some positive integer m, there are unique integers

$c_0, c_1, \cdots, c_m$ such that $a = c_0 + c_1 b + c_2 b^2 + \cdots + c_m b^m$ and $0 \leq c_i < b$ for $i = 0, 1, \cdots, m$ with $c_m \neq 0$.

Proof: Using the division algorithm (Theorem 24) repeatedly, we have

$$a = bq_0 + c_0, \; 0 \leq c_0 < b$$
$$q_0 = bq_1 + c_1, \; 0 \leq c_1 < b$$
$$q_1 = bq_2 + c_2, \; 0 \leq c_2 < b$$
$$\vdots \qquad \vdots \qquad \vdots$$
$$q_{k-1} = bq_k + c_k, \; 0 \leq c_k < b$$
$$q_k = bq_{k+1} + c_{k+1}, \; 0 \leq c_{k+1} < b$$
$$\vdots \qquad \vdots \qquad \vdots$$

Since $a > 0$ and $b > 0$, it follows, from Lemma 19, that $q_0 \geq 0$. (Why is b greater than 0?) Since $q_0 \geq 0$ and $b > 0$, it follows, from Lemma 19, that $q_1 \geq 0$. Similarly, $q_k \geq 0$ for all positive integers k.

Suppose that $q_k > 0$ for all positive integers k. Then, by Lemma 20, we would have $q_0 > q_1 > q_2 > \cdots > q_k > \cdots$. Thus $\{q_0, q_1, \cdots\}$ would be a set of positive integers with no least element. But, by Axiom 9, such a set cannot exist. Hence there is a first integer, say m, such that $q_m = 0$. Therefore, we have (why?) $q_{m-1} = bq_m + c_m = b \cdot 0 + c_m; q_m = b \cdot 0 + 0$.

Returning to the list of equations at the beginning of this proof, if we substitute q_0 from the second equation into the first, we have

$$a = b(bq_1 + c_1) + c_0.$$

Therefore, by Axioms 1, 2, and 3, $a = c_0 + c_1 b + q_1 b^2$. Substituting q_1 from the third equation into the above equation, we have $a = c_0 + c_1 b + (bq_2 + c_2)b^2$. Therefore, by Axioms 1, 2, and 3, $a = c_0 + c_1 b + c_2 b^2 + q_2 b^3$.

By similar reasoning, after m such substitutions, we have $a = c_0 + c_1 b + c_2 b^2 + \cdots + c_m b^m + q_m b^{m+1}$, where $q_m = 0$, $0 \leq c_i < b$ for $i = 0, 1, \cdots, m$, and $c_m \neq 0$. Thus, $a = c_0 + c_1 b + c_2 b^2 + \cdots + c_m b^m$.

Now we must show that this representation of a is unique. Suppose that $a = c_0 + c_1 b + c_2 b^2 + \cdots + c_m b^m = d_0 + d_1 b + d_2 b^2 + \cdots + d_r b^r$, where $0 \leq c_i < b$ for $i = 0, 1, \cdots, m$, and $0 \leq d_j < b$ for $j = 0, 1, \cdots, r$. By repeated use of Axioms 1, 2, and 3, $a = c_0 + b(c_1 + c_2 b + \cdots + c_m b^{m-1}) = d_0 + b(d_1 + d_2 b + \cdots + d_r b^{r-1})$. Therefore, by the uniqueness of the quotient and remainder (Theorem 24), $c_0 = d_0$ and $(c_1 + c_2 b + \cdots + c_m b^{m-1}) = (d_1 + d_2 b + \cdots + d_r b^{r-1}) = q_0$. By repeated use of Axioms 1, 2, and 3, $q_0 = c_1 + b(c_2 + c_3 b + \cdots + c_m b^{m-2}) = d_1 + b(d_2 + d_3 b + \cdots + d_r b^{r-2})$. Therefore, by the uniqueness of the quotient and remainder (Theorem 24), $c_1 = d_1$ and $(c_2 + c_3 b + \cdots + c_m b^{m-2}) = (d_2 + d_3 b + \cdots + d_r b^{r-2}) = q_1$. Continuing in this way, we eventually prove that $c_i = d_i$ for $i = 0, 1, \cdots, m$ and that $m = r$. $Q.E.D.$

EXERCISES

1. Prove Theorem 20, giving all reasons for every step in your proof.
2. Prove Theorem 21, giving all reasons for every step in your proof.
3. Prove Theorem 22, giving all reasons for every step in your proof.
4. Prove Theorem 23, giving all reasons for every step in your proof.
5. Use Theorem 20 to prove the corollary of Theorem 23.
6. Prove that if $c \geq -a$, then $a + c \geq 0$. (See the proof of Theorem 24, page 73.)
7. Let r_1, r_2, and b be elements in **J** such that $0 \leq r_1 < b, 0 \leq r_2 < b$, and $r_1 \leq r_2$. Prove that $0 \leq r_2 - r_1 < b$.

4-6. NUMBER SYSTEMS TO VARIOUS BASES

Theorem 25 justifies the decimal[3] system of notation; that is, the representation of a positive integer a as a sum of multiples of powers of 10, where each multiple is an integer between 0 and 9, inclusive. For example, in the decimal system, the symbol 42059 represents the integer $4(10^4) + 2(10^3) + 0(10^2) + 5(10) + 9$. According to Theorem 25, moreover, we can represent a positive integer a as a sum of multiples of powers of *any* integer b greater than 1, where each multiple is an integer between 0 and $b - 1$ inclusive. When an integer a is thus represented in terms of b, we say that a is represented to the base b. Thus, an integer represented in the decimal system is said to be represented to the base 10.

Once the base b is chosen, an integer can be specified simply by giving the coefficients of the powers of b. We shall use the notation $(c_m, c_{m-1}, \cdots, c_1, c_0)_b$ to denote a certain integer represented to the base b, namely, the integer $c_m b^m + c_{m-1} b^{m-1} + \cdots + c_1 b + c_0$. The subscript b, which indicates the base, will always be written in the decimal system. If $b = 10$, the subscript will be omitted.

Examples   **1.** $(324)_5$ denotes $3(5^2) + 2(5) + 4 = 89$.
               2. $(3012)_4$ denotes $3(4^3) + 0(4^2) + 1(4) + 2 = 198$.
               3. $(892)_{12}$ denotes $8(12^2) + 9(12) + 2 = 1262$.
               4. $(512)_{1000}$ denotes $5(1000^2) + 1(1000) + 2 = 5,001,002$.

One needs only a finite number of distinct symbols (at most, b) to represent any given integer to the base b.

---

[3] From the Latin *decem*, meaning "ten."

Examples
1. When $b = 10$, one needs, at most, ten symbols; we shall use the symbols 0, 1, 2, 3, 4, 5, 6, 7, 8, 9.
2. When $b = 4$, one needs, at most, four symbols; we shall use the symbols 0, 1, 2, 3.
3. When $b = 2$, one needs, at most, two symbols; we shall use the symbols 0, 1.
4. When $b = 12$, one needs, at most, twelve symbols; we shall use the symbols 0, 1, 2, 3, 4, 5, 6, 7, 8, 9, t, e. [t and e were chosen to represent the integers ten and eleven. Notice that the symbols $(10)_{12}$ and $(11)_{12}$ represent (in base 10) the integers 12 and 13 respectively, and not 10 and 11.]

According to the proof of Theorem 25, when a positive integer a is represented in the form $c_m b^m + c_{m-1} b^{m-1} + \cdots + c_1 b + c_0$, the coefficients $c_0, c_1, \cdots, c_m$ may be obtained by repeated use of the division algorithm (page 72). Thus, the proof of Theorem 25 contains an effective method for computing the coefficients of the powers of b.[4]

Examples
1. To represent 1526 to the base 8, we may proceed as follows: $1526 = 8(190) + 6$; that is, $a = bq_0 + c_0$; $q_0 = 190$ and $c_0 = 6$. $190 = 8(23) + 6$; that is, $q_0 = bq_1 + c_1$; $q_1 = 23$ and $c_1 = 6$. $23 = 8(2) + 7$; that is, $q_1 = bq_2 + c_2$; $q_2 = 2$ and $c_2 = 7$. $2 = 8(0) + 2$; that is, $q_2 = bq_3 + c_3$; $q_3 = 0$ and $c_3 = 2$. Therefore, $1526 = 2(8^3) + 7(8^2) + 6(8) + 6 = (2766)_8$.
2. To represent 1526 to the base 12, we may proceed as follows: $1526 = 12(127) + 2$; that is, $c_0 = 2$. $127 = 12(10) + 7$; that is, $c_1 = 7$. $10 = 12(0) + 10$; that is, $c_2 = 10$. Therefore, $1526 = 10(12^2) + 7(12) + 2 = (t72)_{12}$.

To represent $(c_m, c_{m-1}, \cdots, c_1, c_0)_b$ to the base 10, we simply compute $c_m b^m + c_{m-1} b^{m-1} + \cdots + c_1 b + c_0$.

Example. $(t9e)_{12} = 10(12^2) + 9(12) + 11 = 1559$.

We shall now give an example illustrating the addition of integers represented to the base 12. The same procedure applies for adding integers represented to any base b greater than 1.

Example. We may compute $(t9)_{12} + (e8)_{12}$ as follows: By repeated use of Axioms 1, 2, and 3,

---

[4]In the remainder of this chapter, we shall assume the usual addition and multiplication tables for integers represented to the base 10.

$$
\begin{aligned}
(t9)_{12} + (e8)_{12} &= [10(12) + 9] + [11(12) + 8] \\
&= [10(12) + 11(12)] + [9 + 8] \\
&= [10(12) + 11(12)] + [1(12) + 5] \\
&= [10 + 11 + 1](12) + 5 \\
&= [12 + 10](12) + 5 \\
&= 1(12^2) + 10(12) + 5 \\
&= (1t5)_{12}.
\end{aligned}
$$

The work above may be shortened as follows: Listing the integers in a column, we have

$$
\begin{aligned}
(t9)_{12} \\
+(e8)_{12}
\end{aligned}
$$

Adding the right (or unit) column, we have $(9)_{12} + (8)_{12} = 9 + 8 = 17 = (15)_{12}$. We place the 5 in the unit column and carry the 1 to the next (or 12) column:

$$
\begin{aligned}
(10)_{12} \\
(t9)_{12} \\
+(e8)_{12} \\
\hline
(\ 5)_{12}
\end{aligned}
$$

We do this because $(15)_{12}$ means $1(12) + 5$; hence 1 belongs in the 12 column. Adding the integers in the 12 column, we have $(1)_{12} + (t)_{12} + (e)_{12} = 1 + 10 + 11 = 22 = (1t)_{12}$. We place the t in the 12 column and carry the 1 to the next (or 12^2) column:

$$
\begin{aligned}
(100)_{12} \\
(t9)_{12} \\
+\ \ (e8)_{12} \\
\hline
(\ t5)_{12}
\end{aligned}
$$

We do this because we added $[1 + 10 + 11](12)$ to get $[12 + 10](12) = 1(12^2) + 10(12)$; hence 1 belongs in the 12^2 column. Adding the integers in the 12^2 column, we have $(1)_{12} + (0)_{12} + (0)_{12} = 1 + 0 + 0 = 1 = (1)_{12}$, assuming a 0 in the 12^2 column for $(t9)_{12}$ and $(e8)_{12}$. Therefore,

$$
\begin{aligned}
(t9)_{12} \\
+\ \ (e8)_{12} \\
\hline
(1t5)_{12}
\end{aligned}
$$

If one had to do much computing with integers represented to the base 12, it would be advisable to learn the base-12 addition table. In the accompanying table and in the computations which follow, the subscript 12, which belongs after each integer, has been omitted.

+	0	1	2	3	4	5	6	7	8	9	t	e
0	0	1	2	3	4	5	6	7	8	9	t	e
1	1	2	3	4	5	6	7	8	9	t	e	10
2	2	3	4	5	6	7	8	9	t	e	10	11
3	3	4	5	6	7	8	9	t	e	10	11	12
4	4	5	6	7	8	9	t	e	10	11	12	13
5	5	6	7	8	9	t	e	10	11	12	13	14
6	6	7	8	9	t	e	10	11	12	13	14	15
7	7	8	9	t	e	10	11	12	13	14	15	16
8	8	9	t	e	10	11	12	13	14	15	16	17
9	9	t	e	10	11	12	13	14	15	16	17	18
t	t	e	10	11	12	13	14	15	16	17	18	19
e	e	10	11	12	13	14	15	16	17	18	19	$1t$

With this table, $t9 + e8$ may be computed directly as follows: Listing the integers in a column, we have

$$\begin{array}{r} t9 \\ +e8 \end{array}$$

$9 + 8 = 15$. We place 5 in the unit column and carry 1 to the 12 column. $1 + t + e = e + e = 1t$. We place t in the 12 column and 1 in the 12^2 column. Thus, we have

$$\begin{array}{r} t9 \\ +\ e8 \\ \hline 1t5 \end{array}$$

The following example illustrates the multiplication of integers represented to the base 12. The same procedure applies for multiplying integers represented to any base b greater than 1.

Example. We may compute $(7)_{12} \cdot (85e)_{12}$ as follows: By repeated use of Axioms 1, 2, 3, 4, and 5,

$$(7)_{12} \cdot (85e)_{12} = 7[8(12^2) + 5(12) + 11]$$
$$= 56(12^2) + 35(12) + 77$$
$$= [4(12) + 8](12^2) + 35(12) + [6(12) + 5]$$
$$= 4(12^3) + 8(12^2) + [35 + 6](12) + 5$$
$$= 4(12^3) + 8(12^2) + [3(12) + 5](12) + 5$$
$$= 4(12^3) + [8 + 3](12^2) + 5(12) + 5$$
$$= 4(12^3) + 11(12^2) + 5(12) + 5$$
$$= (4e55)_{12}.$$

The work above may be shortened as follows: Listing the integers in a column, we have

$$(85e)_{12}$$
$$\underline{\cdot \quad (7)_{12}}$$

Multiplying the right (or unit) column, we have $(7)_{12} \cdot (e)_{12} = 7(11) = 77 = (65)_{12}$. We place the 5 in the unit column and carry the 6 to the 12 column:

$$(\ 60)_{12}$$
$$(85e)_{12}$$
$$\underline{\cdot \quad (7)_{12}}$$
$$(\ 5)_{12}$$

We do this because $(65)_{12}$ means $6(12) + 5$; hence 6 belongs in the 12 column. Now, $(7)_{12} \cdot (5)_{12} + (6)_{12} = 7(5) + 6 = 41 = (35)_{12}$. We place the 5 in the 12 column and carry the 3 to the 12^2 column:

$$(300)_{12}$$
$$(85e)_{12}$$
$$\underline{\cdot \quad (7)_{12}}$$
$$(\ 55)_{12}$$

We do this because we are actually computing $7[5(12)] + 6(12)$. We get $41(12) = [3(12) + 5](12) = 3(12^2) + 5(12)$; hence 3 belongs in the 12^2 column. Continuing the computation, $(7)_{12} \cdot (8)_{12} + (3)_{12} = 7(8) + 3 = 59 = (4e)_{12}$. We place the e in the 12^2 column and carry the 4 to the 12^3 column (Why?):

$$(4000)_{12}$$
$$(\ 85e)_{12}$$
$$\underline{\cdot \quad (7)_{12}}$$
$$(e55)_{12}$$

Since $(7)_{12} \cdot (0)_{12} + (4)_{12} = 7 \cdot 0 + 4 = 4 = (4)_{12}$, the product of the given numbers is $(4e55)_{12}$. (Why?)

Again, if one had to do much computing with integers represented to the base 12, it would be advisable to learn the base-12 multiplication table (Exercise 6, page 82).

The system of notation in which integers are represented to the base 12 is sometimes called the duodecimal system of notation. This is because *duodecim* is the Latin word for "twelve."

We next consider the system of notation in which integers are represented to the base 2; that is, the binary system of notation. In this system the notation for an integer greater than 1 is longer than in the decimal system. For example, since $41 = 1(2^5) + 0(2^4) + 1(2^3) + 0(2^2) + 0(2) + 1$, we have $41 = (101001)_2$. Computations in the binary system are much simpler than in the decimal system, however, since two symbols, at most, are needed to represent any integer. In the base-2 addition and multiplication tables below, and in the computations following them, the subscript 2, which belongs after each integer, has been omitted.

+	0	1
0	0	1
1	1	10

·	0	1
0	0	0
1	0	1

Examples of computations in the binary system are given below.

Examples   **1.**

$$
\begin{array}{r}
1001101 \\
+ \quad 1010 \\
\hline
1{,}010{,}111
\end{array}
$$

We may check this result as follows: $(1{,}001{,}101)_2 = 1(2^6) + 0(2^5) + 0(2^4) + 1(2^3) + 1(2^2) + 0(2) + 1 = 77$. $(1010)_2 = 1(2^3) + 0(2^2) + 1(2) + 0 = 10$. $(1{,}010{,}111)_2 = 1(2^6) + 0(2^5) + 1(2^4) + 0(2^3) + 1(2^2) + 1(2) + 1 = 87 = 77 + 10$.

2.

$$
\begin{array}{r}
1001101 \\
\cdot \quad 1010 \\
\hline
10011010 \\
10011010 \quad\;\; \\
\hline
1{,}100{,}000{,}010
\end{array}
$$

We may check this result as follows: As shown in Example 1, $(1{,}001{,}101)_2 = 77$; $(1010)_2 = 10$. Moreover, $(1{,}100{,}000{,}010)_2 = 1(2^9) + 1(2^8) + 1(2) = 770 = 10(77)$.

The binary system is frequently used in electronic computers, the two symbols 0 and 1 being represented by the "on" and "off" positions of electrical switches.

EXERCISES

1. Represent 534:
   a) to the base 2;
   b) to the base 5;
   c) to the base 15.
2. Represent $(16te)_{12}$:
   a) to the base 10;
   b) to the base 15.
3. a) What is the greatest integer in the duodecimal system less than $(1000)_{12}$? b) Represent this integer in the decimal system.
4. a) Add and multiply the following integers without converting to the decimal system: $(111)_2$ and $(1010)_2$. b) Check your results by converting to the decimal system.
5. a) Add and multiply the following integers without converting to the decimal system: $(142)_5$ and $(344)_5$. b) Check your results by converting to the decimal system.
6. Write out the base-12 multiplication table.
7. a) Prove that every positive integer can be represented uniquely in the form $c_0 + 3c_1 + 9c_2 + 27c_3 + \cdots$, where $c_0, c_1, c_2, \cdots = -1, 0,$ or 1. b) A druggist has only the five weights of 1, 3, 9, 27, and 81 oz. He also has a two-pan balance. Show how he can weigh any object up to 121 oz in weight.
8. a) What is the remainder when 8057 is divided by 10? b) What is the remainder when $(1022)_3$ is divided by 3? c) What is the remainder when $(11001)_2$ is divided by 2?

4-7. DIVISIBILITY

DEFINITION 9. An integer $a \neq 0$ divides an integer b if there is an integer c such that $b = ac$.

If a divides b, we say that a is a divisor (or factor) of b, and that b is divisible by a, or b is a multiple of a.

If a divides b, we write $a \mid b$. If a does not divide b, we write $a \nmid b$.

Examples   **1.** $2 \mid 12$, since $12 = 2(6)$.
               2. $(-2) \mid 12$, since $12 = (-2)(-6)$.
               3. $2 \nmid 7$, since there is no integer c such that $7 = 2c$.

THEOREM 26. If a divides b, then there is exactly one integer c such that $b = ac$.

Proof: Suppose that c_1 and c_2 are integers such that $b = ac_1$ and $b = ac_2$. Then, by substitution, $ac_1 = ac_2$. By Definition 9, $a \neq 0$. Therefore, by Axiom 7, $c_1 = c_2$.   *Q.E.D.*

The Integers

THEOREM 27. An integer $a \neq 0$ is divisible by a, $-a$, 1, and -1.

Proof: By Axiom 5 and Theorem 9, $a = 1a = (-1)(-a)$. Therefore, by Definition 9 and Axiom 2, a is divisible by a, $-a$, 1, and -1. *Q.E.D.*

THEOREM 28. If $a \mid b$ and $b \mid c$, then $a \mid c$; that is, the relation "divides" is transitive.

Proof: By hypothesis, $a \mid b$ and $b \mid c$. Therefore, by Definition 9, there are integers x and y such that $b = ax$ and $c = by$. Substituting ax for b in the second equation and using Axiom 1, we have $c = (ax)y = a(xy)$. Therefore, by Definition 9, $a \mid c$. *Q.E.D.*

It can be shown (Exercise 1, page 87) that the relation "divides" is neither an equivalence relation nor an order relation.

THEOREM 29. If $a \mid b$ and $a \mid c$, then $a \mid (b + c)$.

Proof: By hypothesis, $a \mid b$ and $a \mid c$. Therefore, by Definition 9, there are integers x and y such that $b = ax$ and $c = ay$. Adding these two equations and using Axiom 3, we have $b + c = ax + ay = a(x + y)$. Therefore, by Definition 9, $a \mid (b + c)$. *Q.E.D.*

COROLLARY 1. If $a \mid b$ and $a \mid c$, then $a \mid (b - c)$.

Proof: Exercise 2, page 87.

COROLLARY 2. An integer represented in the decimal system is divisible by 4 if, and only if, the integer represented by the last two digits of the given integer is divisible by 4.

Proof: Exercise 3, page 87.

Example. Since $4 \mid 27500$ and $4 \mid 36$, it follows, from Theorem 29, that $4 \mid (27500 + 36) = 27536$. Since $4 \mid 36$, it follows, from Corollary 2, that $4 \mid 27536$.

THEOREM 30. If $a \mid (b + c)$ and $a \mid b$, then $a \mid c$.

Proof: Exercise 4, page 87.

THEOREM 31. If $a \mid b$, then $|a| \leq |b|$.

Proof: By hypothesis, $a \mid b$. Therefore, by Definition 9, there is an integer c such that $b = ac$. Hence, by Corollary 2 of Definition 7, $|b| = |ac| = |a||c|$. By Definition 7 (used twice), Definition 9, and Theorem 20, $0 < |a|$ and $1 \leq |c|$. Therefore, by Theorem 17 and Axioms 2 and 5, $|a| = |a| \cdot 1 \leq |a||c| = |b|$. *Q.E.D.*

THEOREM 32. If $a \mid b$ and $b \mid a$, then $a = b$ or $a = -b$. (We denote this by writing "$a = \pm b$.")

Proof: By hypothesis, $a \mid b$ and $b \mid a$. Therefore, by Theorem 31, $|a| \leq |b|$ and $|b| \leq |a|$. Hence, by Theorem 12, $|a| = |b|$. But by Definition 7, this means that $a = \pm b$. *Q.E.D.*

COROLLARY. The only integers which divide 1 are 1 and -1.

Proof: Let a be any nonzero integer. By Theorem 27, $1 \mid a$. Therefore, if $a \mid 1$, it follows, from Theorem 32, that $a = \pm 1$. *Q.E.D.*

THEOREM 33. Let S be a nonempty set of integers such that for all elements a and b in S, $a + b \in S$ and $a - b \in S$; that is, S is closed under addition and subtraction. Then $S = \{0\}$, or there is a positive integer d such that $S = \{nd \mid n \in \mathbf{J}\}$.

Proof: If $S \neq \{0\}$, then S contains an element $a \neq 0$. Since $a \in S$, it follows, from the hypothesis, that $0 = a - a \in S$ and $-a = 0 - a \in S$. By Axiom 8c, either $a \in P$ or $-a \in P$. Thus, S contains a positive integer. Hence, by Axiom 9, S contains a smallest positive integer d.

We now use induction to show that S contains all positive multiples of d. By Axiom 5, $1d \in S$. Suppose $nd \in S$ for some positive integer n. We must show that $(n + 1)d \in S$. Now, by Axioms 2 and 3, $(n + 1)d = nd + d$. By hypothesis, since $d \in S$ and $nd \in S$, it follows that $nd + d \in S$. Therefore, by substitution, $(n + 1)d \in S$. Hence $nd \in S$ for all positive integers n.

We have shown that $0 \in S$ and $nd \in S$, where n is a positive integer. Therefore, by hypothesis, $0 - (nd) \in S$. But, by notation, Axioms 2 and 4, and Theorem 8, $0 - (nd) = -(nd) = (-n)d$. Hence, by substitution, $(-n)d \in S$. Thus, S contains all integral multiples of d.

Now we must show that every element a in S is an integral multiple of d. By the division algorithm, $a = dq + r$, where $0 \leq r < |d| = d$. Since $a \in S$ and $dq = qd \in S$, it follows, from the hypothesis, that $a - dq \in S$. But $a - dq = r$. (Why?) Therefore, $r \in S$. Since $0 \leq r < d$, and since d is the smallest positive integer in S, it follows that $r = 0$. Therefore, $a = dq$, and hence a is a multiple of d. *Q.E.D.*

It can be shown that a nonempty set of integers closed under subtraction must also be closed under addition (Exercise 6b, page 87). Hence the conclusion of Theorem 33 can be established under the weaker hypothesis that S is a nonempty set of integers closed under subtraction.

DEFINITION 10. An integer d is called the greatest common divisor (g.c.d.) of the integers a and b if the following conditions are satisfied:

    a) $d > 0$.

    b) $d \mid a$ and $d \mid b$; that is, d is a common divisor of a and b.

    c) If $c \mid a$ and $c \mid b$, then $c \mid d$; that is, d is a multiple of every other common divisor of a and b.

Examples   **1.** 8 is the g.c.d. of 24 and 32.

          2. 1 is the g.c.d. of 6 and 23.

In Definition 10 we spoke of "the" greatest common divisor of a and b rather than of "a" greatest common divisor of a and b. This is because d is unique. (See the following corollary.)

COROLLARY. If both d and d' are the greatest common divisors of a and b, then $d = d'$.

Proof: By condition c of Definition 10, $d \mid d'$ and $d' \mid d$. Therefore, by Theorem 32, $d = \pm d'$. But, by condition a of Definition 10, this means that $d = d'$.   *Q.E.D.*

We denote the greatest common divisor of a and b by the symbol "(a, b)." It can easily be shown (Exercise 5, page 87) that $(a, b) = (b, a) = (-a, b) = (a, -b) = (-a, -b)$.

THEOREM 34. If a and b are nonzero integers, then the greatest common divisor (a, b) exists. (a, b) can be expressed in the form $ma + nb$, where m and n are integers. ($ma + nb$ is called a linear combination of a and b.)

Proof: Method 1. Let $S = \{ma + nb \mid m, n \in J\}$. By Axioms 2, 4, and 5, and Theorem 7, $a = 1a + 0 \cdot b$ and $b = 0 \cdot a + 1b$. Therefore, S is not empty. By Axioms 1, 2, and 3 and Exercises 4 and 5 (page 66), $(m_1 a + n_1 b) \pm (m_2 a + n_2 b) = (m_1 \pm m_2)a + (n_1 \pm n_2)b$. Therefore, S is closed under addition and subtraction. Hence, by Theorem 33, S consists of all multiples of a smallest positive integer d.

We shall show that $d = (a, b)$. Since a and b are in S, it follows that a and b are multiples of d; that is, $d \mid a$ and $d \mid b$. Since $d \in S$, there are integers m and n such that $d = ma + nb$. Suppose that there is an integer c such that $c \mid a$ and $c \mid b$. Then, by Definition 9, there are integers x and y such that $a = cx$ and $b = cy$. Therefore, by substitution and Axioms 1, 2, and 3, $d = m(cx) + n(cy) = c(mx + ny)$. Hence, by Definition 9, $c \mid d$.   *Q.E.D.* (Method 1)

Method 2 (The Euclidean Algorithm).   Using the division algorithm repeatedly, we obtain

$$a = bq_1 + r_1, 0 < r_1 < |b|;$$
$$b = r_1 q_2 + r_2, 0 < r_2 < r_1;$$
$$r_1 = r_2 q_3 + r_3, 0 < r_3 < r_2;$$
$$r_2 = r_3 q_4 + r_4, 0 < r_4 < r_3;$$
$$\cdots\cdots\cdots\cdots\cdots\cdots\cdots\cdots$$
$$r_{k-3} = r_{k-2} q_{k-1} + r_{k-1}, 0 < r_{k-1} < r_{k-2};$$
$$r_{k-2} = r_{k-1} q_k + r_k, 0 < r_k < r_{k-1};$$
$$r_{k-1} = r_k q_{k+1} + 0.$$

We now must explain why there is a first k such that $r_{k+1} = 0$. If there were no such k, then we would have a sequence of positive integers $r_1 > r_2 > r_3 > \cdots$ with no smallest integer; by Axiom 9, this is impossible.

We next show that $r_k = (a, b)$. From the first equation we have $(a, b) = (b, r_1)$ (Why?) (Exercise 8, page 87). Similarly, from the second equation we have $(b, r_1) = (r_1, r_2)$. From the third equation, $(r_1, r_2) = (r_2, r_3)$. Continuing in this way, $(r_2, r_3) = \cdots = (r_{k-2}, r_{k-1}) = (r_{k-1}, r_k)$. But, from the last equation, it follows that $(r_{k-1}, r_k) = r_k$. Therefore, by substitution, $(a, b) = r_k$.

Now we shall show that there are integers m and n such that $r_k = ma + nb$. From the equation $r_{k-2} = r_{k-1} q_k + r_k$, we have (Why?) $r_k = r_{k-2} - r_{k-1} q_k$. From the equation $r_{k-3} = r_{k-2} q_{k-1} + r_{k-1}$, we have $r_{k-1} = r_{k-3} - r_{k-2} q_{k-1}$. Therefore, by substitution and Axioms 1, 2, and 3, $r_k = r_{k-2} - (r_{k-3} - r_{k-2} q_{k-1}) q_k = (1 + q_{k-1} q_k) r_{k-2} - q_k r_{k-3}$. Similarly, we can express r_{k-2} as a linear combination of r_{k-4} and r_{k-3}. Then, by substitution, r_k can be expressed as a linear combination of r_{k-3} and r_{k-4}. Continuing in this way, we eventually express r_2 as a linear combination of b and r_1, and r_1 as a linear combination of a and b. Substituting for r_{k-3}, $r_{k-4}, \cdots, r_2$, and r_1 in the successive expressions for r_k, we shall finally have r_k expressed as a linear combination of a and b.   *Q.E.D.* (Method 2)

The integers m and n of Theorem 34 are not unique. For example, $(3, 5) = 1; 1 = (-1)5 + 2(3) = 2(5) + (-3)(3) = (-4)(5) + 7(3) = \cdots$. In fact, it can be shown that infinitely many pairs m, n will work for any two nonzero integers a and b.

In the following example we use the Euclidean Algorithm.

Example.   We may compute $(329, 840)$ as follows:

$$840 = 329(2) + 182$$
$$(a = bq_1 + r_1)$$
$$329 = 182(1) + 147$$
$$(b = r_1 q_2 + r_2)$$
$$182 = 147(1) + 35$$
$$(r_1 = r_2 q_3 + r_3)$$
$$147 = 35(4) + 7$$
$$(r_2 = r_3 q_4 + r_4)$$
$$35 = 7(5) + 0$$
$$(r_3 = r_4 q_5 + r_5)$$

Since the last nonzero remainder is 7, it follows that $(329, 840) = 7$.

Moreover, if we use Axioms 1, 2, and 3, and if we start from the fourth equation and continue up the sequence of equations, we have

$$7 = 147 - 35(4) = 147 - (182 - 147)(4) = (-4)(182) +$$
$$[r_4 = r_2 \quad - r_3 q_4 \quad = r_2 \quad - (r_1 - r_2 q_3)q_4 \quad = (-4)r_1 +$$
$$5(147) = 5(329 - 182) + (-4)182 = 5(329) + (-9)182 =$$
$$5r_2 \quad = 5(b - r_1 q_2) \quad + (-4)r_1 \quad = 5b \quad + (-9)r_1 \quad =$$
$$5(329) - 9(840 - 329(2)) = (-9)840 + 23(329).$$
$$5b \quad - 9(a - bq_1) \quad = (-9)a \quad + 23b].$$

Another way of finding (329,840) will be given in Example 1 on page 90.

EXERCISES

1. Prove that the relation "divides" is neither an equivalence relation nor an order relation.

2. Prove Corollary 1 of Theorem 29.

3. Prove Corollary 2 of Theorem 29.

4. Prove Theorem 30.

5. Prove that $(a, b) = (b, a) = (-a, b) = (a, -b) = (-a, -b)$.

6. a) Prove that a set of integers, closed under addition only, need not consist of multiples of one fixed element. b) Prove that a set of integers, closed under subtraction, must be closed under addition.

7. Which of the following sets of integers are closed under both addition and subtraction? For those sets, find the smallest positive integer of the set.

     a) All integers a such that some power of a is divisible by 64.

     b) All integers a such that $(a, 5) = 1$.

     c) All integers a such that $a \mid 48$.

     d) All integers a such that $6 \mid a$ and $24 \mid a^2$.

     e) All integers a such that $9 \mid 21a$.

8. Prove that, for integers a, b, q, and r in **J**, if $a = bq + r$, then $(a, b) = (b, r)$.

9. Use the Euclidean Algorithm to find:

     a) $(14, 35)$.

     b) $(1001, 7655)$.

10. a) Write $(14, 35)$ in the form $m(14) + n(35)$. b) Write $(1001, 7655)$ in the form $m(1001) + n(7655)$.

11. Find three different pairs of integers m and n such that $(5, 7) = m(5) + n(7)$.

12. a) Extend the definition of the greatest common divisor to three integers. b) Use the Euclidean Algorithm to find the g.c.d. $(165,106,210)$.

13. Let a, b, and c be integers. Prove that there are integers r, s, and t such that the g.c.d. $(a, b, c) = ra + sb + tc$.

14. Let a, b, and c be integers such that $a > 0$. Prove that $(ab, ac) = a(b, c)$.

15. Let a and b be integers. Prove that $(a, b) = (a, a + b)$.

16. Let a, b, and c be integers such that $(a, b) = 1$ and $(a, c) = 1$. Prove that $(a, bc) = 1$.

17. Let a, b, m, and n be integers such that $1 = ma + nb$. Prove that $(a, b) = 1$.

18. Let a, b, and c be integers. Prove that, if $(a, b) = 1$, $a \mid c$, and $b \mid c$, then $ab \mid c$.

19. Let a, b, and c be integers. Prove that, if $(a, c) = 1$ and $c \mid ab$, then $c \mid b$.

20. Let a and b be integers. Prove that, if $d = (a, b)$, then there are integers c_1 and c_2 such that $a = dc_1$, $b = dc_2$, and $(c_1, c_2) = 1$.

21. Let a and b be positive integers. Prove that, if ab is a square and if $(a, b) = 1$, then a and b are both squares.

4-8. PRIME NUMBERS

DEFINITION 11. An integer p is called a prime number (or simply a prime) if $p \neq 0$, 1, or -1, and if the only divisors of p are ± 1 and $\pm p$.

Example. The first twenty positive primes are 2, 3, 5, 7, 11, 13, 17, 19, 23, 29, 31, 37, 41, 43, 47, 53, 59, 61, 67, 71.

DEFINITION 12. An integer c is called a composite number if $c \neq 0$, 1, or -1, and if c is not a prime.

Example. The first ten positive composite numbers are 4, 6, 8, 9, 10, 12, 14, 15, 16, 18.

THEOREM 35. If p is a prime number and if $p \mid ab$, then $p \mid a$ or $p \mid b$.

Proof: By hypothesis, the only divisors of p are ± 1 and $\pm p$. Suppose that $p \nmid a$. Then the only common divisors of p and a are ± 1. Therefore, by Theorem 34, there are integers m and n such that $1 = ma + np$. Multiplying both sides of this equation by b and using Axioms 1, 2, 3, and 5, we have $b = mab + npb$. By hypothesis, $p \mid ab$; therefore, there is an integer x such that $ab = px$. Hence, by substitution and Axioms 1, 2, and 3, $b = mpx + npb = p(mx + nb)$. Therefore, by Definition 9, $p \mid b$.

$Q.E.D.$

COROLLARY. If p is a prime number and if $p \mid a_1 \cdot a_2 \cdot \cdots \cdot a_k$, then $p \mid a_1$ or $p \mid a_2$ or $\cdots$ or $p \mid a_k$.

Proof: If $p \nmid a_1$, then, by Theorem 35, $p \mid a_2 \cdot \cdots \cdot a_k$. If also $p \nmid a_2$, then, by Theorem 35, $p \mid a_3 \cdot \cdots \cdot a_k$. Continuing in this way, if $p \nmid a_1$, $p \nmid a_2, \cdots, p \nmid a_{k-1}$, then, by Theorem 35, $p \mid a_k$. *Q.E.D.*

THEOREM 36. Any integer greater than 1 can be expressed as a product of positive prime numbers.

Proof: We shall prove this theorem by using the second principle of finite induction (page 49). Let P_n be the statement "$n + 1$ can be expressed as a product of positive primes." Now if $n + 1$ is a prime, then P_n is valid (with just one factor). Therefore, since 2 is a prime, P_1 is valid. To show that P_n is valid for all positive n, we assume that P_k is valid for all positive $k < m$, and we must show that this assumption implies that P_m is valid. If $m + 1$ is a prime, then P_m is valid and there is nothing more to prove. If $m + 1$ is not a prime, then there are integers a and b such that $1 < a < m + 1$, $1 < b < m + 1$, and $m + 1 = ab$. (Why?) By Theorem 23, since $a < m + 1$ and $b < m + 1$, it follows that $a \leq m$ and $b \leq m$. Therefore, $a - 1 < m$ and $b - 1 < m$. (Why?) Hence, by assumption, both P_{a-1} and P_{b-1} are valid, and thus a and b can be expressed as a product of positive primes. By substituting for a and b in the equation $m + 1 = ab$, we then have $m + 1$ expressed as a product of positive primes. Thus, we have shown that if P_k is valid for all positive $k < m$, then P_m is valid. *Q.E.D.*

The next theorem (37), known as the fundamental theorem of arithmetic, asserts that not only can any integer greater than 1 be expressed as a product of positive primes, but that this expression is unique except for the order in which the prime factors occur. The following example illustrates that this theorem is by no means obvious.

Example. Let $S = \{3n + 1 \mid n \in I\}$; that is, $S = \{1, 4, 7, 10, 13, \cdots\}$. Let us define an S-prime as an integer p, > 1, in S whose only divisors in S are 1 and p. Then 4, 7, 10, and 13 are S-primes; $16 = 4(4)$ is not. The integer 100 is in S and can be expressed as a product of S-primes in two distinct ways, namely, $4(25)$ and $10(10)$. Thus, there is no unique prime factorization theorem for the set S.

THEOREM 37 (Fundamental Theorem of Arithmetic). Any integer greater than 1 can be expressed as a product of positive primes; this expression is unique except for the order of the prime factors.

Proof: By Theorem 36, any integer $n > 1$ can be expressed as a product of positive primes. Now we must show that this expression for n is unique except for the order in which the prime factors occur. Suppose that $n = p_1 \cdot p_2 \cdot \cdots \cdot p_n = q_1 \cdot q_2 \cdot \cdots \cdot q_m$, where $p_1, p_2, \cdots, p_n, q_1, q_2, \cdots, q_m$ are all positive primes. Since $p_1 \mid n$, it follows, by substitution, that $p_1 \mid q_1 \cdot q_2 \cdot \cdots \cdot q_m$. Therefore, by the corollary of Theorem 35, there is an integer q in the set $\{q_1, q_2, \cdots, q_m\}$ such that $p_1 \mid q$. Since both p_1 and q are positive primes, $p_1 = q$. By Axiom 2, we may rearrange the factors in the product $q_1 \cdot q_2 \cdot \cdots \cdot q_m$ so that q appears first. Then we have $p_1 \cdot p_2 \cdot \cdots \cdot p_n = q \cdot q_2^* \cdot \cdots \cdot q_m^*$, where the asterisks denote the new order of the q's. Hence, by Axiom 7, $p_2 \cdot p_3 \cdot \cdots \cdot p_n = q_2^* \cdot q_3^* \cdot \cdots \cdot q_m^*$.

Continuing as above, we shall eventually have no primes remaining on one side of the resulting equation. But then there will be no primes on the other side either; otherwise, we would have a set of integers, each greater than 1, whose product equals 1, which is impossible. (Why?) Thus, we have made the two expressions for n agree simply by rearranging the primes in one of the expressions.   *Q.E.D.*

In representing a positive integer n as a product of positive primes, we often collect the repeated primes and then express n in the form $n = p_1^{\rho_1} \cdot p_2^{\rho_2} \cdot \cdots \cdot p_k^{\rho_k}$, where $0 < p_1 < p_2 < \cdots < p_k$, and the exponents $\rho_1, \rho_2, \cdots, \rho_k$ are positive integers. For example, $5880 = 2^3 \cdot 3 \cdot 5 \cdot 7^2$.

In the following examples, we use the fundamental theorem of arithmetic.

Examples **1.** We may compute $(329,840)$ as follows (see the example on page 86):

$$329 = 7(47)$$
$$840 = 2^3(3)(5)(7)$$

Therefore, $(329,840) = 7$, since 7 is the only factor common to both 329 and 840.

2. We may compute $(700,840)$ as follows:

$$700 = 2^2(5^2)(7)$$
$$840 = 2^3(3)(5)(7)$$

Therefore, $(700,840) = 2^2(5)(7)$.

The proof of the following theorem is due to Euclid.

THEOREM 38. There are infinitely many prime numbers.

Proof: Let $p_1, p_2, \cdots, p_n$ be any distinct prime numbers. Let $a = 1 + p_1 \cdot p_2 \cdot \cdots \cdot p_n$. We first show that none of the primes $p_1, p_2, \cdots, p_n$ divides a. Suppose that a certain prime, say p_k, divides a. Then, since $p_k \mid a$

and $p_k \mid p_1 \cdot p_2 \cdot \cdots \cdot p_n$, it follows, from Theorem 30, that $p_k \mid 1$. But, by the corollary of Theorem 32, this is impossible. Now, by Theorem 36 and Exercise 2 (page 92), a is a prime or a is a product of two or more primes. If a is a prime, then, since $a \neq p_1,\ p_2, \cdots, p_n$, it follows that $\{p_1,\ p_2, \cdots, p_n\}$ cannot be the set of all primes. If a is a product of two or more primes, then, by the argument above, none of these primes can be $p_1,\ p_2, \cdots,$ or p_n. Thus, $\{p_1,\ p_2, \cdots, p_n\}$ cannot be the set of all primes. Therefore, given any finite set of primes, one can always find a prime which is not in the set. Thus, there are infinitely many primes. *Q.E.D.*

There are many simple statements about prime numbers which no one yet has been able to prove or disprove.

Examples

1. Consider pairs of primes differing by 2, such as 3 and 5, 5 and 7, 11 and 13, 17 and 19, 29 and 31, 41 and 43, $\cdots$. Such pairs are called twin primes. It is not yet known whether or not there are infinitely many twin primes.

2. In 1742 a mathematician named Charles Goldbach raised the question: "Can every even positive integer greater than 2 be expressed as the sum of two primes?" (For example, $4 = 2 + 2$; $6 = 3 + 3$; $8 = 3 + 5$; $10 = 5 + 5$; $12 = 5 + 7$.) The answer to this question is still not known.

3. In 1637 Pierre Fermat wrote in the margin of one of his books, "$\cdots$ it is impossible to write a cube as the sum of two cubes, a fourth power as the sum of two fourth powers, and in general any power beyond the second as the sum of two similar powers. For this I have discovered a truly wonderful proof, but the margin is too small to contain it." This is known as Fermat's last theorem. More concisely, it states that if $n > 2$, then there are no nonzero integers x, y, and z such that $x^n + y^n = z^n$. In spite of much effort over the last 300 years, no one yet has been able to prove (or disprove) it.

4. A positive integer n which equals the sum of its positive divisors less than n is called a perfect number. For example, 6 is a perfect number, since $6 = 1 + 2 + 3$. No one knows whether there are odd perfect numbers; no one knows whether there are infinitely many even perfect numbers.

EXERCISES

1. a) Prove that if q is a positive integer which is not a prime, then there is a prime p such that $p \mid q$ and $p^2 < q$. b) Use part a (above) to determine whether 787 is a prime.

2. a) Write a statement analogous to Theorem 36 but applying to all integers $\neq 0, 1$, or -1. b) Prove that your statement is valid.

3. a) Write a statement analogous to Theorem 37 but applying to all integers $\neq 0, 1$, or -1. b) Prove that your statement is valid.

4. In the example on page 89, prove that every element $\neq 1$ in S is an S-prime or is a product of S-primes.

5. Read the following article: Sierpinski, W., "On Some Unsolved Problems of Arithmetic," *Scripta Mathematica*, Vol. 25 (1960), pp. 125–136.

6. List all the articles on prime numbers in the latest issue of *Mathematical Reviews*.

4-9.   CONGRUENCES

DEFINITION 13.   Let a, b, and m be integers such that $m \neq 0$. Then a is said to be congruent to b modulo m if $a - b$ is divisible by m. m is called the modulus of the congruence.

We denote "a is congruent to b modulo m" by $a \equiv b \pmod{m}$. If a is not congruent to b modulo m; that is, if $a - b$ is not divisible by m, we write $a \not\equiv b \pmod{m}$.

Examples   1. $31 \equiv 7 \pmod{12}$, since 12 divides $31 - 7 = 24$.
   2. $31 \equiv 7 \pmod{-3}$, since -3 divides $31 - 7 = 24$.
   3. $31 \not\equiv 7 \pmod{5}$, since 5 does not divide $31 - 7 = 24$.
   4. $a \equiv b \pmod{1}$ for all elements a and b in **J**, since 1 divides every integer $a - b$.

If $a - b$ is divisible by m, then, by Definition 9, there is an integer c such that $a - b = mc$. Hence $a \equiv b \pmod{m}$ if, and only if, there is an integer c such that $a = b + mc$. Thus, all the integers congruent to b modulo m can be obtained by adding multiples of m to b.

Example.   The integers congruent to 5 modulo 3 are of the form $5 + 3c$, where c is an integer. These integers are $\cdots, -4, -1, 2, 5, 8, 11, 14, \cdots$.

THEOREM 39. $a \equiv b \pmod{m}$ if, and only if, a and b when divided by m have the same remainder; that is, if, and only if, $r_1 = r_2$ in the equations $a = mq_1 + r_1$ and $b = mq_2 + r_2$, where $0 \leq r_1 < |m|$ and $0 \leq r_2 < |m|$. (See Theorem 24.)

Proof: Suppose that $a \equiv b \pmod{m}$. Then there is an integer c such that $a = b + mc$. By the division algorithm, there are unique integers q_2 and r_2 such that $b = mq_2 + r_2$, where $0 \leq r_2 < |m|$. Therefore, by substitution and Axioms 1, 2, and 3, $a = (mq_2 + r_2) + mc = m(q_2 + c) + r_2$. By the division algorithm, there are unique integers q_1 and r_1 such that $a = mq_1 + r_1$, where $0 \leq r_1 < |m|$. Hence $r_1 = r_2$.

Conversely, suppose that $a = mq_1 + r$ and $b = mq_2 + r$, where $0 \leq r < |m|$; that is, that a and b, when divided by m, have the same remainder r. Then, by Axioms 1, 2, 3, 4, and 6, $a - b = m(q_1 - q_2)$. Therefore, by Definition 9, $a - b$ is divisible by m; hence, by Definition 13, $a \equiv b \pmod{m}$. $Q.E.D.$

THEOREM 40. For any $m \neq 0$ in $\mathbf{J}$, congruence modulo m is an equivalence relation.

Proof: First we must show that $a \equiv a \pmod{m}$; that is, that $m \mid (a - a)$. Now, by Axiom 6 and Theorem 7, $a - a = 0 = m \cdot 0$. But, by Definition 9, this means that $m \mid (a - a)$.

Next we must show that if $a \equiv b \pmod{m}$, then $b \equiv a \pmod{m}$; that is, that if $m \mid (a - b)$, then $m \mid (b - a)$. If $m \mid (a - b)$, then, by Definition 9, there is an integer c such that $a - b = mc$. Multiplying both sides of this equation by -1, we have (Why?) $b - a = m(-c)$. But then, by Definition 9, $m \mid (b - a)$.

Finally we must show that if $a \equiv b \pmod{m}$ and $b \equiv c \pmod{m}$, then $a \equiv c \pmod{m}$; that is, if $m \mid (a - b)$ and $m \mid (b - c)$, then $m \mid (a - c)$. By Definition 9, since $m \mid (a - b)$ and $m \mid (b - c)$, there are integers c_1 and c_2 such that $a - b = mc_1$ and $b - c = mc_2$. Therefore, by Axioms 1, 2, 3, 4, and 6, $a - c = (a - b) + (b - c) = mc_1 + mc_2 = m(c_1 + c_2)$. But then, by Definition 9, $m \mid (a - c)$. $Q.E.D.$

DEFINITION 14. The equivalence classes determined by the equivalence relation, congruence modulo m, are called residue classes modulo m.

THEOREM 41. If $a \equiv a' \pmod{m}$ and $b \equiv b' \pmod{m}$, then:
  a) $-a \equiv -a' \pmod{m}$.
  b) $a + b \equiv a' + b' \pmod{m}$.
  c) $a - b \equiv a' - b' \pmod{m}$.
  d) $ab \equiv a'b' \pmod{m}$.

Proof: a) Exercise 1, page 100.

b) By hypothesis and Definitions 9 and 13, there are integers c_1 and c_2 such that $a - a' = mc_1$ and $b - b' = mc_2$. Adding these equations and using Axiom 3, we have $(a - a') + (b - b') = mc_1 + mc_2 = m(c_1 + c_2)$. But, by Axioms 1 and 2 and Exercise 5a (page 66), the left side of this equation equals $(a + b) - (a' + b')$. Therefore, by substitution, $(a + b) - (a' + b') = m(c_1 + c_2)$. But then, by Definitions 9 and 13, $a + b \equiv a' + b' \pmod{m}$.

    c) Exercise 1, page 100.

    d) By hypothesis and the discussion on page 92, there are integers c_1 and c_2 such that $a = a' + mc_1$ and $b = b' + mc_2$. Multiplying and using Axioms 1, 2, and 3, we have $ab = (a' + mc_1)(b' + mc_2) = a'b' + m(a'c_2 + b'c_1 + mc_1c_2)$. But then, by Definitions 9 and 13, $ab \equiv a'b'$ $\pmod{m}$.   *Q.E.D.*

Example. $20 \equiv 6 \pmod 7$; $3 \equiv 24 \pmod 7$. Therefore:
    a) $-20 \equiv -6 \pmod 7$.
    b) $20 + 3 \equiv 6 + 24 \pmod 7$; that is, $23 \equiv 30 \pmod 7$.
    c) $20 - 3 \equiv 6 - 24 \pmod 7$; that is, $17 \equiv -18 \pmod 7$.
    d) $20(3) \equiv 6(24) \pmod 7$; that is, $60 \equiv 144 \pmod 7$.

THEOREM 42. If $a \equiv b \pmod m$, then, for any positive integer n, $a^n \equiv b^n \pmod m$.

Proof: We shall prove this theorem by induction. Let P_n be the statement "$a^n \equiv b^n \pmod m$." Then, by hypothesis and Definition 8a, P_1 is valid. We must show that if P_n is valid, then P_{n+1} is valid; that is, we must show that if $a^n \equiv b^n \pmod m$, then $a^{n+1} \equiv b^{n+1} \pmod m$. By Theorem 41d, since (assumption) $a^n \equiv b^n \pmod m$ and since (hypothesis) $a^1 \equiv b^1$ $\pmod m$, it follows that $a^n \cdot a^1 \equiv b^n \cdot b^1 \pmod m$. But, by Definition 8b, this means that $a^{n+1} \equiv b^{n+1} \pmod m$.   *Q.E.D.*

Example. $10 \equiv 1 \pmod 9$. Therefore, $10^6 \equiv 1^6 = 1 \pmod 9$.

THEOREM 43. Suppose that $a \equiv b \pmod m$. Then, for any integers $c_0, c_1, \cdots, c_n$, the following congruence is valid: $c_0 + c_1a + \cdots + c_na^n \equiv c_0 + c_1b + \cdots + c_nb^n \pmod m$.

Proof: The expressions $c_0 + c_1a + \cdots + c_na^n$ and $c_0 + c_1b + \cdots + c_nb^n$ are built up by successive additions and multiplications. Hence, by Theorem 41b and d and Theorem 42, used repeatedly, the conclusion follows.   *Q.E.D.*

    We may use Theorem 43 to devise various tests for divisibility: Let a be any positive integer. According to Theorem 25, there is a positive integer n such that a may be represented in the form $a = c_0 + c_1 10 + c_2 10^2 + \cdots + c_n 10^n$, where $0 \le c_i < 10$ for $i = 0, 1, 2, \cdots, n$ and $c_n \ne 0$. Now $10 \equiv 1 \pmod 9$. Therefore, by Theorem 43, $a \equiv c_0 + c_1 \cdot 1 + c_2 \cdot 1^2 + \cdots + c_n \cdot 1^n = c_0 + c_1 + c_2 + \cdots + c_n \pmod 9$. But, by Theorem 39, this means that a and $c_0 + c_1 + c_2 + \cdots + c_n$ have the same remainder on division by 9. Hence a is divisible by 9 (that is, has remainder 0 on division by 9), if, and only if, $c_0 + c_1 + c_2 + \cdots + c_n$ is

divisible by 9. For example, 12359632 is not divisible by 9, since $2 + 3 +$
$6 + 9 + 5 + 3 + 2 + 1 = 31$ is not divisible by 9. Both integers, when
divided by 9, have a remainder of 4.

The test for divisibility by 3 is exactly the same, since $10 \equiv 1 \pmod 3$.
For example, 12359631 is divisible by 3, since $1 + 3 + 6 + 9 + 5 + 3 +$
$2 + 1 = 30$ is divisible by 3.

Since $10 \equiv (-1) \pmod{11}$, it follows, from Theorem 43, that
$a = c_0 + c_1 10 + c_2 10^2 + \cdots + c_n 10^n \equiv c_0 + c_1(-1) + c_2(-1)^2 +$
$\cdots + c_n(-1)^n = c_0 - c_1 + c_2 - \cdots + (-1)^n c_n. \pmod{11}$. Therefore,
by Theorem 39, a and $c_0 - c_1 + c_2 - \cdots + (-1)^n c_n$ have the same remainder on division by 11. Hence a is divisible by 11 (that is, has remainder 0 on division by 11) if, and only if, $c_0 - c_1 + c_2 - \cdots + (-1)^n c_n$
is divisible by 11. For example, 12359632 is not divisible by 11, since
$2 - 3 + 6 - 9 + 5 - 3 + 2 - 1 = -1$ is not divisible by 11. Since
$-1 \equiv 10 \pmod{11}$, both integers, when divided by 11, have a remainder
of 10.

The test for divisibility by 9 has an application in the process called
"casting out nines." This process is a way of checking addition, subtraction, multiplication, and division. As an illustration, consider the
addition

$$\begin{array}{r} 982 \\ 423 \\ 851 \\ \hline 2256 \end{array}$$

Now,

$$982 \equiv 19 \equiv 10 \equiv 1 \pmod 9;$$
$$432 \equiv 9 \qquad \equiv 0 \pmod 9;$$
$$851 \equiv 14 \qquad \equiv 5 \pmod 9.$$

Therefore, by Theorem 41b, $982 + 432 + 851 \equiv 1 + 0 + 5 = 6 \pmod 9$.
Hence we may check our addition by observing that $2256 \equiv 15 \equiv 6$
$\pmod 9$.[5]

By Theorem 39, 982 and 19 have the same remainder 1 on division
by 9. If we had crossed out the 9 before computing the sum $2 + 8 + 9$,
the remainder 1 would not have changed. Similarly, by Theorem 39,
432 and 9 have the same remainder 0 on division by 9. If we had crossed
out the 2, 3, and 4 (whose sum is 9) before computing the sum $2 + 3 + 4$,
the remainder 0 would not have changed. Again, by Theorem 39, 851
and 14 have the same remainder 5 on division by 9. If we had crossed
out the 1 and 8 (whose sum is 9) before computing the sum $1 + 5 + 8$, the
remainder 5 would not have changed. Finally, by Theorem 39, 2256 and

---

[5] The check by casting out nines is not infallible; see Exercise 4b (page 101).

15 have the same remainder 6 on division by 9. If we had crossed out the 5, 2, and 2 (whose sum is 9) before computing the sum $6 + 5 + 2 + 2$, the remainder 6 would not have changed. Thus, in adding the digits, we may drop out multiples of 9 as we go along; hence the name of the process, "casting out nines."

Congruences are often useful in finding remainders when certain relatively large numbers are divided by small ones.

Examples   1. We wish to find the remainder when 6^{1290} is divided by 7. Now $6 \equiv -1 \pmod 7$; therefore, by Theorem 42, $6^{1290} \equiv (-1)^{1290} = 1 \pmod 7$. Hence, by Theorem 39, 6^{1290}, when divided by 7, has a remainder of 1.

2. We wish to find the remainder when 8^{42} is divided by 5. Now $8^{42} = (8^2)^{21} = 64^{21}$. $64 \equiv 4 \pmod 5$ and $4 \equiv -1 \pmod 5$. Therefore, by Theorem 40, $64 \equiv (-1) \pmod 5$, and by Theorem 42, $64^{21} \equiv (-1)^{21} \pmod 5$. Moreover, $(-1)^{21} = -1 \equiv 4 \pmod 5$. Therefore, by substitution and Theorem 40, $8^{42} \equiv 4 \pmod 5$. Hence, by Theorem 39, 8^{42}, when divided by 5, has a remainder of 4.

THEOREM 44.   Let a, b, c, and m be integers such that $m \neq 0$.   If $(c, m) = 1$, and if $ca \equiv cb \pmod m$, then $a \equiv b \pmod m$; that is, when $(c, m) = 1$, the cancellation law for multiplication holds for congruences.

Proof: By hypothesis and Definition 13, $m \mid (ca - cb)$. Therefore, by Axiom 3, and Exercise 4a (page 66), $m \mid c(a - b)$. Since $(c, m) = 1$ (hypothesis), it follows, from Exercise 19 (page 88), that $m \mid (a - b)$. But, by Definition 13, this means that $a \equiv b \pmod m$.   *Q.E.D.*

Without the restriction $(c, m) = 1$, the cancellation law for multiplication need not hold for congruences. For example, $2(7) \equiv 2(1) \pmod {12}$, but $7 \not\equiv 1 \pmod {12}$. In this case, $c = 2$, $m = 12$, and $(c, m) = (2, 12) = 2 \neq 1$.

The study of equations may be extended to congruences. As an illustration, we shall consider only one theorem concerning the solutions of a congruence—Theorem 45. A more extensive discussion of solutions of congruences may be found in almost any textbook on number theory.

THEOREM 45.   Let a, b, and m be integers such that $m \neq 0$. If $(a, m) = 1$, then the congruence $ax \equiv b \pmod m$ has an integral solution x. If both x_1 and x_2 are solutions, then $x_1 \equiv x_2 \pmod m$. If x_1 is a solution, then any integer x_2 congruent to $x_1 \pmod m$ is also a solution.

Proof: By hypothesis, $(a, m) = 1$. Therefore, by Theorem 34, there are integers r and s such that $1 = ra + sm$. Multiplying by b, and using

Axioms 1, 2, 3, and 5, we have $b = (br)a + (bs)m$. Since $(bs)m$ is a multiple of m, it follows, from Definition 13, that $b \equiv (br)a \pmod{m}$. Therefore, $x = br$ is a solution of $ax \equiv b \pmod{m}$.

Suppose that both x_1 and x_2 are solutions of $ax \equiv b \pmod{m}$. Then, by substitution and Theorem 40, $ax_1 \equiv b \pmod{m}$ and $b \equiv ax_2 \pmod{m}$. Hence, by Theorem 40 again, $ax_1 \equiv ax_2 \pmod{m}$. Since, by hypothesis, $(a, m) = 1$, it follows, from Theorem 44, that $x_1 \equiv x_2 \pmod{m}$.

Suppose that x_1 is a solution of $ax \equiv b \pmod{m}$ and suppose that $x_1 \equiv x_2 \pmod{m}$. Then, by Theorem 41d, $ax_1 \equiv ax_2 \pmod{m}$. But since, by assumption, $ax_1 \equiv b \pmod{m}$, it follows, from Theorem 40, that $ax_2 \equiv b \pmod{m}$. Thus, x_2 is also a solution of the given congruence.

Q.E.D.

When $(a, m) \neq 1$, the congruence $ax \equiv b \pmod{m}$ need not have a solution.

Example. $2x \equiv 3 \pmod 4$ has no solution. In this case, $a = 2$, $m = 4$, and $(a, m) = (2, 4) = 2 \neq 1$.

When $(a, m) \neq 1$, the congruence $ax \equiv b \pmod{m}$ may have two solutions which are not congruent $\pmod m$.

Example. $2x \equiv 2 \pmod{12}$ has solutions $x = 7$ and $x = 13$; but $7 \not\equiv 13 \pmod{12}$. In this case, $(a, m) = (2, 12) = 2 \neq 1$.

The following example illustrates how one may solve a congruence $ax \equiv b \pmod{m}$, where $(a, m) = 1$.

Example.   Solve $3x \equiv 16 \pmod{31}$. Since $(3, 31) = 1$, it follows, from Theorem 34, that there are integers r and s such that $1 = r(3) + s(31)$. These integers r and s may be found by trial and error or else as in the example on page 86. Taking r as -10 and s as 1, we have, by substitution, $1 = (-10)(3) + 1(31)$. Multiplying both sides of this equation by 16, and using Axioms 1, 2, 3, and 5 and Theorem 8, we have $16 = [16(-10)]3 + 16(31) = (-160)3 + 16(31)$. Thus, $16 \equiv (-160)3 \pmod{31}$; hence $x = -160$ is a solution of the given congruence. To get other solutions, we may add any multiple of 31. For example, $\cdots, -129, -98, -67, -36, -5, 26, 57, \cdots$ are solutions.

We shall denote by $\mathbf{J}_m$ the set of equivalence classes of $\mathbf{J}$ with respect to the equivalence relation congruence modulo m; that is, $\mathbf{J}_m$ is the set of all residue classes modulo m.

Examples   1. J_2 is the set of all residue classes modulo 2. These are
$\{\cdots, -2, 0, 2, 4, \cdots\}$ and $\{\cdots, -1, 1, 3, 5, \cdots\}$.
2. J_3 is the set of all residue classes modulo 3. These are
$\{\cdots, -3, 0, 3, 6, \cdots\}$, $\{\cdots, -2, 1, 4, 7, \cdots\}$, and $\{\cdots, -1,$
$2, 5, 8, \cdots\}$.

We shall denote by a_m the residue class of J_m containing the integer a; that is, $a_m = \{x \in J \mid x \equiv a \,(\text{mod}\, m)\}$.

Examples   1. 2_3 is the residue class of J_3 containing the integer 2; thus,
$2_3 = \{\cdots, -1, 2, 5, 8, \cdots\} = 5_3 = 8_3 = (-1)_3$, and so on.
2. 2_5 is the residue class of J_5 containing the integer 2; thus,
$2_5 = \{\cdots, -3, 2, 7, 12, \cdots\} = 7_5 = 12_5 = (-3)_5$, and
so on.
3. $J_2 = \{0_2, 1_2\}$.
4. $J_3 = \{0_3, 1_3, 2_3\}$.
5. It can be shown (Exercise 12, page 101) that for any integer $m > 0$, $J_m = \{0_m, 1_m, \cdots, (m-1)_m\}$. (See Examples 3 and 4 above, where $m = 2$ and 3, respectively.)

DEFINITION 15.   We define addition $(+)$ and multiplication $(\cdot)$ in J_m as follows: $a_m + b_m = (a+b)_m$; $a_m \cdot b_m = (a \cdot b)_m$.

COROLLARY.   Addition and multiplication in J_m are well defined.

Proof: If $a \equiv a' \,(\text{mod}\, m)$ and $b \equiv b' \,(\text{mod}\, m)$, then, by Theorem 41b and d, $a + b \equiv a' + b' \,(\text{mod}\, m)$ and $a \cdot b \equiv a' \cdot b' \,(\text{mod}\, m)$. Therefore, $(a+b)_m = (a'+b')_m$ and $(a \cdot b)_m = (a' \cdot b')_m$.   *Q.E.D.*

Examples   1. The addition table for J_5 is

+	0_5	1_5	2_5	3_5	4_5
0_5	0_5	1_5	2_5	3_5	4_5
1_5	1_5	2_5	3_5	4_5	0_5
2_5	2_5	3_5	4_5	0_5	1_5
3_5	3_5	4_5	0_5	1_5	2_5
4_5	4_5	0_5	1_5	2_5	3_5

Notice that to say that $3_5 + 4_5 = 2_5$ is the same as saying the following: If an integer a has a remainder of 3 when divided by 5 and an integer b has a remainder of 4 when divided by 5, then $a + b$ has a remainder of 2 when divided by 5.

2. The multiplication table for J_5 is

·	0_5	1_5	2_5	3_5	4_5
0_5	0_5	0_5	0_5	0_5	0_5
1_5	0_5	1_5	2_5	3_5	4_5
2_5	0_5	2_5	4_5	1_5	3_5
3_5	0_5	3_5	1_5	4_5	2_5
4_5	0_5	4_5	3_5	2_5	1_5

Notice that to say that $2_5 \cdot 3_5 = 1_5$ is the same as saying the following: If an integer a has a remainder of 2 when divided by 5 and an integer b has a remainder of 3 when divided by 5, then $a \cdot b$ has a remainder of 1 when divided by 5.

THEOREM 46. If m is a prime, then J_m, with addition and multiplication defined as in Definition 15 (page 98), is an integral domain. If m is not a prime, then J_m satisfies all the axioms for an integral domain except Axiom 7, the cancellation law for multiplication.

Proof: By Definition 15 and Axiom 1 for J, $a_m + (b_m + c_m) = a_m + (b + c))_m = (a + (b + c))_m = ((a + b) + c)_m = (a + b)_m + c_m = (a_m + b_m) + c_m$. Thus, the addition part of Axiom 1 holds for J_m.

By Definition 15 and Axiom 2 for J, $a_m + b_m = (a + b)_m = (b + a)_m = b_m + a_m$. Thus, the addition part of Axiom 2 holds for J_m. It is also easy to verify that the multiplication parts of Axioms 1 and 2 hold for J_m (Exercise 14, page 101).

By Definition 15 and Axiom 3 for J, $a_m(b_m + c_m) = a_m(b + c)_m = (a(b + c))_m = (ab + ac)_m = (ab)_m + (ac)_m + a_m b_m + a_m c_m$. Thus, Axiom 3 holds for J_m.

It is easy to verify that the zero element of J_m is 0_m, that the unit element of J_m is 1_m, and that for any element a_m in J_m the inverse element is $(-a)_m = (m - a)_m$ (Exercise 15, page 101).

Suppose that m is a prime and $a_m \cdot b_m = 0_m$. By Definition 15, $a_m \cdot b_m = (ab)_m$. Therefore, by substitution, $(ab)_m = 0_m$, or $ab \equiv 0 \pmod{m}$. By Definition 13, this means that $m \mid ab$. Now, since m is a prime (assumption) and $m \mid ab$, it follows, from Theorem 35, that $m \mid a$ or $m \mid b$. But then $a \equiv 0 \pmod{m}$ or $b \equiv 0 \pmod{m}$; that is, $a_m = 0_m$ or $b_m = 0_m$. Therefore, by Theorem 11, Axiom 7 holds for J_m.

If m is not a prime, then there are integers a and b such that $m = ab$, $1 < a < m$, and $1 < b < m$. Therefore, $a_m \cdot b_m = (ab)_m = m_m = 0_m$, $a_m \neq 0_m$, and $b_m \neq 0_m$. (Why?) Hence, since J_m satisfies Axioms 1 through 6 for an integral domain, it follows, from Theorem 10, that J_m does not satisfy Axiom 7 for an integral domain. *Q.E.D.*

Examples   1. Since 3 is a prime, J_3 is an integral domain. J_3 has no zero divisors (Definition 5, page 65).
2. Since 6 is not a prime, J_6 is not an integral domain. J_6 has the zero divisors 2_6, 3_6, and 4_6. $2_6 \cdot 3_6 = 6_6 = 0_6$; $3_6 \cdot 4_6 = 12_6 = 0_6$.

DEFINITION 16.   A field is an integral domain which contains for every element $a \neq 0$ a multiplicative inverse a^{-1}; that is, an element a^{-1} such that $a \cdot a^{-1} = 1$. (a^{-1} is unique. Why?)

Examples   1. The rational numbers (Chapter 5).
2. The real numbers (Chapter 6).
3. The complex numbers (Chapter 6).
4. J_p, where p is a prime (Theorem 48). Hence J_2 is a field of two elements, J_3 is a field of three elements, J_5 is a field of five elements, and so on. $2_3^{-1} = 2_3$; $2_5^{-1} = 3_5$.
5. The integers J do not form a field. For example, there is no integer c such that $3c = 1$.

THEOREM 47.   Any finite integral domain D is a field.

Proof: Since D is finite, we can list the distinct elements of D: $d_1, d_2, \cdots, d_n$. Let a be any nonzero element in D. We must show that D contains an element a^{-1} such that $a \cdot a^{-1} = 1$. To do this, we form all products ad_1, $ad_2, \cdots, ad_n$. These n products are distinct. Otherwise, if $ad_i = ad_j$ for $i \neq j$, then, by Axiom 7 for an integral domain, $d_i = d_j$, contradicting the assumption that the d's are distinct. Since the list of products contains all the elements of D, 1 must appear somewhere in the list. Thus, $1 = ad_i$ for some i. Therefore, the inverse of a is d_i. *Q.E.D.*

THEOREM 48.   If p is a prime, then J_p is a field.

Proof: Without loss of generality, we may assume that p is a positive prime. (Why?) J_p is finite, since, by Exercise 12 (page 101), J_p contains exactly p elements. J_p is an integral domain, by Theorem 46. Therefore, by Theorem 47, J_p is a field. *Q.E.D.*

EXERCISES

1. Prove that if $a \equiv a'$ (mod m) and $b \equiv b'$ (mod m), then:
   a) $-a \equiv -a'$ (mod m).
   b) $a - b \equiv a' - b'$ (mod m).
2. Prove that if $ab \equiv 1$ (mod m), then $(b, m) = 1$.
3. Prove that the square of any odd integer is congruent to 1 modulo 8.

4. a) Use the process of "casting out nines" to prove that $6/382 \cdot 894356 \neq 4987311782$. b) Does the process of "casting out nines" show that $393 \cdot 952 = 38796$?

5. Use congruences to determine the remainder when $16(18)(15) \cdot (23)(29)(34)$ is divided by 7.

6. Find the last digit in 9^{30}; that is, find the remainder when 9^{30} is divided by 10.

7. Find the remainder when 7^{97} is divided by 8.

8. Is $2^{23} - 2^3$ divisible by 31? Why?

9. Is $(787654321033852312)_{18}$ divisible by 8? Why?

10. Find all integers x satisfying each of the following congruences:
  a) $3x \equiv 2 \pmod 5$.
  b) $7x \equiv 4 \pmod{10}$.
  c) $87x \equiv 15 \pmod 7$.
  d) $2x \equiv 3 \pmod 8$.

11. Let m be a positive integer. Prove that any integer n is congruent modulo m to exactly one of the integers $0, 1, \cdots, m - 1$. (HINT: Use the division algorithm to show that n is congruent modulo m to one of the desired integers. Then show that n cannot be congruent modulo m to two different integers a and b such that $0 \leq a \leq m - 1$ and $0 \leq b \leq m - 1$.)

12. Use Exercise 11 (above) to prove that for any positive integer m, $\mathbf{J}_m = \{0_m, 1_m, \cdots, (m - 1)_m\}$.

13. Let m be a positive integer and let a_m be a residue class modulo m. Prove that if there is an integer b in a_m such that $(b, m) = 1$, then $(x, m) = 1$ for all integers x in a_m.

14. Prove that $\mathbf{J}_m$, with multiplication defined as in Definition 15, satisfies the associative and commutative laws of multiplication. (See Theorem 46.)

15. Verify that:
  a) The unit element of $\mathbf{J}_m$ is 1_m.
  b) The zero element of $\mathbf{J}_m$ is 0_m.
  c) for any element a_m in $\mathbf{J}_m$ the additive inverse element is $(-a)_m = (m - a)_m$. (See Theorem 46.)

16. a) Construct the multiplication table for $\mathbf{J}_8$. b) Find the additive inverses of $2_8, 3_8, 5_8,$ and 7_8 in $\mathbf{J}_8$.

17. Find all zero divisors in $\mathbf{J}_{48}$.

18. Let $S = \{1_5, 2_5, 3_5, 4_5\}$ be a set of elements of $\mathbf{J}_5$. Let $a_5 \mathfrak{R} b_5$ if, and only if, $a_5 \mid b_5$, where a_5 and b_5 are in S.
  a) Is $\mathfrak{R}$ an order relation? Why?
  b) Is $\mathfrak{R}$ an equivalence relation? Why?

19. Prove that $\mathbf{J}_p$, where p is a prime, cannot be an ordered integral domain.

5 / The Rational Numbers

5-1. CONSTRUCTION OF THE RATIONAL NUMBERS FROM THE INTEGERS

We shall begin by constructing the rational numbers (Definition 3, page 103) from the integers. We shall then investigate some of the properties of the rational numbers. Throughout the chapter we shall assume the usual rules of addition and multiplication for the integers.

DEFINITION 1. Let a and b be integers such that $b \neq 0$. Let S be the set of all ordered pairs (a, b). Define a relation $\sim$ on $S \times S$ as follows: $(a, b) \sim (a', b')$ if, and only if, $ab' = ba'$.

LEMMA 1. $\sim$ is an equivalence relation on S.

Proof: By Definition 1 and Axiom 2, Chapter 4, for **J**, $(a, b) \sim (a, b)$. Thus, $\sim$ is reflexive.

By Definition 1, if $(a, b) \sim (a', b')$, then $ab' = ba'$. But then, by Axiom 2 for **J**, $a'b = b'a$. Therefore, by Definition 1, $(a', b') \sim (a, b)$. Thus, $\sim$ is symmetric.

If $(a, b) \sim (a', b')$ and $(a', b') \sim (a'', b'')$, then, by Definition 1, $ab' = ba'$ and $a'b'' = b'a''$. We must show that $(a, b) \sim (a'', b'')$; that is, that $ab'' = ba''$. Multiplying the first equation by b'', using Axiom 1 for **J**, and substituting from the second equation, we have $(ab')b'' = (ba')b'' = b(a'b'') = b(b'a'')$. Therefore, by Axioms 1 and 2 for **J**, $b'(ab'') = b'(ba'')$. Since by Definition 1, $b' \neq 0$, it follows, from Axiom 7 for **J**, that $ab'' = ba''$. Thus, $\sim$ is transitive. Q.E.D.

We now use the equivalence relation $\sim$ to partition the set S into disjoint equivalence classes. We denote the equivalence class containing the pair (a, b) by $(a, b)^\sim$; that is, $(a, b)^\sim = \{(x, y) \mid (x, y) \sim (a, b)\}$.

DEFINITION 2. Consider the set of equivalence classes of S under $\sim$. Define addition ($+$) and multiplication ($\cdot$) on this set as follows: $(a, b)^{\sim} + (c, d)^{\sim} = (ad + bc, bd)^{\sim}$; $(a, b)^{\sim} \cdot (c, d)^{\sim} = (ac, bd)^{\sim}$.

Examples   1. $(3, 4)^{\sim} + (2, 3)^{\sim} = (3(3) + 4(2), 4(3))^{\sim} = (17, 12)^{\sim}$.
           2. $(3, 4)^{\sim} \cdot (2, 3)^{\sim} = (3(2), 4(3))^{\sim} = (6, 12)^{\sim} = (1, 2)^{\sim}$.
           3. $(2, 1)^{\sim} + (3, 1)^{\sim} = (2(1) + 1(3), 1(1))^{\sim} = (5, 1)^{\sim}$.
           4. $(2, 1)^{\sim} \cdot (3, 1)^{\sim} = (2(3), 1(1))^{\sim} = (6, 1)^{\sim}$.
           5. $(2, 3)^{\sim} \cdot (3, 2)^{\sim} = (2(3), 3(2))^{\sim} = (6, 6)^{\sim} = (1, 1)^{\sim}$.

LEMMA 2. Addition and multiplication are well defined.

Proof: Suppose that $(a, b) \sim (a', b')$ and $(c, d) \sim (c', d')$. Then, by Definition 1, $ab' = ba'$ and $cd' = dc'$. To show that addition is well defined, we must show that $(ad + bc, bd) \sim (a'd' + b'c', b'd')$; that is, that $(ad + bc)b'd' = bd(a'd' + b'c')$. But, using Axioms 1, 2, and 3 for **J** and substituting from the first two equations, $(ad + bc)b'd' = ab'dd' + cd'bb' = ba'dd' + dc'bb' = bd(a'd' + b'c')$.

To show that multiplication is well defined, we must show that $(ac, bd) \sim (a'c', b'd')$; that is, that $(ac)(b'd') = (bd)(a'c')$. But, using Axioms 1 and 2 for **J** and substituting from the first two equations, $(ac)(b'd') = (ab')(cd') = (ba')(dc') = (bd)(a'c')$.   *Q.E.D.*

DEFINITION 3. The set **R** of rational numbers is the set of equivalence classes of S, under $\sim$, together with addition and multiplication as defined in Definition 2.

According to Theorem 10, Chapter 4, **J** contains no zero divisors. Hence, in the ordered pairs (a, b) and (c, d), since $b \neq 0$ and $d \neq 0$, it follows that $b(d) \neq 0$. Therefore, by Definition 2, **R** is closed under addition and multiplication.

We sometimes use the notation $\dfrac{a}{b}$ to denote the equivalence class $(a, b)^{\sim}$. For example, by $\dfrac{3}{4}$, we mean the equivalence class $(3, 4)^{\sim}$. Thus, when we write $\dfrac{3}{4} = \dfrac{6}{8}$, we mean that $(3, 4)^{\sim} = (6, 8)^{\sim}$ or $(3, 4) \sim (6, 8)$. Indeed, in accordance with Definition 1, $(3, 4) \sim (6, 8)$, since $3(8) = 4(6)$. Similarly, in accordance with Definition 1, $\dfrac{6}{8} = \dfrac{-9}{-12}$, since $6(-12) = 8(-9)$. The name "rational number" was derived from the notion of "ratio" of integers.

In ordinary usage, $\dfrac{3}{4}$ sometimes means the fraction $\dfrac{3}{4}$ [that is, the ordered pair $(3, 4)]$ and sometimes means the equivalence class $\frac{3}{4}$ [that is,

$(3, 4)^\sim]$. As fractions, $\frac{3}{4}$ and $\frac{6}{8}$ are not equal: $(3, 4) \neq (6, 8)$, since $3 \neq 6$

and $4 \neq 8$. (See Sec. 2-4.) As equivalence classes, $\frac{3}{4}$ and $\frac{6}{8}$ are equal, as

shown above. In this book we shall consistently use $\frac{a}{b}$ to denote the

equivalence class $(a, b)^\sim$.

Example. $\frac{3}{4} + \frac{2}{3} = \frac{17}{12}$, since, by Definition 2, $(3, 4)^\sim + (2, 3)^\sim = (17, 12)^\sim$.

5-2. THE RATIONAL NUMBERS AS AN ORDERED FIELD

THEOREM 1. The set **R** of rational numbers is a field.

Proof: On page 103 we proved that **R** is closed under addition and multiplication. We now must prove that **R** satisfies all the axioms for a field; that is, the seven axioms for an integral domain plus the additional axiom: Every element $a \neq 0$ has a multiplicative inverse; that is, an element a^{-1} such that $aa^{-1} = 1$.

By Definition 2 and Axioms 1, 2, and 3 for **J**, $(a, b)^\sim + [(c, d)^\sim + (e, f)^\sim] = (a, b)^\sim + (cf + de, df)^\sim = (a(df) + b(cf + de), b(df))^\sim = ((ad + bc)f + (bd)e, (bd)f)^\sim = (ad + bc, bd)^\sim + (e, f)^\sim = [(a, b)^\sim + (c, d)^\sim] + (e, f)^\sim$.

By Definition 2 and Axiom 1 for **J**, $(a, b)^\sim \cdot [(c, d)^\sim \cdot (e, f)^\sim] = (a, b)^\sim \cdot (ce, df)^\sim = (a(ce), b(df))^\sim = ((ac)e, (bd)f)^\sim = (ac, bd)^\sim \cdot (e, f)^\sim = [(a, b)^\sim \cdot (c, d)^\sim] \cdot (e, f)^\sim$. Thus, **R** satisfies Axiom 1 for an integral domain.

The proof that **R** satisfies Axiom 2 for an integral domain is left as an exercise (Exercise 1, page 107).

By Definition 2, Axioms 1, 2, and 3 for **J**, and Definition 1, $(a, b)^\sim \cdot [(c, d)^\sim + (e, f)^\sim] = (a, b)^\sim \cdot (cf + de, df)^\sim = (a(cf + de), b(df))^\sim = ((ba)(cf + de), (bb)(df))^\sim = ((ac)(bf) + (bd)(ae), (bd)(bf))^\sim = (ac, bd)^\sim + (ae, bf)^\sim = (a, b)^\sim \cdot (c, d)^\sim + (a, b)^\sim \cdot (e, f)^\sim$. Thus, **R** satisfies Axiom 3 for an integral domain.

The zero element of **R** is $(0, 1)^\sim$, since, by Definition 2, Theorem 7 of Chapter 4, and Axioms 2, 4, and 5 for **J**, $(a, b)^\sim + (0, 1)^\sim = (a(1) + b(0), b(1))^\sim = (a, b)^\sim$. Thus, **R** satisfies Axiom 4 for an integral domain.

The unit element of **R** is $(1, 1)^\sim$, since, by Definition 2 and Axiom 5 for **J**, $(1, 1)^\sim \cdot (a, b)^\sim = (1(a), 1(b))^\sim = (a, b)^\sim$. Thus, **R** satisfies Axiom 5 for an integral domain.

By Definition 2, Axioms 2 and 6 for **J**, Theorem 8 of Chapter 4, and Definition 1, $(a, b)^{\sim} + (-a, b)^{\sim} = (ab + b(-a), bb)^{\sim} = (0, bb)^{\sim} = (0, 1)^{\sim}$. Therefore, we shall call $(-a, b)^{\sim}$ the negative of $(a, b)^{\sim}$, and shall write $(-a, b)^{\sim} = -(a, b)^{\sim}$. By Exercise 2 (page 107), the negative of $(a, b)^{\sim}$ is well defined. Thus, **R** satisfies Axiom 6 for an integral domain.

Suppose that $(a, b)^{\sim} \neq (0, 1)^{\sim}$ and $(a, b)^{\sim} \cdot (c, d)^{\sim} = (a, b)^{\sim} \cdot (c', d')^{\sim}$. Now $(a, b)^{\sim} \cdot (c, d)^{\sim} = (ac, bd)^{\sim}$ and $(a, b)^{\sim} \cdot (c', d')^{\sim} = (ac', bd')^{\sim}$. Therefore, by hypothesis and substitution, $(ac, bd)^{\sim} = (ac', bd')^{\sim}$. Hence, by Definition 1, $(ac)(bd') = (bd)(ac')$. Therefore, by Axioms 1, 2, and 7 for **J**, $cd' = dc'$. But by Definition 1, this means that $(c, d)^{\sim} = (c', d')^{\sim}$. Thus **R** satisfies Axiom 7 for an integral domain.

It only remains to show that every element $(a, b)^{\sim} \neq (0, 1)^{\sim}$ has a multiplicative inverse in **R**. Now it can be shown that $(0, 1) \sim (x, y)$ if, and only if, $x = 0$ (Exercise 3, page 107). Hence, since by assumption $(a, b) \not\sim (0, 1)$, it follows that $a \neq 0$. Therefore, $(b, a)^{\sim}$ is in **R**. By Definitions 1 and 2 and Axiom 2 for **J**, $(a, b)^{\sim} \cdot (b, a)^{\sim} = (ab, ba)^{\sim} = (ab, ab)^{\sim} = (1, 1)^{\sim}$. Therefore, we shall call $(b, a)^{\sim}$ the multiplicative inverse of $(a, b)^{\sim}$ and shall write $(b, a)^{\sim} = [(a, b)^{\sim}]^{-1}$. By Exercise 4 (page 107), the multiplicative inverse of $(a, b)^{\sim}$ is well defined. Thus, **R** satisfies all the axioms for a field. *Q.E.D.*

DEFINITION 4. We say that $(0, 1)^{\sim}$ is less than $(a, b)^{\sim}$, and write $(0, 1)^{\sim} < (a, b)^{\sim}$ if, and only if, $ab > 0$.

Examples 1. $(0, 1)^{\sim} < (3, 4)^{\sim}$, or $\dfrac{0}{1} < \dfrac{3}{4}$, since $3(4) = 12 > 0$.

2. $(0, 1)^{\sim} < (-3, -4)^{\sim}$, or $\dfrac{0}{1} < \dfrac{-3}{-4}$, since $-3(-4) = 12 > 0$.

3. $(0, 1)^{\sim} \not< (-3, 4)^{\sim}$, or $\dfrac{0}{1} \not< \dfrac{-3}{4}$, since $-3(4) = -12 \not> 0$.

LEMMA 3. The relation "$(0, 1)^{\sim} < (a, b)^{\sim}$" is well defined.

Proof: Suppose that $(a, b) \sim (c, d)$ and $ab > 0$. We must show that $cd > 0$. By hypothesis and Definition 1, $ad = bc$. Using this equation and Axioms 1 and 2 for **J**, we have $(ab)d^2 = (ad)(bd) = (bc)(bd) = (cd)b^2$. Hence $(ab)d^2$ and $(cd)b^2$ are both greater than 0 or both less than 0. But, by Theorem 19 of Chapter 4 and by Corollaries 1 and 2 of Theorem 17 of Chapter 4, the sign of $(ab)d^2$ is the same as the sign of ab; similarly, the sign of $(cd)b^2$ is the same as the sign of cd. Therefore, since, by hypothesis, $ab > 0$, it follows that $cd > 0$. *Q.E.D.*

DEFINITION 5. $(a, b)^{\sim}$ is said to be positive if, and only if, $(0, 1)^{\sim} < (a, b)^{\sim}$; that is, if, and only if, $ab > 0$.

DEFINITION 6. $(a, b)^{\sim}$ is said to be negative if, and only if, $(a, b)^{\sim} \neq$

$(0, 1)\tilde{}$ and $(a, b)\tilde{}$ is not positive. By Exercise 5 (page 107), this means that $(a, b)\tilde{}$ is negative if, and only if, $ab < 0$.

Examples   1. $(2, 3)\tilde{}$, or $\frac{2}{3}$, is positive, since $2(3) = 6 > 0$.

            2. $(-2, 3)\tilde{}$, or $\frac{-2}{3}$, is negative, since $(-2)3 = -6 < 0$.

DEFINITION 7. An ordered field is a field which, considered as an integral domain, is an ordered integral domain.

THEOREM 2. The set **R** of rational numbers is an ordered field.

Proof: By Theorem 1, **R** is a field. Hence, by Definition 7, we need prove only that **R** satisfies Axiom 8 for an ordered integral domain. Let P be the subset of **R** consisting of all the positive elements of **R**; that is, $P = \{(a, b)\tilde{} \mid ab > 0\}$. Now suppose that $(a, b)\tilde{} \in P$ and $(c, d)\tilde{} \in P$. Then, by Exercise 6 (page 107), $(a, b)\tilde{} + (c, d)\tilde{} \in P$, and $(a, b)\tilde{} \cdot (c, d)\tilde{} \in P$.

Let $(a, b)\tilde{}$ be any element of **R**. By Theorem 12 of Chapter 4, exactly one holds: $ab > 0$; $ab = 0$; $-(ab) > 0$. If $ab > 0$, then $(a, b)\tilde{} \in P$. If $ab = 0$, then, since $b \neq 0$, it follows, from Theorem 10 of Chapter 4, that $a = 0$. Therefore, by Exercise 3 (page 107), $(a, b)\tilde{} = (0, 1)\tilde{}$, the zero element of **R**. Suppose that $-(ab) > 0$. By Theorem 8 of Chapter 4, $-(ab) = (-a)b$. Therefore, by substitution, $(-a)b > 0$. Hence, by the definition of P, $(-a, b)\tilde{} \in P$. But $(-a, b)\tilde{} = -(a, b)\tilde{}$. Therefore, $-(a, b)\tilde{} \in P$. Thus, **R** satisfies Axiom 8 for an ordered integral domain.

Q.E.D.

We shall denote $(c, d)\tilde{} + (-a, b)\tilde{}$—that is, $(c, d)\tilde{} + [-(a, b)\tilde{}]$ by $(c, d)\tilde{} - (a, b)\tilde{}$.

DEFINITION 8. We say that $(a, b)\tilde{}$ is less than $(c, d)\tilde{}$, and write $(a, b)\tilde{} < (c, d)\tilde{}$ if, and only if, $(0, 1)\tilde{} < (c, d)\tilde{} - (a, b)\tilde{}$.

Thus, by Definition 5, $(a, b)\tilde{} < (c, d)\tilde{}$ if, and only if, $(c, d)\tilde{} - (a, b)\tilde{}$ is positive; that is, if, and only if, there is an element $(e, f)\tilde{} \in P$ such that $(c, d)\tilde{} = (a, b)\tilde{} + (e, f)\tilde{}$. (Why?) Compare this with Definition 2 of Chapter 4. Moreover, by Definition 5, Theorem 8 of Chapter 4, and Axiom 2 for **J**, $(a, b)\tilde{} < (c, d)\tilde{}$ if, and only if, $(cb - ad)bd > 0$.

Examples   1. $(2, 3)\tilde{} < (5, 6)\tilde{}$, or $\frac{2}{3} < \frac{5}{6}$, since $[5(3) - 2(6)](3)(6) = 54 > 0$.

            2. $(0, 1)\tilde{} < (3, 4)\tilde{}$, or $\frac{0}{1} < \frac{3}{4}$, since $[3(1) - 0(4)](1)(4) = 12 > 0$.

3. $(1, 2)^\sim \not< (1, 4)^\sim$, or $\frac{1}{2} \not< \frac{1}{4}$, since $[1(2) - 1(4)](2)(4) = -16 \not> 0$.

LEMMA 4. The relation "$(a, b)^\sim < (c, d)^\sim$" is well defined.

Proof: Exercise 7 (page 108).

THEOREM 3. The set **R** of rational numbers is linearly ordered by the relation "less than."

Proof: By Theorem 2, **R** is an ordered integral domain. The order relation "less than" (Definition 8) on **R** × **R** is analogous to the order relation "less than" (Definition 2 of Chapter 4) on **J** × **J**. Since all the theorems in Sec. 4-4 are valid for any ordered integral domains whatever (see page 66), it follows, from Theorems 12 and 13 of Sec. 4-4, that **R** is linearly ordered by the relation "less than." *Q.E.D.*

THEOREM 4. There is an isomorphism ψ between the elements a of **J** and the elements $(a, 1)^\sim$ of **R** such that $\psi(a) = (a, 1)^\sim$; that is, the integer a corresponds to the rational number $(a, 1)^\sim$, or $\frac{a}{1}$, under the isomorphism ψ.

Proof: ψ is a 1:1 correspondence, since, by Definition 1 and Axioms 2 and 4 for **J**, if $(a, 1)^\sim = (b, 1)^\sim$, then $a = b$. By Definition 2 and Axioms 2 and 4 for **J**, $\psi(a + b) = (a + b, 1)^\sim = (a(1) + 1(b), 1(1))^\sim = (a, 1)^\sim + (b, 1)^\sim = \psi(a) + \psi(b)$. By Definition 2 and Axiom 5 for **J**, $\psi(ab) = (ab, 1)^\sim = (a, 1)^\sim \cdot (b, 1)^\sim = \psi(a) \cdot \psi(b)$. Suppose that $\psi(a) < \psi(b)$. Then, by substitution, $(a, 1)^\sim < (b, 1)^\sim$. By the discussion following Definition 8 and by Axioms 2 and 5 for **J**, this means that $(b(1) - a(1))(1)(1) > 0$ or that $b - a > 0$. But then, $a < b$. Conversely, if $a < b$, then $(b(1) - a(1))(1)(1) = b - a > 0$. Therefore, $\psi(a) < \psi(b)$. Thus, $\psi(a) < \psi(b)$ if, and only if, $a < b$. *Q.E.D.*

EXERCISES

1. Prove that the set **R** of rational numbers satisfies Axiom 2 for an integral domain.

2. Prove that the negative of $(a, b)^\sim$ is well defined. (See page 105.)

3. Prove that $(0, 1) \sim (x, y)$ if, and only if, $x = 0$.

4. Prove that the multiplicative inverse of $(a, b)^\sim$ is well defined. (See page 105.)

5. Prove that $(a, b)^\sim$ is negative if, and only if, $ab < 0$.

6. Prove that if $(a, b)^\sim \in P$ and $(c, d)^\sim \in P$, then a) $(a, b)^\sim + (c, d)^\sim \in P$ and b) $(a, b)^\sim \cdot (c, d)^\sim \in P$.

7. Prove that the relation "$(a, b)^\sim < (c, d)^\sim$" is well defined. [HINT: "$(c, d)^\sim + (-a, b)^\sim$" is well defined, by Lemma 2. "$(0, 1)^\sim < (c, d)^\sim + (-a, b)^\sim$" is well defined, by Lemma 3.]

8. Prove Theorem 3 by using the equivalence classes $(a, b)^\sim$ of **R**.

5-3.   UNIQUENESS OF THE RATIONAL NUMBERS

Suppose that $b \neq 0$. Then $[(b, 1)^\sim]^{-1} = (1, b)^\sim$. (See page 105.) Therefore, by Definition 2, every element $(a, b)^\sim$ in the field **R** can be expressed as a product $[(b, 1)^\sim]^{-1} \cdot (a, 1)^\sim$.

Examples   **1.** $(2, 3)^\sim = (1, 3)^\sim \cdot (2, 1)^\sim = [(3, 1)^\sim]^{-1} \cdot (2, 1)^\sim$.

            2. $(1, 2)^\sim = (1, 2)^\sim \cdot (1, 1)^\sim = [(2, 1)^\sim]^{-1} \cdot (1, 1)^\sim$.

By Theorem 4, there is an isomorphism ψ associating each integer a in **J** with the equivalence class $(a, 1)^\sim$ in **R**. Since the integers are defined by their axioms only up to an isomorphism, we may identify each integer a with the equivalence class $(a, 1)^\sim$. Accordingly, we may think of every element in the field **R** as a product of two elements—the inverse of an integer times an integer.

It can be shown that there is exactly one field (up to an isomorphism) which contains **J** and in which every element can be expressed as the inverse of an element in **J** times an element in **J**. Thus, the set **R** of rational numbers is unique up to an isomorphism.

In view of the above discussion, we could have defined the rational numbers, without directly resorting to equivalence classes, as follows:

The set **R** of rational numbers is the field (up to an isomorphism) of elements containing **J** such that every element in the field can be expressed in the form $b^{-1}a$, where a and b are in **J** and $b \neq 0$.

The set of rational numbers so defined is isomorphic to the set **R** of rational numbers (Definition 3) under the isomorphism in which $b^{-1}a$ corresponds to $(a, b)^\sim$.

Because of the isomorphism associating a in **J** with $(a, 1)^\sim$ in **R**, instead of writing $\frac{a}{1}$ to denote $(a, 1)^\sim$, we often simply write a. Then since

$(1, a)^\sim = [(a, 1)^\sim]^{-1}; (1, a)^\sim$, or $\frac{1}{a}$, can be denoted by a^{-1}. $b^{-1}a = \frac{a}{b}$, since,

by our notation and substitution, $(1, b)^\sim \cdot (a, 1)^\sim = (a, b)^\sim = \frac{a}{b}$.

DEFINITION 9.   For any elements $\frac{a}{b}$ and m in **R**:   a) $\left(\frac{a}{b}\right)^1 = \frac{a}{b}$; and

b) $\left(\frac{a}{b}\right)^{m+1} = \left(\frac{a}{b}\right)^m \cdot \left(\frac{a}{b}\right)^1$.

In particular, when $m = -1$, $\left(\dfrac{a}{b}\right)^0 = \left(\dfrac{a}{b}\right)^{-1} \cdot \left(\dfrac{a}{b}\right) = 1$. When

$m = -2$, $\left(\dfrac{a}{b}\right)^{-2+1} = \left(\dfrac{a}{b}\right)^{-1} = \left(\dfrac{b}{a}\right)$. Moreover, by substitution, $\left(\dfrac{a}{b}\right)^{-2+1} =$

$\left(\dfrac{a}{b}\right)^{-2} \cdot \left(\dfrac{a}{b}\right)^{1} = \left(\dfrac{b}{a}\right)$. Therefore, $\left(\dfrac{a}{b}\right)^{-2} = \left(\dfrac{b}{a}\right)^{2}$. (Why?)

5-4. PROPERTIES OF THE RATIONAL NUMBERS

According to Theorem 2, the set $\mathbf{R}$ of rational numbers is an ordered field; that is, a field which, considered as an integral domain, is an ordered integral domain. Hence all the theorems which have been proved about ordered integral domains (Sec. 4-3 and 4-4) and the theorems to be proved about ordered fields (Exercises 4 and 6, page 110) are valid for the set $\mathbf{R}$ of rational numbers. We shall now consider one additional theorem.

THEOREM 5. Let $\dfrac{a}{b}$ and $\dfrac{c}{d}$ be rational numbers such that $\dfrac{a}{b} < \dfrac{c}{d}$. Then

there is a rational number $\dfrac{i}{j}$ such that $\dfrac{a}{b} < \dfrac{i}{j} < \dfrac{c}{d}$.

Proof: Let $\dfrac{i}{j} = \dfrac{1}{2}\left(\dfrac{a}{b} + \dfrac{c}{d}\right)$. Then $\dfrac{i}{j} - \dfrac{a}{b} = \left(\dfrac{1}{2}\dfrac{a}{b} + \dfrac{1}{2}\dfrac{c}{d}\right) - \dfrac{a}{b} = \dfrac{1}{2}\dfrac{c}{d} +$

$\left(\dfrac{1}{2} - 1\right)\dfrac{a}{b} = \dfrac{1}{2}\dfrac{c}{d} - \dfrac{1}{2}\dfrac{a}{b} = \dfrac{1}{2}\left(\dfrac{c}{d} - \dfrac{a}{b}\right) > 0$. (Give all reasons. Exercise 1, page 110.)

Similarly, $\dfrac{c}{d} - \dfrac{i}{j} = \dfrac{c}{d} - \left(\dfrac{1}{2}\dfrac{a}{b} + \dfrac{1}{2}\dfrac{c}{d}\right) = \left(1 - \dfrac{1}{2}\right)\dfrac{c}{d} - \dfrac{1}{2}\dfrac{a}{b} = \dfrac{1}{2}\dfrac{c}{d} -$

$\dfrac{1}{2}\dfrac{a}{b} = \dfrac{1}{2}\left(\dfrac{c}{d} - \dfrac{a}{b}\right) > 0$. (Give all reasons. Exercise 1, page 110.) Since

$\dfrac{i}{j} - \dfrac{a}{b} > 0$ and $\dfrac{c}{d} - \dfrac{i}{j} > 0$, it follows, from Definition 8, that $\dfrac{a}{b} < \dfrac{i}{j} < \dfrac{c}{d}$.

                                                                         Q.E.D.

COROLLARY 1. There are infinitely many rational numbers between any two distinct rational numbers.[1]

Proof: Let r_1 and r_2 be two rational numbers such that $r_1 < r_2$. By Theorem 5, there is a rational number r_3 such that $r_1 < r_3 < r_2$. Also, there is a rational number r_4 such that $r_1 < r_3 < r_4 < r_2$; there is a rational number r_5 such that $r_1 < r_3 < r_4 < r_5 < r_2$; and so on.   *Q.E.D.*

---

[1] See page 16 or page 137.

COROLLARY 2. The rational numbers are not well ordered.[2]

Proof: Method 1. Let $S = \{r \mid r \in \mathbf{R} \text{ and } 0 < r < 1\}$. Then S does not contain a greatest lower bound. Otherwise, suppose there is an element r_0 in S such that $r_0 \leq r$ for all r in S. Then, by Theorem 5, there is a rational number r_1 such that $0 < r_1 < r_0$. But then r_1 is in S, contradicting the assumption that r_0 is the smallest element in S.

Method 2. $\mathbf{R}$ contains a subset isomorphic to $\mathbf{J}$. $\mathbf{J}$ is not well ordered; therefore, $\mathbf{R}$ is not well ordered.   *Q.E.D.*

Theorem 5 asserts that there is at least one rational number between any two distinct rational numbers. To describe this situation, we sometimes say that the rational numbers are dense. The integers are not dense; by the corollary of Theorem 23 of Chapter 4, for any integer b there is no integer a such that $b < a < b + 1$.

EXERCISES

1. Give all reasons for each of the steps in the proof of Theorem 5.

2. a) Use the definition of addition to compute $\dfrac{89}{113} + \dfrac{87}{111}$. b) Use the definition of "less than" to determine whether $\dfrac{89}{113}$ is less than $\dfrac{87}{111}$.

c) Find a rational number between $\dfrac{89}{113}$ and $\dfrac{87}{111}$.

3. Prove that every rational number contains exactly one ordered pair (x, y) such that $y > 0$, and the greatest common divisor of x and y is 1. Prove that, therefore, every positive rational number contains exactly one ordered pair (x, y) such that $x > 0$, $y > 0$, and the greatest common divisor of x and y is 1.

4. Prove that if a and b are any elements in a field F such that $b \neq 0$, there there is exactly one element x in F such that $bx = a$. (HINT: Take x as $b^{-1}a$.)

5. Prove that if a and b are any two rational numbers, then a is a factor of b and b is a factor of a.

6. Prove that if a and b are elements of an ordered field F, then:

a) $0 < \dfrac{1}{a}$ if, and only if, $a > 0$.

b) If $0 < a < b$, then $0 < \dfrac{1}{b} < \dfrac{1}{a}$.

c) If $a < b < 0$, then $0 > \dfrac{1}{a} > \dfrac{1}{b}$.

[2] See page 35.

5-5.   DECIMAL EXPANSIONS OF RATIONAL NUMBERS

Consider the rational number $\frac{15}{8}$. By using the division algorithm repeatedly, we have

$$15 = 8(1) + 7 \qquad 7 < 8$$
$$10(7) = 8(8) + 6 \qquad 6 < 8$$
$$10(6) = 8(7) + 4 \qquad 4 < 8$$
$$10(4) = 8(5) + 0$$

Dividing both sides of the first equation by 8 (that is, multiplying by 8^{-1} in the field **R** of rational numbers), we have $\frac{15}{8} = 1 + \frac{7}{8}$. Dividing both sides of the second equation by 8(10) and substituting, we have $\frac{7}{8} = \frac{8}{10} + \frac{6}{8}\left(\frac{1}{10}\right)$; therefore, $\frac{15}{8} = 1 + \frac{8}{10} + \frac{6}{8}\left(\frac{1}{10}\right)$. Dividing both sides of the third equation by $8(10^2)$ and substituting, we have $\frac{6}{8}\left(\frac{1}{10}\right) = \frac{7}{10^2} + \frac{4}{8}\left(\frac{1}{10^2}\right)$; therefore, $\frac{15}{8} + 1 + \frac{8}{10} + \frac{7}{10^2} + \frac{4}{8}\left(\frac{1}{10^2}\right)$. Dividing both sides of the fourth equation by $8(10^3)$ and substituting, we have $\frac{4}{8}\left(\frac{1}{10^2}\right) = \frac{5}{10^3}$; therefore, $\frac{15}{8} = 1 + \frac{8}{10} + \frac{7}{10^2} + \frac{5}{10^3}$.

The equations above yield the following inequalities:

$$1 + \frac{8}{10} \leq \frac{15}{8} \leq 1 + \frac{9}{10}$$

$$1 + \frac{8}{10} + \frac{7}{10^2} \leq \frac{15}{8} \leq 1 + \frac{8}{10} + \frac{8}{10^2}$$

$$1 + \frac{8}{10} + \frac{7}{10^2} + \frac{5}{10^3} \leq \frac{15}{8} \leq 1 + \frac{8}{10} + \frac{7}{10^2} + \frac{6}{10^3}$$

$$1 + \frac{8}{10} + \frac{7}{10^2} + \frac{5}{10^3} + \frac{0}{10^4} \leq \frac{15}{8} \leq 1 + \frac{8}{10} + \frac{7}{10^2} + \frac{5}{10^3} + \frac{1}{10^4}$$

We shall see the significance of these inequalities presently.

We use the notation 1.875 to denote the expression $1 + \frac{8}{10} + \frac{7}{10^2} + \frac{5}{10^3}$, and call 1.875 a decimal expansion of the rational number $\frac{15}{8}$. We have just shown that $\frac{15}{8}$ and its decimal expansion 1.875 are equal; that is, $\frac{15}{8} = 1.875$.

Notice how the repeated use, above, of the division algorithm justi-fies the usual procedure for long division.

$$
\begin{array}{r}
1.875 \\
8)\overline{15.0000} \\
\underline{8} \\
70 \\
\underline{64} \\
60 \\
\underline{56} \\
40 \\
\underline{40}
\end{array}
$$

Now consider the rational number $\dfrac{35}{11}$. By using the division algo-rithm repeatedly, we have

$$
\begin{array}{ll}
35 = 11(3) + 2 & 2 < 11 \\
10(2) = 11(1) + 9 & 9 < 11 \\
10(9) = 11(8) + 2 & 2 < 11 \\
10(2) = 11(1) + 9 & 9 < 11 \\
\qquad \vdots & \vdots
\end{array}
$$

Dividing both sides of the first equation by 11 (that is, multiplying by 11^{-1} in the field **R** of rational numbers), we have $\dfrac{35}{11} = 3 + \dfrac{2}{11}$. Dividing both sides of the second equation by 11(10) and substituting, we have $\dfrac{2}{11} = \dfrac{1}{10} + \dfrac{9}{11}\left(\dfrac{1}{10}\right)$; therefore, $\dfrac{35}{11} = 3 + \dfrac{1}{10} + \dfrac{9}{11}\left(\dfrac{1}{10}\right)$. Dividing both sides of the third equation by $11(10^2)$ and substituting, we have $\dfrac{9}{11}\left(\dfrac{1}{10}\right) = \dfrac{8}{10^2} + \dfrac{2}{11}\left(\dfrac{1}{10^2}\right)$; therefore, $\dfrac{35}{11} = 3 + \dfrac{1}{10} + \dfrac{8}{10^2} + \dfrac{2}{11}\left(\dfrac{1}{10^2}\right)$. Dividing both sides of the fourth equation by $11(10^3)$ and substituting, we have $\dfrac{2}{11}\left(\dfrac{1}{10^2}\right) = \dfrac{1}{10^3} + \dfrac{9}{11}\left(\dfrac{1}{10^3}\right)$; therefore, $\dfrac{35}{11} = 3 + \dfrac{1}{10} + \dfrac{8}{10^2} + \dfrac{1}{10^3} + \dfrac{9}{11}\left(\dfrac{1}{10^3}\right)$, and so on.

Since the remainders $2, 9, 2, 9, \cdots$, from the use of the division algorithm above, repeat indefinitely, the equations above yield the follow-ing infinite set of inequalities:

$$3 + \frac{1}{10} \leq \frac{35}{11} \leq 3 + \frac{2}{10}$$

$$3 + \frac{1}{10} + \frac{8}{10^2} \leq \frac{35}{11} \leq 3 + \frac{1}{10} + \frac{9}{10^2}$$

$$3 + \frac{1}{10} + \frac{8}{10^2} + \frac{1}{10^3} \leq \frac{35}{11} \leq 3 + \frac{1}{10} + \frac{8}{10^2} + \frac{2}{10^3}$$

$$\vdots \qquad \vdots$$

We use the notation $3.\overline{18}\cdots$ to denote the expression $3 + \frac{1}{10} + \frac{8}{10^2} + \frac{1}{10^3} + \frac{8}{10^4} + \cdots$, and call $3.\overline{18}\cdots$ a decimal expansion of the rational number $\frac{35}{11}$. By this, we mean that $\frac{35}{11}$ satisfies each of the inequalities in the infinite set of inequalities above. The bar over the block of digits 18 indicates that this block of digits is repeated indefinitely.

The above considerations are formalized in the following definition.

DEFINITION 10. Let $d, d_1, d_2, \cdots$ be integers such that $d \geq 0$ and $0 \leq d_i \leq 9$ for $i = 1, 2, \cdots$. The expression $d.d_1 d_2 d_3 \cdots$ (called a decimal) is said to be a decimal expansion of a positive rational number r if, for every positive integer n, $d + \frac{d_1}{10} + \frac{d_2}{10^2} + \cdots + \frac{d_n}{10^n} \leq r \leq d + \frac{d_1}{10} + \frac{d_2}{10^2} + \cdots + \frac{d_n + 1}{10^n}$. A decimal is said to be terminating if there is a positive integer N such that $d_i = 0$ for all integers $i > N$.

Example. 1.875 is a terminating decimal. In this case, $N = 3$, $d = 1$, $d_1 = 8$, $d_2 = 7$, $d_3 = 5$, and $d_4 = d_5 = d_6 = \cdots = 0$.

A decimal is said to be periodic, or repeating, if there are two integers p and N such that $d_{i+p} = d_i$ for all integers $i > N$.

Examples   1. $3.\overline{18}\cdots$ is a periodic, or repeating, decimal. In this case, $p = 2$ and $N = 0$; $d_{i+2} = d_i$ for all integers $i > 0$. Thus, $d_{1+2} = d_3 = d_1 = 1$, $d_{2+2} = d_4 = d_2 = 8$, $d_{3+2} = d_5 = d_3 = 1$, and so on.

      2. $376.2567\overline{372}\cdots$ is a periodic, or repeating, decimal. In this case, $p = 3$ and $N = 4$; $d_{i+3} = d_i$ for all integers $i > 4$. Thus, $d_{5+3} = d_8 = d_5 = 3$, $d_{6+3} = d_9 = d_6 = 7$, $d_{7+3} = d_{10} = d_7 = 2$, and so on.

      3. Any terminating decimal is periodic. For example, for the terminating decimal 1.875, $p = 1$ and $N = 3$. Thus, $d_{4+1} = d_5 = d_4 = 0$, $d_{5+1} = d_6 = d_5 = 0$, and so on.

THEOREM 6.   Every positive rational number has a periodic decimal expansion.

Proof: Let $\dfrac{a}{b}$ be any positive rational number, where a and b are positive integers. (See Exercise 3, page 110.)   Using the division algorithm repeatedly, we have

$$a = bd + r_0 \qquad\qquad 0 \le r_0 < b$$
$$10r_0 = bd_1 + r_1 \qquad\qquad 0 \le r_1 < b$$
$$10r_1 = bd_2 + r_2 \qquad\qquad 0 \le r_2 < b$$
$$\vdots \qquad\qquad\qquad \vdots$$
$$10r_{n-1} = bd_n + r_n \qquad\qquad 0 \le r_n < b$$
$$10r_n = bd_{n+1} + r_{n+1} \qquad\qquad 0 \le r_{n+1} < b$$
$$\vdots \qquad\qquad\qquad \vdots$$

Dividing both sides of the first equation by b, we have $\dfrac{a}{b} = d + \dfrac{r_0}{b}$.
Dividing both sides of the second equation by $b(10)$ and substituting, we
have $\dfrac{r_0}{b} = \dfrac{d_1}{10} + \dfrac{r_1}{b}\left(\dfrac{1}{10}\right)$; therefore, $\dfrac{a}{b} = d + \dfrac{d_1}{10} + \dfrac{r_1}{b}\left(\dfrac{1}{10}\right)$. Dividing both
sides of the third equation by $b(10^2)$ and substituting, we have

$$\dfrac{r_1}{b}\left(\dfrac{1}{10}\right) = \dfrac{d_2}{10^2} + \dfrac{r_2}{b}\left(\dfrac{1}{10^2}\right); \text{ therefore, } \dfrac{a}{b} = d + \dfrac{d_1}{10} + \dfrac{d_2}{10^2} + \dfrac{r_2}{b}\left(\dfrac{1}{10^2}\right)$$
$$\vdots \qquad\qquad \vdots$$

Dividing both sides of the $(n + 1)$st equation by $b(10^n)$ and substituting,
we have $\dfrac{r_{n-1}}{b}\left(\dfrac{1}{10^{n-1}}\right) = \dfrac{d_n}{10^n} + \dfrac{r_n}{b}\left(\dfrac{1}{10^n}\right)$; therefore, $\dfrac{a}{b} = d + \dfrac{d_1}{10} +$

$\dfrac{d_2}{10^2} + \cdots + \dfrac{d_n}{10^n} + \dfrac{r_n}{b}\left(\dfrac{1}{10^n}\right)$, and so on.

Since $0 \le \dfrac{r_i}{b} < 1$ for $i = 1, 2, \cdots$, (Why?) the equations above yield
the following infinite set of inequalities:

$$d + \dfrac{d_1}{10} \le \dfrac{a}{b} \le d + \dfrac{d_1 + 1}{10}$$

$$d + \dfrac{d_1}{10} + \dfrac{d_2}{10^2} \le \dfrac{a}{b} \le d + \dfrac{d_1}{10} + \dfrac{d_2 + 1}{10^2}$$

$$\vdots \qquad\qquad \vdots$$

$$d + \frac{d_1}{10} + \frac{d_2}{10^2} + \cdots + \frac{d_n}{10^n} \le \frac{a}{b} \le d + \frac{d_1}{10} + \frac{d_2}{10^2} + \cdots + \frac{d_n + 1}{10^n}$$

$$\vdots \qquad \vdots$$

Now for any d_n, $bd_n = 10r_{n-1} - r_n \le 10r_{n-1} < 10b$ and, therefore, $d_n < 10$. (Why?) Moreover, by Exercise 1 (page 119), $d \ge 0$ and $d_n \ge 0$ for all positive integers n. Thus, by Definition 10, $d.d_1 d_2 d_3 \cdots$ is a decimal expansion of $\frac{a}{b}$.

Since $0 \le r_i < b$ for $i = 0, 1, 2, \cdots$, it follows that each r_i is one of the b integers $0, 1, 2, \cdots, b - 1$. Therefore, after applying the division algorithm at most b times, a remainder r_{i+p} must equal one of the previous remainders r_i. When this happens, the computations start repeating.

$$Q.E.D.$$

Certain rational numbers have more than one decimal expansion. For example, the rational number 1 has the decimal expansion $1.\overline{0}\cdots$. But 1 also has the decimal expansion $.\overline{9}\cdots$, since

$$\frac{9}{10} \le 1 \le \frac{10}{10}$$

$$\frac{9}{10} + \frac{9}{100} \le 1 \le \frac{9}{10} + \frac{10}{100} = \frac{10}{10}$$

$$\frac{9}{10} + \frac{9}{100} + \frac{9}{1000} \le 1 \le \frac{9}{10} + \frac{9}{100} + \frac{10}{1000} = \frac{10}{10}$$

$$\vdots \qquad \vdots$$

Moreover, it can be shown (Exercise 4, page 119) that $d.d_1 d_2 \cdots d_{N-1} d_N \overline{0} \cdots$ and $d.d_1 d_2 \cdots d_{N-1} (d_N - 1)\overline{9} \cdots$ are both decimal expansions of the rational number $\frac{dd_1 d_2 \cdots d_N}{10^N}$.

Examples 1. $2.643\overline{0}\cdots$ and $2.642\overline{9}\cdots$ are both decimal expansions of the rational number $\frac{2643}{1000}$.

2. $5.\overline{0}\cdots$ and $4.\overline{9}\cdots$ are both decimal expansions of the rational number 5.

3. $872.234537\overline{0}\cdots$ and $872.234536\overline{9}\cdots$ are both decimal expansions of the rational number $\frac{872,234,537}{1,000,000}$.

The next theorem, which we shall not prove, is the converse of our last statement.

THEOREM 7.   Let D and D' be two different decimal expansions of the same rational number r. Then one of these decimal expansions, say D, must have the form $d.d_1 d_2 \cdots d_{N-1} d_N \overline{0} \cdots$, and the other D' must have the form $d.d_1 d_2 \cdots d_{N-1}(d_N - 1)\overline{9} \cdots$.

THEOREM 8.   Every periodic decimal is a decimal expansion of a positive rational number.

Theorem 8 is the converse of Theorem 6. We shall prove Theorem 8 on page 117. First, however, we shall illustrate, in the following examples, a technique for obtaining the rational number whose existence is asserted by Theorem 8. We shall not justify this technique because we have not, in this book, developed the mathematical background necessary for doing so. Nevertheless, this technique can be justified and does indeed give us the unique rational number r determined by any given periodic decimal.

Examples   **1.** Let $D = 39.4\overline{713}\cdots$.   Here $p = 3$ and $N = 1$.   Then $10^{N+p}D = 10^4 D = 394{,}713.\overline{713}\cdots;^3 \quad 10^N D = 10D = 394.\overline{713}\cdots;^3 \quad 10^{N+p}D - 10^N D = 10^4 D - 10D = 394{,}319.^3$

Therefore, $D(10^4 - 10) = 394{,}319$ and $D = \dfrac{394{,}319}{10^4 - 10} = \dfrac{394{,}319}{9990}$.

We now claim that $39.4\overline{713}\cdots$ is the decimal expansion of the rational number $\dfrac{394{,}319}{9990}$. We may check this result by applying the division algorithm repeatedly to $\dfrac{394{,}319}{9990}$, as in the proof of Theorem 6.

2. Let $D = .\overline{3}\cdots$. Here $p = 1$ and $N = 0$. Then $10^{N+p}D = 10D = 3.\overline{3}\cdots;^3 \quad 10^N D = D = .\overline{3}\cdots; \quad 10^{N+p}D - 10^N D = 10D - D = 3.^3$ Therefore, $9D = 3$ and $D = \dfrac{3}{9} = \dfrac{1}{3}$.

We now claim that $.\overline{3}\cdots$ is the decimal expansion of the rational number $\dfrac{1}{3}$. We may check this result by applying the division algorithm repeatedly to $\dfrac{1}{3}$, as in the proof of Theorem 6.

---

^{3}We have not justified this step.

3. Let $D = d.d_1 d_2 \cdots d_N \overline{d_{N+1} \cdots d_{N+p}} \cdots$. Then

$$10^{N+p}D = dd_1 d_2 \cdots d_{N+p} . \overline{d_{N+1} d_{N+2} \cdots d_{N+p}} \cdots;[4]$$
$$10^N D = dd_1 d_2 \cdots d_N . \overline{d_{N+1} d_{N+2} \cdots d_{N+p}} \cdots;[4]$$
$$10^{N+p}D - 10^N D = dd_1 d_2 \cdots d_{N+p} - dd_1 d_2 \cdots d_N.[4]$$

Therefore,

$$D = \frac{dd_1 d_2 \cdots d_{N+p} - dd_1 d_2 \cdots d_N}{10^{N+p} - 10^N}.$$

We now claim that $d.d_1 d_2 \cdots d_N \overline{d_{N+1} \cdots d_{N+p}} \cdots$ is a decimal expansion of the rational number

$$\frac{dd_1 d_2 \cdots d_{N+p} - dd_1 d_2 \cdots d_N}{10^{N+p} - 10^N}.$$

Once we check this result, we have a proof of Theorem 8.

Proof of Theorem 8: Let $d.d_1 d_2 \cdots d_N \overline{d_{N+1} \cdots d_{N+p}} \cdots$ be any periodic decimal. We shall show that this decimal is a decimal expansion of the rational number $\dfrac{dd_1 d_2 \cdots d_{N+p} - dd_1 d_2 \cdots d_N}{10^{N+p} - 10^N}$. First let us consider the special case $p = 2$ and $N = 2$. There we must show that $d.d_1 d_2 \overline{d_3 d_4} \cdots$ is a decimal expansion of the rational number $\dfrac{dd_1 d_2 d_3 d_4 - dd_1 d_2}{10^4 - 10^2}$. Let $a = dd_1 d_2 d_3 d_4 - dd_1 d_2$. Thus, $a = (10^4 - 10^2)d + (10^3 - 10)d_1 + (10^2 - 1)d_2 + 10d_3 + d_4$. Let $b = (10^4 - 10^2)$. Then

$$a = bd + (10^3 - 10)d_1 + (10^2 - 1)d_2 + 10d_3 + d_4.$$
$$10[(10^3 - 10)d_1 + (10^2 - 1)d_2 + 10d_3 + d_4]$$
$$= bd_1 + (10^3 - 10)d_2 + 10^2 d_3 + 10d_4.$$
$$10[(10^3 - 10)d_2 + 10^2 d_3 + 10d_4] = bd_2 + 10^3 d_3 + 10^2 d_4.$$
$$10[10^3 d_3 + 10^2 d_4] = bd_3 + 10^3 d_4 + 10^2 d_3.$$
$$10[10^3 d_4 + 10^2 d_3] = bd_4 + 10^3 d_3 + 10^2 d_4$$

and so on. (Why are all the remainders less than b?) Now, continuing exactly as in the proof of Theorem 6, we see that $d.d_1 d_2 d_3 d_4 \cdots$ is a decimal expansion of $\dfrac{dd_1 d_2 d_3 d_4 - dd_1 d_2}{10^4 - 10^2}$. When p and N are arbitrary positive integers a similar proof may be given, except for the case where from some point on the d's all equal 9. Then, (Exercise 5, page 120) when we apply the division algorithm to the rational number r obtained from our formula, we get the corresponding terminating decimal expansion of r rather than the decimal expansion consisting of 9's from a certain point on.   *Q.E.D.*

[4] We have not justified this step.

In the preceding discussions we used only positive rational numbers. To include negative rational numbers, we simply place minus signs before the appropriate decimal expansions.

Now let us consider the following: Must we use only decimal expansions for rational numbers? Can we use expansions, say to the base 2 or to the base 12? For example, can we represent a positive rational number r in the form $d.d_1 d_2 d_3 \cdots$ where $d \geq 0$, $0 \leq d_i \leq 1$ for $i = 1, 2, \cdots$, and this representation means that $d + \dfrac{d_1}{2} + \dfrac{d_2}{2^2} + \cdots + \dfrac{d_n}{2^n} \leq r \leq d + \dfrac{d_1}{2} + \dfrac{d_2}{2^2} + \cdots + \dfrac{d_n + 1}{2^n}$ for every positive integer n? Or, can we represent r in the form $d.d_1 d_2 d_3 \cdots$ where $d \geq 0$, $0 \leq d_i \leq e$ for $i = 1, 2, \cdots$, and this representation means that $d + \dfrac{d_1}{12} + \dfrac{d_2}{12^2} + \cdots + \dfrac{d_n}{12^n} \leq r \leq d + \dfrac{d_1}{12} + \dfrac{d_2}{12^2} + \cdots + \dfrac{d_n + 1}{12^n}$ for every positive integer n? The answer, of course, is yes.

Examples   1. We shall obtain the expansion to the base 2 of $\dfrac{15}{8}$ by successively subtracting 1, $\dfrac{1}{2}$, and $\dfrac{1}{4}$ from $\dfrac{15}{8}$. $\dfrac{15}{8} - 1 = \dfrac{7}{8}$; therefore, $\dfrac{15}{8} = 1 + \dfrac{7}{8}$. $\dfrac{7}{8} - \dfrac{1}{2} = \dfrac{3}{8}$; therefore, $\dfrac{15}{8} = 1 + \dfrac{1}{2} + \dfrac{3}{8}$. $\dfrac{3}{8} - \dfrac{1}{4} = \dfrac{1}{8}$; therefore, $\dfrac{15}{8} = 1 + \dfrac{1}{2} + \dfrac{1}{4} + \dfrac{1}{8}$. Hence $\dfrac{15}{8} = (1.111)_2$.

2. We could obtain the expansion to the base 5 of $\dfrac{1}{3}$ by successively subtracting integral multiples (between 0 and 4) of $\dfrac{1}{5}, \dfrac{1}{5^2}, \dfrac{1}{5^3}, \cdots$ from $\dfrac{1}{3}$. Instead, we shall obtain the expansion to the base 5 of $\dfrac{1}{3}$ by using the division algorithm.

$$1 = 3(0) + 1$$
$$5(1) = 3(1) + 2$$
$$5(2) = 3(3) + 1$$
$$5(1) = 3(1) + 2$$
$$\vdots$$

Dividing both sides of the first equation by 3, we have $\frac{1}{3} = 0 + \frac{1}{3}$. Dividing both sides of the second equation by 3(5), we have $\frac{1}{3} = \frac{1}{5} + \frac{2}{3}\left(\frac{1}{5}\right)$. Dividing both sides of the third equation by $3(5^2)$ and substituting, we have $\frac{2}{3}\left(\frac{1}{5}\right) = \frac{3}{5^2} + \frac{1}{3}\left(\frac{1}{5^2}\right)$; therefore, $\frac{1}{3} = \frac{1}{5} + \left(\frac{3}{5^2}\right) + \frac{1}{3}\left(\frac{1}{5^2}\right)$. Dividing both sides of the fourth equation by $3(5^3)$ and substituting, we have $\frac{1}{3}\left(\frac{1}{5^2}\right) = \frac{1}{5^3} + \frac{2}{3}\left(\frac{1}{5^3}\right)$; therefore,

$\frac{1}{3} = \frac{1}{5} + \frac{3}{5^2} + \frac{1}{5^3} + \frac{2}{3}\left(\frac{1}{5^3}\right)$, and so on. Hence (Why?),

$\frac{1}{3} = (0.\overline{13}\cdots)_5$.

3. $\frac{1}{3} = (0.1\overline{0}\cdots)_3$.

4. $\frac{15}{8} = (1.7\overline{0}\cdots)_8$.

5. $\frac{71}{64} = (1.07\overline{0}\cdots)_8$.

We return now to decimal expansions of rational numbers. Theorem 6 asserts that every positive rational number has a periodic decimal expansion; Theorem 8 asserts that every periodic decimal is a decimal expansion of a positive rational number. It is now natural to wonder whether an expression of the form $d.d_1d_2\cdots$ with $d \geq 0$, $0 \leq d_1 \leq 9$, and with no repeating block of digits, makes any kind of sense; that is, is it a decimal expansion of any kind of number? This question leads us to the next chapter.

EXERCISES

1. In the proof of Theorem 6, integers d and d_n are obtained. Prove that $d \geq 0$ and $d_n \geq 0$ for all n. (HINT: Use Lemma 20 of Chapter 4.)

2. Find the rational number whose decimal expansion is $54.296\overline{181}\cdots$.

3. Find the rational number whose decimal expansion is a) $54.296110\overline{9}\cdots$; b) $54.296118\overline{9}\cdots$.

4. Show that $d.d_1d_2\cdots d_{N-1}d_N\overline{0}\cdots$ and $d.d_1d_2\cdots d_{N-1}(d_N - 1)\overline{9}\cdots$ are both decimal expansions of the rational number $\dfrac{dd_1d_2\cdots d_N}{10^N}$.

5. According to the formula of Example 3 (page 117), $d.d_1 d_2 \overline{9} \cdots$ is a decimal expansion of the rational number $\dfrac{dd_1 d_2 9 - dd_1 d_2}{10^3 - 10^2}$. Prove that the decimal expansion of this rational number, obtained by repeated use of the division algorithm, is $d.d_1(d_2 + 1)\overline{0} \cdots$.

6. Represent $(.3102)_4$ to the base 10.

7. a) Obtain the expansion to the base 2 of $\dfrac{1}{3}$. b) Prove that this expansion is not terminating.

8. Obtain the expansion to the base 5 of $\dfrac{15}{8}$ by using the division algorithm.

9. Prove that if a rational number is represented by an expansion to any base b, where b is an integer greater than 1, then that expansion is periodic.

10. Prove that $(d.d_1 \overline{d_2 d_3 d_4} \cdots)_7$ is an expansion to the base 7 of the rational number $\dfrac{dd_1 d_2 d_3 d_4 - dd_1}{7^4 - 7}$.

11. State a theorem about expansions to the base 8 which is analogous to Theorem 7.

6 / The Real Numbers

6-1. EXISTENCE OF IRRATIONAL NUMBERS

In this chapter we shall discuss briefly an axiomatic theory of the real numbers.

First, however, let us consider the following question: Is there a rational number x such that $x^2 = 2$? This question arises from the geometric problem of finding the length x of a diagonal of a square whose sides have length 1 (Fig. 6-1). Now the Pythagorean theorem asserts that if the lengths of the sides of a right triangle are given by the numbers a, b, and c, as in Fig. 6-2, then $a^2 + b^2 = c^2$. Hence, applying the Pythagorean theorem to the square of side 1, we have $1^2 + 1^2 = x^2$ or $x^2 = 2$.

For a long time the Pythagorean school of Greek mathematicians believed that all numbers are ratios of integers; that is, are rational numbers. Eventually, however, using the theory of even and odd integers, the Greeks proved that there is no rational number whose square is 2.

In the proof which follows, we use the Fundamental Theorem of Arithmetic (Theorem 37, Chapter 4).

THEOREM 1. There is no rational number whose square is 2.

Proof: Suppose that there is a rational number $\dfrac{m}{n}$ such that $\left(\dfrac{m}{n}\right)^2 = 2$.

Then $\dfrac{m^2}{n^2} = 2$, and hence, $m^2 = 2n^2$. (Why?) By the Fundamental Theorem of Arithmetic, m^2 contains 2 as a factor an even number of times; that is, twice the number of times that 2 is a factor of m.[1] By this same theorem,

---

[1] If 2 is not a factor of m, then m^2 contains 2 as a factor 0 times—still an even number of times and still twice the number of times that 2 is a factor of m.

FIG. 6-1

$2n^2$ contains 2 as a factor an odd number of times; that is, twice the number of times that 2 is a factor of n plus one time more for the multiplier 2 in the expression $2n^2$. But, since m^2 and $2n^2$ denote the same integer, this situation is impossible—again by the Fundamental Theorem of Arithmetic. Thus, the assumption that there is a rational number $\frac{m}{n}$ such that $\left(\frac{m}{n}\right)^2 = 2$ leads to a contradiction and hence must be invalid.   *Q.E.D.*

Theorem 1 leads to the creation of a new type of number. Let x be a number whose square is 2. Since, by Theorem 1, x is not a rational number, we call x an irrational number; that is, a number which is not rational. It can be shown that the set consisting of all rational and irrational numbers is the set of all real numbers (Definition 3, page 125). Thus, a real number which is not rational is irrational. It can also be shown that there are actually two real numbers whose squares are 2—one positive and one negative. We call the positive number whose square is 2 "the square root of two" and denote it by $\sqrt{2}$. We call the negative number whose square is 2 "the negative square root of 2" and denote it by $-\sqrt{2}$.

Let us find some other irrational numbers. By Exercise 1 (page 124), if $m \neq 0$ is a rational number, then $m(\sqrt{2})$ is irrational. Thus, for example, $\frac{1}{3}\sqrt{2}$, $\frac{9}{16}\sqrt{2}$, $\frac{-3}{11}\sqrt{2}$, and $175\sqrt{2}$ are all irrational numbers. We shall see that the following generalization of Theorem 1 asserts the existence of additional irrational numbers.

THEOREM 2.   If a is a positive integer such that for no integer b does $a = b^2$, then there is no rational number whose square is a.

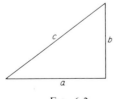

FIG. 6-2

Proof: Suppose that there is a rational number $\frac{m}{n}$ such that $\left(\frac{m}{n}\right)^2 = a$.

Then $\frac{m^2}{n^2} = a$, and hence, $m^2 = an^2$. (Why?) By the Fundamental Theorem of Arithmetic, if p is a prime factor of m^2, then m^2 contains p an even number of times; similarly, if q is a prime factor of n^2, then n^2 contains q an even number of times. We claim that there is a prime factor s of a which a contains an odd number of times. Otherwise, $a = p_1^{\rho_1} p_2^{\rho_2} \cdots p_k^{\rho_k}$, where $p_1, p_2, \cdots, p_k$ are primes such that $p_1 < p_2 < \cdots < p_k$ and the exponents $\rho_1, \rho_2, \cdots, \rho_k$ are all even positive integers. But then, by Axioms 1 and 2 for **J**, $a = (p_1^{\rho_1/2} p_2^{\rho_2/2} \cdots p_k^{\rho_k/2})^2$. Moreover, $\frac{\rho_1}{2}, \frac{\rho_2}{2}, \cdots, \frac{\rho_k}{2}$ are all positive integers. Therefore, $(p_1^{\rho_1/2} p_2^{\rho_2/2} \cdots p_k^{\rho_k/2})$ is some integer, say b, and thus $a = b^2$, contradicting the hypothesis.

Since there is a prime number s which a contains an odd number of times and which n^2 contains an even number of times, it follows that there is a prime number s which an^2 contains an odd number of times. But, by the Fundamental Theorem of Arithmetic, this is impossible, since m^2 and an^2 denote the same integer and m^2 contains s an even number of times. Thus, the assumption that there is a rational number $\frac{m}{n}$ such that $\left(\frac{m}{n}\right)^2 = a$ leads to a contradiction and hence must be invalid. *Q.E.D.*

It can be shown that there are two real numbers whose squares are a where a is a positive integer. One of these is positive and the other negative. We call the positive number whose square is a "the square root of a" and denote it by $\sqrt{a}$. We call the negative number whose square is a "the negative square root of a" and denote it by $-\sqrt{a}$. If there is no integer b such that $a = b^2$, then, by Theorem 2, $\sqrt{a}$ and $-\sqrt{a}$ are irrational.

Example. $\sqrt{3}, \sqrt{5}, \sqrt{7}, \sqrt{8}, \sqrt{10}, \sqrt{11}, \sqrt{12},$ and $\sqrt{13}$ are all irrational.

The following is a generalization of Theorem 2.

THEOREM 3. If a and n are positive integers such that for no integer b does $a = b^n$, then there is no rational number x such that $x^n = a$.

Proof: Exercise 3, page 124.

It can be shown that if a and n are positive integers, then there is exactly one positive real number x such that $x^n = a$. We call this positive real number "the nth root of a" and denote it by $\sqrt[n]{a}$. If there is no integer b such that $a = b^n$, then, by Theorem 3, $\sqrt[n]{a}$ is irrational.

Example. $\sqrt[3]{2}$, $\sqrt[3]{3}$, $\sqrt[5]{4}$, and $\sqrt[9]{26}$ are all irrational.

Notice that all the irrational numbers discussed above are numbers x such that $bx^n = a$ where a and b are integers. For example, $x = 3\sqrt{2}$ satisfies the equation $x^2 = 18$, where $a = 18$ and $b = 1$. It can be shown that π is an irrational number not satisfying such an equation, where π is defined to be the length of the circumference of a circle of unit diameter. Moreover, in 1882 Lindemann proved that π does not satisfy any equation of the form $a_n x^n + a_{n-1} x^{n-1} + \cdots + a_1 x + a_0 = 0$, where $a_0, a_1, \cdots,$ a_n are integers such that $a_n \neq 0$. Indeed, in Chapter 7 it will be shown that "most" irrational numbers do not satisfy such an equation.

EXERCISES

1. Prove that if $m \neq 0$ is a rational number, then $m(\sqrt{2})$ is irrational. [HINT: Assume that $m(\sqrt{2})$ is rational and obtain a contradiction.]

2. a) Prove that the sum of a rational number and an irrational number is an irrational number. b) Can the sum of two irrational numbers ever be rational? Why?

3. Prove Theorem 3.

6-2.   AXIOMS FOR THE REAL NUMBERS

We now discuss an axiomatic theory of the real numbers. To do this, we need some definitions.

DEFINITION 1.   If a subset of a field F (domain D) is itself a field (domain) under the addition and multiplication of F (D), then that subset is called a subfield of F (subdomain of D).

Example.   The set **J** of integers is a subdomain of the set **R** of rational numbers.

DEFINITION 2.   An ordered field F is said to be complete if, and only if, every nonempty subset of F which has an upper bound in F has a least upper bound in F.[2]

Example.   The field **R** of rational numbers is an ordered field (Theorem 2, Chapter 5) but is not complete. Let $S = \{r \mid r \in \mathbf{R}$ and $r^2 < 2\}$. By Exercise 2 (page 128), S does not have a least upper bound in **R**.

---

[2] See page 33.

By Exercise 3 (page 35), if a least upper bound exists, then it is unique. Hence we may speak of "the" least upper bound rather than of "a" least upper bound.

It can be shown that there exists a complete ordered field and that any two complete ordered fields are isomorphic. Therefore, there is "up to an isomorphism" only one set of elements satisfying all the axioms for a complete ordered field.

DEFINITION 3. The set R of real numbers is the set of elements satisfying all the axioms for a complete ordered field.

It can be shown that any ordered field contains a subfield isomorphic to the field **R** of rational numbers. Hence the field R of real numbers contains the field **R** of rational numbers as a subfield.

EXERCISES

1. Make a list of all the axioms for the real numbers.
2. Let S and S' be two subfields of a given field F. Prove that $S \cap S'$ is a subfield of F.

6-3. PROPERTIES OF THE REAL NUMBERS

From Definition 3 one can deduce all the properties of the real numbers. Since the real numbers form a complete ordered field, all the theorems which have been proved about ordered integral domains (Secs. 4-3 and 4-4, Exercises 4 and 5 of Sec. 4-3, and Exercise 11 of Sec. 4-4) and all the theorems which have been proved about fields (Exercises 4 and 6 of Sec. 5-4) are valid for the set R of real numbers. We shall now consider some additional theorems.

THEOREM 4 (The Archimedean Property).   Let a and b be any positive real numbers. Then there is an integer n such that $na > b$.

Proof: Suppose that a and b are positive real numbers such that for every integer n, $b \geq na$. Then the set $S = \{na \mid n \in \mathbf{J}\}$ has b as an upper bound. Hence, by Definition 3, S has a least upper bound b'. Thus, $b' \geq na$ for all n in **J**. Now if n is in **J**, then $n + 1$ is in **J** also. Therefore, $(n + 1)a$ is in S, and hence $(n + 1)a \leq b'$. By Axioms 2, 3, and 5 for **J**, this means that $na + a \leq b'$. Therefore, for all n in **J**, $na \leq b' - a$. (Why?) Hence $b' - a$ is an upper bound of S. But since a is positive, $b' - a < b'$. Thus, $b' - a$ is an upper bound of S which is less than the least upper bound of S, which is impossible. Therefore, the original assumption that $b \geq na$ for every integer n must be invalid.   *Q.E.D.*

THEOREM 5.   Every real number r is the least upper bound of a set of rational numbers.

Proof: Let $S = \left\{ \dfrac{m}{n} \,\middle|\, \dfrac{m}{n} \in \mathbf{R} \text{ and } \dfrac{m}{n} < r \right\}$. By Exercise 3 (page 128), S is not empty. Since r is an upper bound of S, it follows, from Definitions 2 and 3, that S has a least upper bound $x \leq r$. Suppose that $x < r$. Then $r - x > 0$, and, by Theorem 4, there is an integer n such that $n(r - x) > 1$. Therefore, $(r - x) > n^{-1} = \dfrac{1}{n}$ (Why?), and $x + \dfrac{1}{n} < r$. (Why?) Since x is the least upper bound of S, there is an element $\dfrac{m'}{n'}$ in S such that $x - \dfrac{1}{n} < \dfrac{m'}{n'} \leq x$. (Otherwise $x - \dfrac{1}{n}$ would be an upper bound of S less than the least upper bound of S, which is impossible.) Therefore, $x < \dfrac{m'}{n'} + \dfrac{1}{n} \leq x + \dfrac{1}{n} < r$. (Why?) Now $\dfrac{m'}{n'} + \dfrac{1}{n}$ is in S, since it is a rational number less than r. Hence $\dfrac{m'}{n'} + \dfrac{1}{n} \leq x$, the least upper bound of S. But this is impossible because we proved above that $x < \dfrac{m'}{n'} + \dfrac{1}{n}$. Thus, the assumption that $x < r$ leads to a contradiction and hence must be invalid. Therefore $x = r$.   *Q.E.D.*

THEOREM 6.   Let a and b be any two real numbers such that $a < b$. Then there is a rational number $\dfrac{m}{n}$ such that $a < \dfrac{m}{n} < b$.

Proof: Let $S = \left\{ \dfrac{m}{n} \,\middle|\, \dfrac{m}{n} \in \mathbf{R} \text{ and } \dfrac{m}{n} < b \right\}$. Then, by the proof of Theorem 5, b is the least upper bound of S. Moreover, there is an element $\dfrac{m'}{n'}$ in S such that $a < \dfrac{m'}{n'} < b$. Otherwise, a would be an upper bound of S less than the least upper bound of S, which is impossible.   *Q.E.D.*

We may associate each point on a line with exactly one real number, as follows: Arbitrarily choose a point on the line and label that point 0. Choose a unit of distance on the line. Let points one unit, two units, three units, $\cdots$ in one direction from 0 be labeled $1, 2, 3, \cdots$, respectively. Let points one unit, two units, three units, $\cdots$ in the opposite direction from 0 be labeled $-1, -2, -3, \cdots$, respectively. Label as $\dfrac{1}{2}$ the point halfway between 0 and 1; label as $\dfrac{-1}{2}$ the point halfway between 0 and -1; label as $\frac{1}{3}$ the point one third of the distance from 0 to 1; label as $\frac{-4}{3}$ the point one third of the distance from -1 to -2; and so on. In this way we may associate each rational number with exactly one point on the line and two distinct rational numbers with two distinct points. (See Fig. 6-3.)

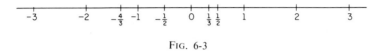

FIG. 6-3

Now suppose that P is a point on the line which is not associated with a rational number. Let M be the set of all rational numbers associated with points on one side of P and let N be the set of all rational numbers associated with points on the other side of P. Thus, each rational number belongs to M or to N but not to both. Without loss of generality we may assume that the rational numbers in N are greater than the rational numbers in M. Then M has an upper bound and N has a lower bound. Let m be the least upper bound of M; let n be the greatest lower bound of N. By Theorem 12 of Chapter 4, for integral domains exactly one holds: $m < n$, $m = n$, or $m > n$.

Suppose that $m < n$. Then, by Theorem 6, there is a rational number $\frac{a}{b}$ such that $m < \frac{a}{b} < n$. Since $\frac{a}{b}$ is rational, $\frac{a}{b}$ is in M or in N. But this is impossible, since $\frac{a}{b}$ is greater than the least upper bound of M and less than the greatest lower bound of N. Thus, the assumption that $m < n$ leads to a contradiction and hence must be invalid.

Suppose that $m > n$. Then, by Theorem 6, there is a rational number $\frac{a}{b}$ such that $n < \frac{a}{b} < m$. Since $\frac{a}{b} < m$, it follows that $\frac{a}{b}$ is in M. Since $\frac{a}{b} > n$, it follows that $\frac{a}{b}$ is in N. But this is impossible, since M and N are disjoint. Thus, the assumption that $m > n$ leads to a contradiction and hence must be invalid.

The only remaining alternative is that $m = n$. We shall let the real number $r = m = n$ be associated with P.

Thus, since the least upper bound of a set is unique, we have associated each point on a line with exactly one real number. Conversely, it can be shown that this association pairs each real number with exactly one point on the line. In other words, there is a 1:1 correspondence between the set of all real numbers and the set of all points on a line.

EXERCISES

1. Show why the following are applications of the Archimedean property: a) One may mark off any length (however large) by repeatedly marking off a given length (however small) so that each successive marking off starts where the preceding one ended. b) (Supposedly due to Archimedes) One may remove all the grains of sand on a beach by carrying away a cupful of sand a sufficient number of times.

2. Prove that the set $S = \{r \mid r \in \mathbf{R} \text{ and } r^2 < 2\}$ does not have a least upper bound in $\mathbf{R}$. (HINT: Assume the contrary and use Theorem 6.)

3. Let r be a fixed real number. Prove that the set $S = \left\{ \dfrac{m}{n} \,\middle|\, \dfrac{m}{n} \in \mathbf{R} \right.$ and $\left. \dfrac{m}{n} < r \right\}$ is not empty.

4. Give all reasons for each of the steps in the proof of Theorem 5.

5. Prove that between every two rational numbers there is an irrational number.

6. Prove that between every two irrational numbers there is an irrational number.

6-4. DECIMAL EXPANSIONS OF REAL NUMBERS

DEFINITION 4. Let $d, d_1, d_2, \cdots$ be integers such that $d \geq 0$ and $0 \leq d_i \leq 9$ for $i = 1, 2, \cdots$. The expression $d.d_1 d_2 d_3 \cdots$ (called a decimal) is said to be a decimal expansion of a positive real number r if, for every positive integer n,

$$d + \frac{d_1}{10} + \frac{d_2}{10^2} + \cdots + \frac{d_n}{10^n} \leq r \leq d + \frac{d_1}{10} + \frac{d_2}{10^2} + \cdots + \frac{d_n + 1}{10^n}.$$

The following theorems are proved in more advanced texts:

THEOREM 7. Every decimal is a decimal expansion of a positive real number.

THEOREM 8. Every positive real number has a decimal expansion.[3]

Suppose that $d.d_1 d_2 d_3 \cdots$ is any decimal. A proof of Theorem 7 consists in showing that this decimal is a decimal expansion of the least upper bound of the set $\left\{ d, \dfrac{d_1}{10}, \dfrac{d_2}{10^2}, \dfrac{d_3}{10^3}, \cdots \right\}$. Notice that proving Theorems 7 and 8 is equivalent to proving that the set of all decimals together with the set of all negative decimals[3] constitutes a complete ordered field.

---

[3] To include negative real numbers, we place minus signs before the appropriate decimal expansions.

In the preceding chapter we proved (Theorem 6) that every positive rational number has a periodic decimal expansion and (Theorem 8) that every periodic decimal is a decimal expansion of a positive rational number. Thus, we can distinguish rational numbers from irrational numbers by their decimal expansions. A real number is rational if, and only if, its decimal expansion is periodic; a real number is irrational if, and only if, its decimal expansion is not periodic.

6-5. CONSTRUCTION OF THE REAL NUMBERS FROM THE RATIONAL NUMBERS

You will recall that in Chapter 4 we showed (Theorem 1) how we could construct the set J of integers from the set I of positive integers. In Chapter 5 we showed how we could construct the set R of rational numbers from the set J of integers. It is now natural to wonder whether we can construct the set R of real numbers from the set R of rational numbers. The answer is yes. In fact, we can do so in several ways, each of which, however, is considerably more complicated than constructing J from I, or R from J. We list references for four different methods of constructing the real numbers from the rational numbers and promise the interested reader many delightful hours becoming acquainted with them.

1. Method of Nested Intervals: R. Courant and H. Robbins, *What Is Mathematics?* New York: Oxford University Press, Inc., 1941, pp. 68–71.

2. Method of Decimal Representation: J. F. Ritt, *Theory of Functions*, rev. ed. New York: King's Crown Press, 1947, Chapter I.

3. Cantor's Method: C. Goffman, *Real Functions.* New York: Holt, Rinehart & Winston, Inc., 1953, pp. 31–41.

4. Dedekind's Method: *ibid.* pp. 41–45.

6-6. THE COMPLEX NUMBERS

Next we turn to the question of the existence of other numbers besides the real numbers.

According to Theorem 19 of Chapter 4, if $x \neq 0$ is an element in an ordered integral domain, then x^2 is positive. Hence, since the set R of real numbers is an ordered integral domain, there is no real number x such that $x^2 = -1$. This leads to the creation of a new type of number. Let i be a number whose square is -1; that is, $i^2 = -1$. We call this number i an imaginary number. This does not mean that i is imaginary in the sense that i does not exist; i exists in the same sense that the irrational number $\sqrt{2}$ exists. If a and b are real numbers, then we also call bi an imaginary number and we call $a + bi$ a complex number.

Cardan, in 1545, was the first to use imaginary numbers. For a long time, however, mathematicians were rather uncomfortable with the notion of imaginary numbers; they felt that these numbers had a somewhat mystic quality. In 1702, Leibnitz said "Imaginary numbers are a fine and wonderful refuge of the divine spirit, almost an amphibian between being and non-being."

In the 1830's Hamilton developed a theory of complex numbers in which a complex number was simply considered to be an ordered pair of real numbers. From this point of view there is certainly nothing mysterious about complex numbers. He defined a complex number as follows:

DEFINITION 5. The set C of complex numbers consists of all ordered pairs (a, b) of real numbers with addition $(+)$ and multiplication $(\cdot)$ defined as:

$$(a, b) + (a', b') = (a + a', b + b')$$

and

$$(a, b) \cdot (a', b') = (aa' - bb', ab' + ba').$$

Using this definition, we can prove Theorem 9.

THEOREM 9. The complex numbers form a field. This field contains a subfield, $\{(a, b) \mid b = 0\}$, isomorphic [under the correspondence $\psi(a, 0) = a$] to the field R of real numbers. The field of complex numbers also contains a solution of the equation $x^2 = -1$.

Under the isomorphism ψ of Theorem 9, we may identify the real number 1 with the ordered pair $(1, 0)$; the real number -1 with the ordered pair $(-1, 0)$; and so on. Then the solution of $x^2 = -1$ is $i = (0, 1)$ since, by Definition 5, $i^2 = (0, 1) \cdot (0, 1) = (0 - 1, 0) = (-1, 0) = -1$.

Moreover, by Definition 5, $(a, b) = (a, 0) + (0, b) = (a, 0) + [(b, 0) \cdot (0, 1)] = a + bi$.

According to Corollary 1 of Theorem 19, Chapter 4, the complex numbers do not form an ordered integral domain; hence they do not form an ordered field. Moreover, it can be shown that any integral domain, containing the set R of real numbers as well as a solution of $x^2 = -1$, contains a subdomain isomorphic to C. Hence, if we wish to use ordered number systems only, the set R of real numbers cannot be extended to include i.

It can be shown, however, that every equation of the form $a_n x^n + a_{n-1} x^{n-1} + \cdots + a_1 x + a_0 = 0$ with real coefficients $a_0, a_1, \cdots, a_n$ (and every such equation with complex coefficients) is satisfied by a complex number. Thus, if we are interested in having solutions of equations even if we must sacrifice ordering our numbers, we can use the complex numbers.

The set C of complex numbers need not be obtained by means of the real numbers. The complex numbers can also be defined by a suitable set of axioms.[4]

EXERCISES

1. Prove that for the set C of complex numbers, multiplication is commutative, associative, and distributive over addition.

2. Let $(1, 1)$ and $(1, 2)$ be complex numbers. Find the complex number (x, y) which satisfies the equation $(1, 1) \cdot (x, y) = (1, 2)$.

6-7. THE HIGHER COMPLEX NUMBERS

Now let us consider the possibility of extending the complex number system to a system of "higher" complex numbers containing additional units besides 1 and i. A system of higher complex numbers consists of n units: $1, i_1, i_2, \cdots, i_{n-1}$, the set $\{x(1) + x_1 i_1 + x_2 i_2 + \cdots + x_{n-1} i_{n-1} \mid x, x_1, x_2, \cdots, x_{n-1} \in R\}$, and an addition and multiplication to be "suitably" defined.

In 1843 Hamilton considered a higher complex number system containing four units, $1, i_1, i_2$, and i_3. In this system each element has the form $x + x_1 i_1 + x_2 i_2 + x_3 i_3$, where x, x_1, x_2, and x_3 are real numbers. Addition and multiplication can be defined in this system so that all the requirements for a field, excepting the commutativity of multiplication, are satisfied. The sum of two elements is defined as follows: $(a + a_1 i_1 + a_2 i_2 + a_3 i_3) + (b + b_1 i_1 + b_2 i_2 + b_3 i_3) = [(a + b) + (a_1 + b_1)i_1 + (a_2 + b_2)i_2 + (a_3 + b_3)i_3]$. $1, i_1, i_2$, and i_3 are multiplied (row element times column element) according to the following table:

	1	i_1	i_2	i_3
1	1	i_1	i_2	i_3
i_1	i_1	-1	i_3	$-i_2$
i_2	i_2	$-i_3$	-1	i_1
i_3	i_3	i_2	$-i_1$	-1

The set $\{x + x_1 i_1 + x_2 i_2 + x_3 i_3 \mid x, x_1, x_2, x_3 \in R\}$, together with this addition and multiplication, is called the set Q of quaternions. It can be shown that the subset $\{x + x_1 i_1 + 0(i_2) + 0(i_3)\}$ of Q is isomorphic

---

[4] E. V. Huntington, *Monographs on Topics of Modern Mathematics Relevant to the Elementary Field*, edited by J. W. A. Young. New York: Dover Publications, Inc., 1955.

to C and that the subset $\{x + O(i_1) + O(i_2) + O(i_3)\}$ of Q is isomorphic to R. Quaternions have many applications in physics and mathematics.

Frobenius and Pierce proved that only for systems with one, two, and four units can addition and multiplication be defined so as to satisfy all the requirements for a field excepting, at most, the commutativity of multiplication. In 1958 Bott, Kervaire, and Milnor proved that only for systems with one, two, four, and eight units can addition and multiplication be defined so as to satisfy all the requirements for a field excepting, at most, the commutativity and associativity of multiplication.

6-8. ALGEBRAIC AND TRANSCENDENTAL NUMBERS

In using the following definitions we should recall that the set C of complex numbers contains the set R of real numbers as a subset.

DEFINITION 6. An algebraic number is a complex number x which satisfies an equation of the form $a_n x^n + a_{n-1} x^{n-1} + \cdots + a_1 x + a_0 = 0$, where the coefficients $a_0, a_1, \cdots, a_n$ are integers and $a_n \neq 0$.

Examples

1. All rational numbers are algebraic. Any rational number $\dfrac{p}{q}$ satisfies the equation $qx - p = 0$, in which $a_0 = -p$ and $a_1 = q$.

2. Many irrational numbers are algebraic. For example, $\sqrt{2}$ satisfies the equation $x^2 - 2 = 0$, in which $a_0 = -2$, $a_1 = 0$, and $a_2 = 1$; $\sqrt[5]{3}$ satisfies the equation $x^5 - 3 = 0$, in which $a_0 = -3$, $a_1 = a_2 = a_3 = a_4 = 0$, and $a_5 = 1$.

3. Many complex numbers are algebraic. For example, i satisfies the equation $x^2 + 1 = 0$, in which $a_0 = 1$, $a_1 = 0$, and $a_2 = 1$. $-1 + \sqrt{2}i$ satisfies the equation $x^2 + 2x + 3 = 0$, in which $a_0 = 3$, $a_1 = 2$, and $a_2 = 1$.

DEFINITION 7. A transcendental number is a complex number which is not algebraic.

Example. π is a transcendental number.

The preceding two definitions will be of especial interest in the next chapter.

EXERCISE

Ascribe all possible names from the list (real, rational, irrational, integer, algebraic, transcendental, periodic decimal, complex number) to each of the following numbers:

   a) $\sqrt[3]{-8}$.

   b) $\dfrac{22}{7}$.

   c) π.

   d) -3.

   e) $.679\overline{1251}\cdots$.

   f) $.32332333233332\cdots$.

   g) $\sqrt[5]{4}$.

   h) 0.

   i) $\sqrt{2} + \sqrt{3}i$.

7 / Cardinal Numbers

7-1. FINITE, DENUMERABLE, AND NONDENUMERABLE SETS

In the preceding chapters we were concerned with various sets of numbers—the set **I** of positive integers, the set **J** of integers, the set **R** of rational numbers, and the set R of real numbers. In this chapter we shall be concerned with comparing the "sizes" of two different sets. To do this, we shall use the notion of 1:1 correspondence (page 24). The theory which we shall discuss was formulated by Georg Cantor in the late 1800's, and constitutes one of the great achievements of mathematics.

DEFINITION 1. Two sets A and B are said to have the same number of elements or to have the same cardinal number if there is a 1:1 correspondence between A and B. If the sets A and B have the same cardinal number, we write "$A \approx B$."

It is easy to show that the relation "having the same cardinal number" is an equivalence relation (Exercise 1, page 142).

Examples   1. The sets $A = \{\circ, \triangle, \square\}$, $B = \{\rho, \lambda, \mu\}$, and $\mathbf{J}_3$ (page 98) all have the same cardinal number. Thus, $A \approx B$, $A \approx \mathbf{J}_3$, and $B \approx \mathbf{J}_3$.

2. The set **I** of positive integers, $\{1, 2, 3, \cdots\}$, and the set **I**′ of even positive integers, $\{2, 4, 6, \cdots\}$, have the same cardinal number, since the correspondence

$$
\begin{array}{ccccccc}
1 & 2 & 3 & 4 & \cdots & n & \cdots \\
\updownarrow & \updownarrow & \updownarrow & \updownarrow & & \updownarrow & \\
2 & 4 & 6 & 8 & \cdots & 2n & \cdots
\end{array}
$$

is 1:1. Similarly, the set **I** and the set **I**″ = $\{10, 20, 30, \cdots\}$ have the same cardinal number, since the correspondence

134

is 1:1. Thus, $\mathbf{I} \approx \mathbf{I}'$, $\mathbf{I} \approx \mathbf{I}''$, and (Why?) $\mathbf{I}' \approx \mathbf{I}''$.

3. Let $\mathbf{I}_p = \mathbf{I} - \{p\}$, where p is any positive integer. Then $\mathbf{I} \approx \mathbf{I}_p$, since the correspondence

$$
\begin{array}{ccccccccc}
1 & 2 & 3 & \cdots & p-1 & p & p+1 & \cdots \\
\updownarrow & \updownarrow & \updownarrow & & \updownarrow & \updownarrow & \updownarrow & \\
1 & 2 & 3 & \cdots & p-1 & p+1 & p+2 & \cdots
\end{array}
$$

is 1:1.

4. The set $\mathbf{I}$ of positive integers and the set $\mathbf{J}$ of integers have the same cardinal number, since the correspondence

$$
\begin{array}{ccccccccccccc}
\cdots & -n & \cdots & -3 & -2 & -1 & 0 & 1 & 2 & 3 & \cdots & n & \cdots \\
& \updownarrow & & \updownarrow & \updownarrow & \updownarrow & \updownarrow & \updownarrow & \updownarrow & \updownarrow & & \updownarrow & \\
\cdots & 2n & \cdots & 6 & 4 & 2 & 1 & 3 & 5 & 7 & \cdots & 2n+1 & \cdots
\end{array}
$$

is 1:1. Thus, $\mathbf{I} \approx \mathbf{J}$.

5. The set of all points on any line segment L has the same cardinal number as the set of all points on any line segment L'. For example, Fig. 7-1 illustrates a 1:1 correspondence between the points x on the line segment $L = AB$ and the points x' on the line segment $L' = A'B'$. According to Fig. 7-1, if P is the point of intersection of the lines AA' and BB', then each point x on L corresponds to the point x' on L' obtained by intersecting line Px with L'. Moreover, each point x' on L' corresponds to the point x on L obtained by intersecting line Px' with L.

6. The set of all points on any line L has the same cardinal number as the set of all points on any open segment of L; that is, any segment of L with the end points excluded.

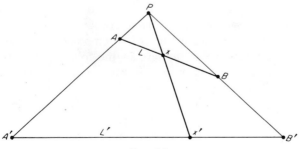

FIG. 7-1

For example, Fig. 7-2 illustrates a 1:1 correspondence between the points on the line L and the points on the open segment AB of L. According to Fig. 7-2, if C is the center of a semicircle of radius equal to half the distance between

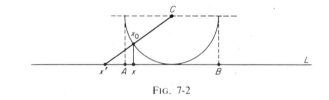

Fig. 7-2

points A and B and tangent to the segment AB at its midpoint, then each point x on the open segment AB corresponds to the point x' on L obtained as follows: Construct a perpendicular to AB at x. This perpendicular will intersect the semicircle at a point x_0. Then x' is the point of intersection of line Cx_0 with line L. Moreover, each point x' on line L corresponds to the point x on AB obtained as follows: Let x_0 be the point of intersection of line Cx' with the semicircle. Then x is the foot of the perpendicular from x_0 to the segment AB. Under the correspondence described above, the point of tangency of the semicircle with AB corresponds to itself.

7. The set **I** of positive integers has the same cardinal number as the set **R** of rational numbers. We may obtain a 1:1 correspondence between **I** and **R** as follows: By Exercise 3 (page 110), every rational number contains exactly one ordered pair (x, y) where x and y are integers such that $y > 0$ and the greatest common divisor of x and y is 1. Take a set of horizontal and vertical lines and label them as in Fig. 7-3. Starting at the point of intersection of lines $x = 0$ and $y = 0$ and continuing along a spiral path, assign a positive integer to each point of intersection of an x line and a y line, except the following: those points of intersection corresponding to a pair (x, y) with the greatest common divisor of x and y not equal to 1; those points of intersection with $y \leq 0$. The points assigned an integer are indicated in Fig. 7-3 by the dots and the corresponding integer. In this way we obtain the following 1:1 correspondence between **I** and **R**:

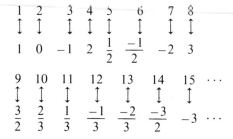

in which each positive integer is paired with exactly one rational number and each rational number is paired with exactly one positive integer.

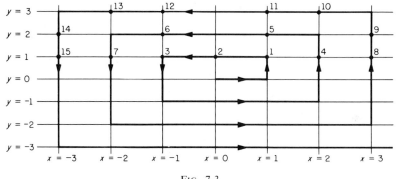

FIG. 7-3

DEFINITION 2. A nonempty set S is said to be finite if, and only if, there is a positive integer n such that S has the same cardinal number as the set $\{1, 2, \cdots, n\}$.

Examples   1. The set of books in this room is finite.
                 2. J_3 is finite.

It can be shown that if S_m and S_n are any two finite sets having the same cardinal numbers as the sets $\{1, 2, \cdots, m\}$ and $\{1, 2, \cdots, n\}$ respectively, then $S_m \approx S_n$ if, and only if, $m = n$.

DEFINITION 3. A nonempty set which is not finite is said to be infinite.

DEFINITION 4. A set S is said to be denumerable if, and only if, S has the same cardinal number as the set **I** of positive integers; that is, if, and only if, there is a 1:1 correspondence between S and **I**.

Examples   1. **I** is denumerable.
                 2. **J** is denumerable. (See Example 4, page 135.)
                 3. **R** is denumerable. (See Example 7, page 136.)

THEOREM 1. If A is a denumerable set and B is a finite set, then $A \cup B$ is denumerable.

Proof: Let $A = \{a_1, a_2, \cdots, a_i, \cdots\}$ and let $B = \{b_1, b_2, \cdots, b_n\}$. Without loss of generality, we may assume that A and B are disjoint. Then $A \cup B = \{b_1, b_2, \cdots, b_n, a_1, a_2, \cdots, a_i, \cdots\}$. We may construct a 1:1 correspondence between $A \cup B$ and **I** as follows:

$$
\begin{array}{ccccccccc}
1 & 2 & \cdots & n & n+1 & n+2 & \cdots & n+i & \cdots \\
\updownarrow & \updownarrow & & \updownarrow & \updownarrow & \updownarrow & & \updownarrow & \\
b_1 & b_2 & \cdots & b_n & a_1 & a_2 & \cdots & a_i & \cdots \qquad Q.E.D.
\end{array}
$$

THEOREM 2. The union of a finite number of denumerable sets is denumerable.

Proof: Let

$$
\begin{aligned}
A_1 &= \{a_{11}, a_{12}, \cdots, a_{1i}, \cdots\} \\
A_2 &= \{a_{21}, a_{22}, \cdots, a_{2i}, \cdots\} \\
&\ \ \vdots \qquad\qquad\ \ \vdots \\
A_n &= \{a_{n1}, a_{n2}, \cdots, a_{ni}, \cdots\}
\end{aligned}
$$

Without loss of generality, we may assume that $A_1 \cap A_2 \cap \cdots \cap A_n = \emptyset$. We may construct a 1:1 correspondence between $A_1 \cup A_2 \cup \cdots \cup A_n$ and I according to the following scheme:

$$
\begin{array}{ccccc}
a_{11} & a_{12} & a_{13} & \cdots & a_{1i} \quad \cdots \\
\downarrow & \downarrow & \downarrow & & \downarrow \\
a_{21} & a_{22} & a_{23} & \cdots & a_{2i} \quad \cdots \\
\downarrow & \downarrow & \downarrow & & \downarrow \\
a_{31} & a_{32} & a_{33} & \cdots & a_{3i} \quad \cdots \\
\vdots & \vdots & \vdots & & \vdots \\
\downarrow & \downarrow & \downarrow & & \downarrow \\
a_{n1} & a_{n2} & a_{n3} & \cdots & a_{ni} \quad \cdots
\end{array}
$$

Thus,

$$
\begin{array}{cccccccc}
1 & 2 & 3 & \cdots & n & n+1 & n+2 & \cdots & 2n \\
\updownarrow & \updownarrow & \updownarrow & & \updownarrow & \updownarrow & \updownarrow & & \updownarrow \\
a_{11} & a_{21} & a_{31} & \cdots & a_{n1} & a_{12} & a_{22} & \cdots & a_{n2}
\end{array}
$$

$$
\begin{array}{ccccccc}
2n+1 & 2n+2 & \cdots & kn & kn+1 & kn+2 & \cdots \\
\updownarrow & \updownarrow & & \updownarrow & \updownarrow & \updownarrow & \\
a_{13} & a_{23} & \cdots & a_{nk} & a_{1,k+1} & a_{2,k+1} & \cdots \qquad Q.E.D.
\end{array}
$$

THEOREM 3. The union of a denumerable collection of denumerable sets is denumerable.

Proof: Let

$$A_1 = \{a_{11}, a_{12}, \cdots, a_{1i}, \cdots\}$$
$$A_2 = \{a_{21}, a_{22}, \cdots, a_{2i}, \cdots\}$$
$$\vdots \qquad \vdots$$
$$A_k = \{a_{k1}, a_{k2}, \cdots, a_{ki}, \cdots\}$$
$$\vdots \qquad \vdots$$

Without loss of generality, we may assume that no two sets in the collection have an element in common. We may construct a 1:1 correspondence between $\bigcup_{i \in \mathbf{I}} A_i$ and $\mathbf{I}$ according to the scheme below, where, along each diagonal, the sum of the two indices is constant:

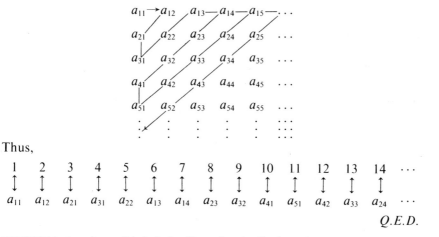

Thus,

1	2	3	4	5	6	7	8	9	10	11	12	13	14	$\cdots$
$\updownarrow$	$\updownarrow$	$\updownarrow$	$\updownarrow$	$\updownarrow$	$\updownarrow$	$\updownarrow$	$\updownarrow$	$\updownarrow$	$\updownarrow$	$\updownarrow$	$\updownarrow$	$\updownarrow$	$\updownarrow$	
a_{11}	a_{12}	a_{21}	a_{31}	a_{22}	a_{13}	a_{14}	a_{23}	a_{32}	a_{41}	a_{51}	a_{42}	a_{33}	a_{24}	$\cdots$

$$Q.E.D.$$

THEOREM 4. A set S is infinite if, and only if, there is a 1:1 correspondence between S and a proper subset of S.

Proof: If S is finite, then, by Definition 2, there is a 1:1 correspondence between S and the set $S_n = \{1, 2, \cdots, n\}$. Hence, by the statement following Definition 2, there cannot be a 1:1 correspondence between S and a proper subset of S. Therefore, if there is a 1:1 correspondence between S and a proper subset of S, then, by Definition 3, S must be infinite.

Conversely, if S is infinite, then, by Exercise 4 (page 142), S contains a denumerable subset $S' = \{s_1, s_2, \cdots, s_i, \cdots\}$. The correspondence associating each s_i with s_{i+1} and each element of $S - S'$ with itself is a 1:1 correspondence between S and a proper subset of S. $\qquad Q.E.D.$

Examples   1. **I** is infinite, since, by Example 2 (page 134), there is a 1:1
                   correspondence between **I** and $\mathbf{I}' = \{2, 4, 6, \cdots\}$.
                2. **J** is infinite, since, by Example 4 (page 135), there is a
                   1:1 correspondence between **J** and **I**, and **I** is a proper
                   subset of **J**.
                3. By Exercise 5 (page 142), any set S having the same cardi-
                   nal number as **I** is infinite.
                4. The set **R** of real numbers is infinite. The correspondence
                   associating each real number r with the real number $2r$ is
                   a 1:1 correspondence between **R** and a proper subset of **R**.

DEFINITION 5.   An infinite set which is not denumerable is said to be
nondenumerable.

THEOREM 5.   The set **R** of real numbers is nondenumerable.

Proof: By Example 4 above, **R** is infinite. The proof that **R** is not denumerable depends upon the so-called diagonal process by which, given
any denumerable set of real numbers, a real number is constructed which
cannot possibly be contained in the set.

By Theorem 8, Chapter 6, every positive real number has a decimal
expansion. By Theorems 6, 7, and 8 of Chapter 5, every positive real
number has exactly one decimal expansion which does not consist of 9's
from a certain point on. Let us represent each positive real number r in
its decimal expansion not consisting of 9's from a certain point on. Now
suppose that there is a 1:1 correspondence between the set **I** of positive
integers and the set **R** of positive real numbers:

$$1 \leftrightarrow d_1.d_{11}d_{12}d_{13}d_{14} \cdots$$

$$2 \leftrightarrow d_2.d_{21}d_{22}d_{23}d_{24} \cdots$$

$$3 \leftrightarrow d_3.d_{31}d_{32}d_{33}d_{34} \cdots$$

$$\vdots \qquad \vdots$$

$$n \leftrightarrow d_n.d_{n1}d_{n2}d_{n3}d_{n4} \cdots$$

$$\vdots \qquad \vdots$$

Construct a real number $r_0 = .a_1a_2a_3a_4 \cdots$ as follows: Let a_1 be a digit
which does not equal d_{11} or 9; let a_2 be a digit which does not equal d_{22}
or 9; $\cdots$; let a_n be a digit which does not equal d_{nn} or 9; $\cdots$. Thus, r_0 is
a real number which differs from each of the real numbers in the above
list, since $a_1 \neq d_{11}$, $a_2 \neq d_{22}$, $a_3 \neq d_{33}$; and so on. Hence the assumption
that there is a 1:1 correspondence between the set **I** and the set **R** leads to
a contradiction and must be invalid. Therefore, **R** is not denumerable.
                                                                    Q.E.D.

At this point one might wonder whether we can use a similar argument to show that the rational numbers are not denumerable, thus contradicting the statement in Example 3, page 137. Now, by Theorem 6 of Chapter 5, every rational number has a periodic decimal expansion. Therefore, in attempting to construct a rational number r_0 by the method used in the proof of Theorem 5, we must allow the digits to start repeating from a certain decimal place on. Hence we can no longer freely assign values to the digits in the subsequent decimal places, as we did in the case of the real numbers. Thus, the argument used for the real numbers is not valid for the rational numbers.

COROLLARY. The set of all irrational numbers is nondenumerable.

Proof: The set R of real numbers consists of all the rational numbers and all the irrational numbers. By Theorem 5, R is nondenumerable and, by Example 3 (page 137), the set R of rational numbers is denumerable. Therefore, by Exercise 7 (page 142), the set of all irrational numbers is nondenumerable. *Q.E.D.*

We shall now consider two other subsets of R—the set A of algebraic real numbers (Definition 6, Chapter 6) and the set T of transcendental real numbers (Definition 7, Chapter 6). We shall prove (Theorem 7) that A is denumerable and (Exercise 8, page 142) that T is nondenumerable. We shall need the following theorem which we shall not prove.

THEOREM 6. There are, at most, n real numbers satisfying an equation of the form $a_n x^n + a_{n-1} x^{n-1} + \cdots + a_1 x + a_0 = 0$, where the coefficients $a_0, a_1, \cdots, a_n$ are integers and $a_n \neq 0$. (These real numbers are called the real roots of the given equation.)

THEOREM 7. The set A of algebraic real numbers is denumerable.

Proof: We shall describe a method of enumerating all the algebraic real numbers. Consider the set of all equations of the form $a_n x^n + a_{n-1} x^{n-1} + \cdots + a_1 x + a_0 = 0$, where the coefficients $a_0, a_1, \cdots, a_n$ are integers and $a_n \neq 0$. Without loss of generality, we may assume that $a_n > 0$. Assign to each equation in the set a positive integer N, called its index, and defined as $N = n + a_n + |a_{n-1}| + \cdots + |a_1| + |a_0|$. N is always a positive integer. (Why?) There is no equation of index 1, since n and a_n are both at least 1. The only equation of index 2 is $x = 0$; its only root is 0. The only equations of index 3 are $2x = 0$, $x + 1 = 0$, $x - 1 = 0$, and $x^2 = 0$; their real roots are 0, -1, and 1. The only equations of index 4 are $3x = 0$, $2x + 1 = 0$, $2x - 1 = 0$, $x + 2 = 0$, $x - 2 = 0$, $x^2 + 1 = 0$, $x^2 - 1 = 0$, and $x^3 = 0$. Their real roots are 0, $\frac{-1}{2}$, $\frac{1}{2}$, -2, 2, 1, and -1. Thus, for each index N, there are only a finite number of equations and hence, by Theorem 6, only a finite number of corresponding real roots. We may order the roots for each index according to the order relation "less than," omitting any number that is a root of an equation of lower index. Then we may arrange these finite sets of roots according to the sizes of their indices. In this way all the algebraic real numbers can be placed in a 1:1 correspondence with the set **I** of positive integers. According to the procedure just described, the first seven pairs in this correspondence are

$$
\begin{array}{ccccccc}
1 & 2 & 3 & 4 & 5 & 6 & 7 \\
\updownarrow & \updownarrow & \updownarrow & \updownarrow & \updownarrow & \updownarrow & \updownarrow \\
0 & -1 & 1 & -2 & \dfrac{-1}{2} & \dfrac{1}{2} & 2
\end{array}
\qquad Q.E.D.
$$

COROLLARY. The set T of transcendental real numbers is nondenumerable.

Proof: Exercise 8, page 142.

This corollary actually proves that transcendental numbers exist and, moreover, that nondenumerably many transcendental numbers exist. What is very remarkable is that all this is proved without exhibiting a single transcendental number.

EXERCISES

✳1. Prove that "having the same cardinal number" (Definition 1) is an equivalence relation.

2. Prove that $\mathbf{J} \approx \mathbf{R}$.

3. a) Prove that $\{r \mid r \in \mathbf{R} \text{ and } r > 0\} \approx \mathbf{I}$.
   b) Prove that $\{r \mid r \in \mathbf{R} \text{ and } r > 0\} \approx \mathbf{R}$.

4. Prove that any infinite set contains a denumerable subset.

5. Prove that any set having the same cardinal number as **I** is infinite.

6. Let A be an infinite set and B a denumerable set. Prove that $A \approx A \cup B$.

7. Prove that if A, B, and C are sets such that $A - B = C$, A is nondenumerable, and B is denumerable, then C is nondenumerable.

8. Prove that the set T of transcendental real numbers is nondenumerable.

9. Prove that if A, B, and C are sets such hat $A \supset B$, $A - B \supset C$, and B and C are denumerable, then $A \approx A - B$.

10. Exhibit a 1:1 correspondence between the set R of real numbers and the set $R - \mathbf{I}$, where **I** is the set of positive integers.

11. List all equations of index 7. (See proof of Theorem 7.)

7-2. THE CARDINAL NUMBER OF A SET

DEFINITION 6. The cardinal number of a set S is the equivalence class of all sets that have the same cardinal number as S.

Since we previously defined (Definition 1) "having the same cardinal number," Definition 6 is not circular.

DEFINITION 7. a) The cardinal number **1** is the equivalence class $\{\{0\},$ $\{1\}, \{2\}, \{\triangle\}, \{\square\}, \cdots\}$; the cardinal number **2** is the equivalence class $\{\{0, 1\}, \{1, 2\}, \{0, 2\}, \{\triangle, \square\}, \{\alpha, \beta\}, \cdots\}$; and so on.

b) The cardinal number $\aleph_0$[1] (read alef null) is the equivalence class of all denumerable sets.

c) The cardinal number **c** is the equivalence class of all sets having the same cardinal number as the set R of real numbers. This equivalence class contains, for example, the set of all irrational numbers, the set of all transcendental numbers, the set of all points on a line, and so on.

Thus, we say that the cardinal number of a set S is $\aleph_0$ or that S has cardinal number $\aleph_0$ or that S has $\aleph_0$ elements if S is in the equivalence class $\aleph_0$ (that is, if S is in the equivalence class containing the set I of positive integers).

We say that the cardinal number of a set S is **c** or that S has cardinal number **c** or that S has **c** elements if S is in the equivalence class **c** (that is, if S is in the equivalence class containing the set R of real numbers). Since there is a 1:1 correspondence between the set R of real numbers and the set of all points on a line, the set R of real numbers is said to have the cardinal number of the continuum—hence the symbol **c** for the cardinal number of R.

DEFINITION 8. Let α and β be cardinal numbers. α is said to be less than or equal to β, and we write "$\alpha \leq \beta$" if there is a set A in α and a set B in β such that A has the same cardinal number as a subset of B. α is said to equal β, and we write "$\alpha = \beta$" if there is a set A in α and a set B in β such that A has the same cardinal number as B. α is said to be less than β, and we write "$\alpha < \beta$" if $\alpha \leq \beta$ and $\alpha \neq \beta$.

By Exercise 1 (page 145), the relations "less than or equal to," "equals," and "less than" are well defined.

Example. For every positive integer n, $n < \aleph_0 < c$.

THEOREM 8. (Schroeder-Cantor-Bernstein). Let α and β be cardinal numbers. If $\alpha \leq \beta$ and $\beta \leq \alpha$, then $\alpha = \beta$.

---

[1]The symbol $\aleph$ (alef) is the first letter of the Hebrew alphabet.

We shall not prove Theorem 8.[2] Using Theorem 8, however, we may prove the following corollary.

COROLLARY.   The relation "less than" (Definition 8) is an order relation.

Proof: Exercise 2, page 145.

DEFINITION 9.   A cardinal number α is said to be infinite if there is a set A in α such that A is infinite.

THEOREM 9. $\aleph_0$ is the smallest infinite cardinal number.

Proof: By Example 1 (page 140), I is infinite; therefore, by Definition 9, since I is in $\aleph_0$, $\aleph_0$ is infinite. By Exercise 4 (page 142), any infinite set S contains a denumerable subset. Let σ be the cardinal number of S. Then, by Definition 8, $\aleph_0 \leq \sigma$, since there is a set I in $\aleph_0$ and a set S in σ such that I has the same cardinal number as a subset of S. $Q.E.D.$

Cantor conjectured that there is no set A having a cardinal number α such that $\aleph_0 < \alpha < c$. This conjecture is called the Continuum Hypothesis. Paul J. Cohen, in 1963, proved that the Continuum Hypothesis is unprovable from the other axioms of set theory.

DEFINITION 10.   Let A and B be two nonempty sets. Let α be the cardinal number of A; let β be the cardinal number of B. Then A^B is defined to be the set of all functions from B to A. α^β is defined to be the cardinal number of A^B.

By Exercise 3 (page 145), if A, B, A', and B' are sets with cardinal numbers α, β, α', β', respectively, and if $A \approx A'$ and $B \approx B'$, then $\alpha^\beta = \alpha'^{\beta'}$; that is, α^β is well defined.

Example.   If $A = \{0, 1\}$ and $B = \{1, 2, 3\}$, then $\alpha = 2$, $\beta = 3$, and A^B consists of the following eight functions:

$$\{(1, 0), \ (2, 0), \ (3, 0)\}$$
$$\{(1, 0), \ (2, 0), \ (3, 1)\}$$
$$\{(1, 0), \ (2, 1), \ (3, 0)\}$$
$$\{(1, 0), \ (2, 1), \ (3, 1)\}$$
$$\{(1, 1), \ (2, 0), \ (3, 0)\}$$
$$\{(1, 1), \ (2, 0), \ (3, 1)\}$$
$$\{(1, 1), \ (2, 1), \ (3, 0)\}$$
$$\{(1, 1), \ (2, 1), \ (3, 1)\}$$

---

[2] A proof may be found in G. Birkhoff and S. Maclane, *A Survey of Modern Algebra*, 3d ed. New York: The Macmillan Company, 1965.

The cardinal number of A^B = 8; that is, $\alpha^\beta = 2^3 = 8$.

We shall not prove the following two theorems.[3]

THEOREM 10. For any cardinal number α, $\alpha < 2^\alpha$.

Examples 1. $1 < 2^1$; $2 < 2^2$; $3 < 2^3$; $\cdots$.

2. $\aleph_0 < 2^{\aleph_0}$.

3. $c < 2^c$.

THEOREM 11. $2^{\aleph_0} = c$.

Thus, by Theorems 10 and 11,

$$\aleph_0 < 2^{\aleph_0} (= c) < 2^{(2^{\aleph_0})} < 2^{\left(2^{(2^{\aleph_0})}\right)} < \cdots,$$

where $2^{(2^{\aleph_0})}$ is the cardinal number of the set of all functions from a set S to the set $\{0, 1\}$ such that S is the set of all functions from a denumerable set to the set $\{0, 1\}$; and so on. Thus, there are a denumerable number of cardinal numbers α such that $c < \alpha$. The Generalized Continuum Hypothesis states that for any cardinal number α there does not exist a cardinal number β such that $\alpha < \beta < 2^\alpha$. According to this hypothesis, the sequence $\aleph_0$, $2^{\aleph_0}$, $2^{(2^{\aleph_0})}, \cdots$ lists all the infinite cardinal numbers.

EXERCISES

1. Prove that the relations "less than or equal to," "equals," and "less than" (Definition 8) are well defined.

2. Prove that the relation "less than" is an order relation.

3. Let α and β be cardinal numbers. Prove that α^β is well defined.

7-3. ARITHMETIC OF CARDINAL NUMBERS

Cardinal numbers may be added and multiplied as follows:

DEFINITION 11. Let α and β be cardinal numbers. Let A be a set in α and let B be a set in β. Then $\alpha + \beta$ is the cardinal number of $A \cup B$, providing that $A \cap B = \emptyset$. $\alpha \cdot \beta$ is the cardinal number of $A \times B$, where $A \times B$ is the Cartesian product of A and B.

By Exercise 1 (page 146), addition and multiplication are well defined.

Examples 1. $\aleph_0 + \aleph_0 = \aleph_0$. This is because $I \in \aleph_0$, $I_0^- = \{\cdots, -2, -1, 0\} \in \aleph_0$, $I \cap I_0^- = \emptyset$, and $I \cup I_0^- = J \in \aleph_0$.

---

[3] A proof may be found in G. Birkhoff and S. MacLane, *A Survey of Modern Algebra*, 3d ed. New York: The Macmillan Company, 1965.

2. $\aleph_0 \cdot \aleph_0 = \aleph_0$. This can be shown as follows: $\aleph_0 \cdot \aleph_0$ is the cardinal number of $\mathbf{I} \times \mathbf{I}$. But $\mathbf{I} \times \mathbf{I}$ consists of all ordered pairs (m, n) of positive integers. A 1:1 correspondence between $\mathbf{I} \times \mathbf{I}$ and $\mathbf{I}$ be constructed exactly as in the proof of Theorem 3. Under this correspondence,

$$
\begin{array}{cccccc}
1 & 2 & 3 & 4 & 5 & 6 \\
\updownarrow & \updownarrow & \updownarrow & \updownarrow & \updownarrow & \updownarrow \\
(1,1) & (1,2) & (2,1) & (3,1) & (2,2) & (1,3)
\end{array}
$$

$$
\begin{array}{ccccc}
7 & 8 & 9 & 10 & \cdots \\
\updownarrow & \updownarrow & \updownarrow & \updownarrow & \\
(1,4) & (2,3) & (3,2) & (4,1) & \cdots
\end{array}
$$

By Exercises 2, 3, 4, and 5 (page 147), for any cardinal numbers α, β, and γ:

1. $\alpha + \beta = \beta + \alpha$.
2. $\alpha \cdot \beta = \beta \cdot \alpha$.
3. $\alpha + (\beta + \gamma) = (\alpha + \beta) + \gamma$.
4. $\alpha \cdot (\beta \cdot \gamma) = (\alpha \cdot \beta) \cdot \gamma$.
5. $\alpha \cdot (\beta + \gamma) = \alpha \cdot \beta + \alpha \cdot \gamma$.
6. $1 \cdot \alpha = \alpha$.
7. $\alpha^\beta \cdot \alpha^\gamma = \alpha^{\beta + \gamma}$.
8. $(\alpha \cdot \beta)^\gamma = \alpha^\gamma \cdot \beta^\gamma$.
9. $(\alpha^\beta)^\gamma = \alpha^{\beta \cdot \gamma}$.
10. $\alpha^1 = \alpha$.
11. $1^\alpha = 1$.

THEOREM 12. The cancellation laws of addition and multiplication do not hold for infinite cardinal numbers.

Proof: By Theorem 1 and Definition 11, $\aleph_0 = \aleph_0 + 1$. Therefore, by substitution and identity 3 above, $\aleph_0 + 1 = (\aleph_0 + 1) + 1 = \aleph_0 + (1 + 1) = \aleph_0 + 2$. Since $1 \neq 2$, the cancellation law of addition does not hold.

By Example 1 (page 145), $\aleph_0 + \aleph_0 = \aleph_0$. Using this equality and identities 5, 2, and 6 above, we have $\aleph_0(2) = \aleph_0(1 + 1) = \aleph_0(1) + \aleph_0(1) = 1\aleph_0 + 1\aleph_0 = \aleph_0 + \aleph_0 = \aleph_0 = 1\aleph_0 = \aleph_0(1)$. Since $2 \neq 1$, the cancellation law of multiplication does not hold. *Q.E.D.*

EXERCISES

1. Prove that addition and multiplication of cardinal numbers are well defined.

2. Prove that the commutative laws of addition and multiplication hold for cardinal numbers.

3. Prove that the associative laws of addition and multiplication hold for cardinal numbers.

4. Prove that, for cardinal numbers, multiplication is distributive over addition.

5. Prove that for any cardinal numbers α, β, and γ:
  a) $1 \cdot \alpha = \alpha$.
  b) $\alpha^\beta \cdot \alpha^\gamma = \alpha^{\beta+\gamma}$.
  c) $(\alpha \cdot \beta)^\gamma = \alpha^\gamma \cdot \beta^\gamma$.
  d) $(\alpha^\beta)^\gamma = \alpha^{\beta \cdot \gamma}$.
  e) $\alpha^1 = \alpha$.
  f) $1^\alpha = 1$.

6. Prove that:
  a) $\aleph_0 + c = c$.
  b) $c + c = c$.
  c) $\aleph_0 \cdot c = c$.

7. Let α, β, and γ be cardinal numbers. Prove that, if $\alpha \leq \beta$, then:
  a) $\alpha + \gamma \leq \beta + \gamma$.
  b) $\alpha \cdot \gamma \leq \beta \cdot \gamma$.
  c) $\alpha^\gamma \leq \beta^\gamma$.
  d) $\gamma^\alpha \leq \gamma^\beta$.

Bibliography

Bell, E. T. *The Development of Mathematics.* New York: McGraw-Hill Book Company, Inc., 1945.

Birkhoff, G., and S. MacLane. *A Survey of Modern Algebra*, 3d ed. New York: The Macmillan Company, 1965.

Courant, R., and H. Robbins. *What Is Mathematics?* New York: Oxford University Press, Inc., 1941.

Dantzig, Tobias. *Number, the Language of Science.* New York: The Macmillan Company, 1954.

Eves, H., and C. V. Newsom. *An Introduction to the Foundations and Fundamental Concepts of Mathematics*, rev. ed. New York: Holt, Rinehart & Winston, Inc., 1965.

Fine, Nathan J. *Introduction to Modern Mathematics.* Chicago: Rand McNally & Co., 1965.

Gamow, G. *One, Two, Three, ···, Infinity.* New York: The Viking Press, Inc., 1948.

Goffman, C. *Real Functions.* New York: Holt, Rinehart & Winston, Inc., 1953.

Haag, Vincent H. *Structure of Algebra.* Reading, Mass.: Addison-Wesley Publishing Co., Inc., 1964.

Hafstrom, J. E. *Basic Concepts in Modern Mathematics.* Reading, Mass.: Addison-Wesley Publishing Co., Inc., 1961.

Hamilton, N. T., and J. Landin. *The Structure of Arithmetic.* Boston: Allyn & Bacon, Inc., 1961.

Henkin, L., W. N. Smith, V. J. Varineau, and M. J. Walsh. *Retracing Elementary Mathematics.* New York: The Macmillan Company, 1962.

Huntington, E. V. *Monographs on Topics of Modern Mathematics Relevant to the Elementary Field*, edited by J. W. A. Young. New York: Dover Publications, Inc., 1955.

Jones, B. W. *Elementary Concepts of Mathematics*, 2d ed. New York: The Macmillan Company, 1963.

Keedy, Mervin L. *Number Systems: A Modern Introduction.* Reading, Mass.: Addison-Wesley Publishing Co., Inc., 1965.

Kershner, R. B., and L. R. Wilcox. *The Anatomy of Mathematics.* New York: The Ronald Press Company, 1950.

Mostow, G. D., J. H. Sampson, and J.-P. Meyer. *Fundamental Structures of Algebra.* New York: McGraw-Hill Book Company, Inc., 1963.

Olmsted, J. H. M. *The Real Number System.* New York: Appleton-Century-Crofts, 1962.

Ore, O. *Number Theory and Its History.* New York: McGraw-Hill Book Company, Inc., 1948.

Polya, G. *How to Solve It,* 2d ed. Garden City, N.Y.: Anchor Books, Doubleday & Company, Inc., 1957.

Ritt, J. F. *Theory of Functions,* rev. ed. New York: King's Crown Press, 1947.

Roberts, J. B. *The Real Number System in an Algebraic Setting.* San Francisco: W. H. Freeman & Co., Publishers, 1962.

Rosser, J. B. *Logic for Mathematicians.* New York: McGraw-Hill Book Company, Inc., 1953.

Sierpinski, W. "On Some Unsolved Problems of Arithmetic." *Scripta Mathematica,* Vol. 25 (1960), pp. 125–136.

Stein, S. K. *Mathematics, the Man-Made Universe.* San Francisco: W. H. Freeman & Co., Publishers, 1963.

Wilder, R. L. *Introduction to the Foundations of Mathematics.* New York: John Wiley & Sons, Inc., 1952.

Index